Class in Britain

The book is dedicated to all the members of my family – past, present and new generations

Class in Britain

Ivan Reid

Polity Press

First published 1998 by Polity Press in association with Blackwell Publishers Ltd.

Editorial office:
Polity Press
65 Bridge Street
Cambridge CB2 1UR, UK

Marketing and production:
Blackwell Publishers Ltd
108 Cowley Road
Oxford OX4 1JF, UK

Published in the USA by
Blackwell Publishers Inc.
Commerce Place
350 Main Street
Malden, MA 02148, USA

ISBN 0–7456–1891–X
ISBN 0–7456–1892–8 (pbk)

A catalogue record for this book is available from the British Library and has been applied for from the Library of Congress.

Typeset in 10 on 11.5 pt Times
by Wearset, Boldon, Tyne and Wear
Printed in Great Britain by T. J. International, Padstow, Cornwall

This book is printed on acid-free paper.

Contents

List of Tables

Acknowledgements

The author expresses his gratitude to all those who, directly or indirectly, helped and supported him during the preparation of this book. Since there is such a large number it would be difficult and perhaps invidious to name them. The following lists the sources of help and support from which I and the book have benefited. They are not associated however with any shortcomings of either, all of which I claim for myself. All those researchers and writers whose work is reviewed in this book. Several 'generations' of students at the four universities and a college I have taught in. Various members of the staff of: the Department of Education, Loughborough University; the Loughborough University and Leeds University, the British Lending and the Office of National Statistics libraries; BBC, Broadcasting Research; British Market Research Bureau (BMRB) International; the Cathy Marsh Centre for Census and Survey Research, University of Manchester; The Gallup Organisation Inc.; Market and Opinion Research International (MORI); NOP Research Group Ltd; National Readership Surveys Ltd; Northern Ireland Statistics and Research Agency; Office of National Statistics (and, prior to redesignation, Office of Population Surveys and Censuses, Social Surveys Department); Quantime Ltd; and the staff of Polity Press for their delightful professionalism. Finally, but in fact in pride of place, my wife Pat, whose support has continued to be essential and much more than deserved.

The author and publisher thank the following for permission to use data presented in this book (full details of publications can be found in the References): Ashgate Publishing Ltd, Aldershot and Social and Community Planning Research (SCPR), London for data from the annual British Social Attitudes surveys contained in: Young, K. (1992)

Class, race and opportunity, in *British Social Attitudes, The 9th Report*; Hedges, B. (1994) Work in a changing climate, in *British Social Attitudes, The 11th Report*; Airey, C. and Brook, L. (1986) Interim report: social and moral issues, in *British Social Attitudes, The 1986 Report*; and Taylor-Goodby, P. (1991) Attachment to the welfare state, in *British Social Attitudes, The 8th Report*; the British Broadcasting Corporation, Radio Joint Audience Research Ltd (RAJAR) and Broadcasting Audience Research Bureau (BARB), London, for unpublished data from their audience research for 1995; the British Market Research Bureau International, London, for data from and special analyses of their *Target Group Index 1994*; N.R. Butler for data from British Lending Library Supplementary Publication no. 90, being an unpublished appendix to Butler, N.R. and Golding, J. (1986) *From Birth to Five*; Cambridge University Press for data from Goldthorpe, J.H., Llewellyn, C. and Payne, C. (1980) *Social Mobility and Class Structure in Modern Britain* and from Haskey, J. (1986) Grounds for divorce in England and Wales – a social and demographic analysis, *Journal of Biosocial Science*, 18; the Cathy Marsh Centre for Census and Survey Research, University of Manchester, for a special analysis of data from *Housing Deprivation and Social Change* (1994) (Crown Copyright); The Centre for Educational Sociology, The University of Edinburgh, for data from Burnhill, P. (1981) The relationship between examination performance and social class, *Centre for Educational Sociology Collaborative Research Newsletter*, no. 8; The Centre for Survey Research (CSR), Queen's University, Belfast and Social and Community Planning Research (SCPR), London for data from the 1990 Northern Ireland Social Attitudes (NISA) survey contained in Cairns, E. (1992) Political violence, social values and the generation gap, in Stringer, P. and Robinson, G. (1992) *Social Attitudes in Northern Ireland: The Second Report 1991–92*; Leslie J. Francis of Trinity College, Carmarthen for data from his ongoing research on school children's religious beliefs; Anthony Heath of Nuffield College, Oxford for data from Heath, A., Jowell, R. and Curtice, J (1985) *How Britain Votes*; David Fulton Publishers, London for data from Benn, C. and Chitty, C. (1996) *Thirty Years On: Is Comprehensive Education Alive and Well or Struggling to Survive?*; The Gallup Organisation Inc., London for published and unpublished data from their surveys based on face-to-face interviews with 1000 or more persons; the Controller of Her Majesty's Stationery Office, Norwich, for unpublished data from the 1991 Census for Northern Ireland, the *General Household Surveys* of 1982, 1994 and 1995, *Housing Deprivation and Social Change* (1994) and from the *Labour Force Survey* of Spring 1996. Crown Copyright data are reproduced with the permission of the Controller of Her Majesty's Stationery Office from: *Birth Statistics 1994* (1994); *Day Care Services for Children* (1994); Drever, F., Whitehead, M. and Roden, M. (1996) Current patterns and trends in male mortality by social class (based on occupation). *Population Trends*, no. 86; *Drug Misuses Declared: Results of the 1994 British Crime Survey* (1996), Home Office Research Study no. 151; *Economic Activity, 1991 Census, Great Britain* (1994); *Ethnic Group and Country of Birth, 1991 Census, Great Britain* (1993); *Family Spending: A Report on the 1993 Family Expenditure Survey* (1995); *General Household Surveys 1977* (1979), *1979* (1981), *1982* (1984), *1983* (1985), *1988* (1990), *1989* (1991), *1991* (1993), *1992* (1994), *1993* (1995), *1994* (1996) and *1995* (1997); Haskey, J. (1983) Social class patterns of marriage, *Population Trends*, no. 34; Haskey, J. (1984) Social class and socio-economic differentials in divorce in England and Wales, *Population Trends*, no. 38; Haskey, J. (1987) Social class differentials in remarriage after divorce: results from a forward linkage study, *Population Trends*, no. 47; *Health in England 1995* (1996); *Health Survey for England 1994* (1996), *Volume 1: Findings*; *Anxiety about Crime: Findings from the 1994 British Crime Survey* (1995), Home Office Research and Planning Unit Report no. 147; *Household and Family Composition, 1991 Census, Great Britain* (1994); *Housing Deprivation and Social Change* (1994); *Infant Feeding 1990* (1992); Knight, I. and Eldridge, J. (1984) *The Heights and Weights of Adults in Great Britain*; *Migration, 1991 Census, Great Britain* (1994); *Labour Force Survey 1996*; *Morbidity Statistics from General Practice 1981–82* (1990); *Mortality and Geography* (1990); *Mortality Statistics, Perinatal and Infant 1991* (1993); *New Earnings Survey 1996* (1996) Part D, Analysis by Occupation; *Occupational Mortality, Childhood Supplement* (1988); *Occupational Mortality* (1986); *Population Trends* no. 86 (1996); *Psychiatric Morbidity amongst Homeless People* (1996); *Report for Great Britain, 1991 Census* (1993); *Retirement and Retirement Plans* (1992); Robertson, D. and Hillman, J. (1997) *Widening Participation in Higher Education for Students from Lower Socio-Economic Groups and Students with disabilities*, Report no. 6, National Committee of Enquiry into Higher Education; *Royal Commission on the Distribution of Income and Wealth, Report no. 9* (1979); *Social Trends no. 17* (1987); *Social Trends no. 25* (1995); *The Health of our Children* (1995); *The National Prison Survey 1991* (1992); *Voluntary Work* (1993); *Young People's Intentions to Enter Higher Education* (1987); Hodder Headline and Peters Fraser and Dunlop, London for data from Sampson, A. (1982) *The Changing Anatomy of Britain*; The Institute of Actuaries, Oxford for data from Bloomfield, D.S.F. and Haberman, S. (1992) Male social class mortality differences around 1981: an extension to include ages, *Journal of the Institute of Actuaries*, 119 (III); Macmillan Press Ltd, London for data from Butler, D. and Kavanagh, D. (1984) *The British General Election of 1983*; Butler, D. and Kavanagh, D. (1992) *The British General Election of 1992*; and Routh, G. (1980) *Occupation and Pay in Great Britain 1906–79*; MORI for published and unpublished data from their surveys;

NOP Research Group Ltd, London, for published and unpublished data from their surveys; National Readership Surveys Ltd, London, for data from their *National Readership Survey 1996*; Oxford University Press, Oxford for data from Halsey, A.H., Heath, A.F. and Ridge, J.M. (1980) *Origins and Destinations*; Penguin Books Ltd, Harmondsworth, for data from Townsend, P. (1979) *Poverty in the United Kingdom*; Peters, Fraser and Dunlop Group Ltd, London for data from Wellings, K., Field, J., Johnson, A. and Wadsworth, J. (1994) *Sexual Behaviour in Britain: The National Survey of Sexual Attitudes and Lifestyles*; Routledge, London for data from Abbott, P. and Sapsford, R. (1987) *Women and Social Class*; Mack, J. and Lansley, S. (1985) *Poor Britain*; Marshall, G., Rose, D., Newby, H. and Vogler, C. (1988) *Social Class in Modern Britain*; and Newson, J. and Newson, E. (1976) *Seven Years Old in the Home Environment.*; Quantime Ltd, London for special analyses of data from the *Labour Force Survey*, Spring 1996 (Crown Copyright); Tyrell Burgess Associates Ltd, Croydon, for data from Edwards, E.G. and Roberts, I.J. (1980) British higher education: long term trends in student enrolment, *Higher Education Review*, 12; The Universities and Colleges Admissions Systems, Cheltenham, for data from UCAS (1996) *Annual Report 1995 Entry* and UCCA (1994) *31st Report 1992–3.*

Every effort has been made to trace all the copyright holders in respect to the data in this book; should any others have been inadvertently overlooked the author and publisher will be pleased to make the necessary arrangements at the first opportunity.

Preface

This book, like my previous ones in the field, arises from my continuing recognition of the need of students, teachers and others for a review of contemporary British social class reality based on empirical research data. The reception of the books has not only vindicated my belief in that need, but also established that others, outside the academic realm, have a use for such a book. This book therefore has the same aim and approach, both of which are fully outlined in chapter 1.

In purposefully sustaining a singular concern with the empirical reality of social class differences, I have been aware of how much has had to be left unsaid and unexplored. For this I make no apology. Empirical data are but one part of an extremely broad and complex literature on social class: hence interested readers will experience no difficulty in moving from or on to literature more specific to their interests, or that which complements the concern of this book.

In several ways writing about empirical research on social class is more challenging in the late 1990s than it was in the mid 1970s and the 1980s. Social class differences and inequalities have become less central concerns both politically and socially and within social science, perhaps because of developing interest in these features of gender and ethnicity, and/or because the popularity of class has declined owing to its intransigence. By analogy perhaps the situation is not unlike coal mining, the decline in which is related neither to the lack of coal nor to its utility, but to the changing and comparative attraction of other fuels. However, this book takes social class as the fundamental form of stratification in society while not ignoring the interrelationships of all forms. Consequently, it is clearly and straightforwardly a commentary on social class differences as revealed in empirical research in contemporary Britain.

Somebody remarked about my first venture into this field that its publication was timely. My feeling is that, given the social and political changes, together with those in the disciplines which provide the data, the present one may be even more so. This book provides, I believe, considerable food for thought and reflection, not only in academic but also in social and political terms. I trust that readers and users will find it useful.

Ivan Reid

1

Social Class and This Book

This book is about social class differences and inequalities in contemporary Britain. In particular it examines in detail one aspect of the vast, complex and controversial topic of social class – the empirical evidence concerning class differences in Britain today. As such it follows earlier books by its author (Reid, 1977; 1981; 1989a) in continuing to fill a gap identified in the considerable literature on social class. That gap lay, and still lies, between rather grand generalizations concerning social class differences and the very detailed, though often inaccessible, data and findings of empirical studies. Many accounts, for example textbooks, are misleading about social class, their oversimplification amounting to misrepresentation or even inaccuracy when compared with contemporary sources. Moreover, some treatments of class simultaneously present data from different societies and times and from a range of types and scales of research sources: their juxtaposition implies a similar degree of reliability and importance, which may well be inappropriate. The overall effect of such literature can be misleading and confusing, and lead to the rejection of the concept and reality of social class because of a lack of appropriate material. Further, contact with contemporary statistics and research findings demands not only access to a university library or its equivalent, but also very real efforts of searching and interpretation. This is because their presentation is normally designed for purposes other than communication with, or use by, students or the public.

This book provides easy access to the empirical data on social class in Britain, using a standardized format (see 'Criteria for inclusion and presentation' later in this chapter). It provides not only a comprehensive view of the nature and extent of class in our society, but also the basis or vehicle for discussions about how the concept of social class has been used in empirical research (operationalized), and it reveals something of the actual state of knowledge in the field. In so doing it should lead to a more realistic appraisal by a wide-ranging readership.

As Monk (1970) has pointed out:

> Social class is a concept readily understood by the average man [*sic*], but relatively difficult to define ... in recognizing that social class is not a simple factor, but an amalgam of factors that operate in different ways in different circumstances, such a person has arrived at the same view as the professional sociologist.

Hence this introductory chapter has three purposes. First, it places social class in its public context by outlining something of the breadth of usage of the idea in society at large. Second, it outlines how class is seen and used by researchers and how that use relates to the everyday. Third, it describes this book's distinctive and particular approach.

Social Class: a Subject for All Seasons

A commonly held idea

In general terms social differences, based on social class, sex, age and ethnicity, or allusions to them, are very familiar and frequent in our society. At the everyday level they can be discerned in conversation, attitudes and behaviour both public and private. Differences are recognized in people's appearance and speech, where they live and come from, what they do for a living, how they spend time and money and what their interests are, to name but a few examples. Such differences provide much rich material for discussion, emulation, condemnation and, indeed, humour. In turn these differences are used to characterize, or make assumptions about, people of different types. The nature of this common and essential characteristic of social differentiation varies from place to place. At work the distinction between employers and employees and, within these, differences of rank and skill, can be seen as a more formalized idea of social class. In politics it is often difficult to escape social class connotations in what the parties and politicians stand for, or in their assumptions, words and actions.

Everyday life provides many further examples. One of the earliest and most common inquiries made in a casual meeting is, 'What job do you do?' – a question which usually brings a response, and rarely leads to an end of the conversation, or to embarrassment. From this 'knowledge' (of another's occupation) people are likely to make a number of assumptions about that person, their interests, attitudes, and so on. These assumptions, based on previous experience of similar people and/or what has been seen or heard about them, will affect the conversation and one's reactions to it. Surprises and mistakes do occur, but on the whole our assumptions are borne out. Significantly, when they are not, we do not discard them, but merely dust them off and retain them for the future. The experience is accommodated as an oddity. This happens because our categories are resilient, and indeed they probably need to be. Life would be socially and psychologically intolerable if every new encounter had to be built up from scratch.

Outside the purely social encounter, many commercial and government organizations require to know our occupation. Since few of us change our jobs dramatically, we may not realize what a crucial role our job plays in the way people and organizations react to us. It is possible to test this by pretending to be something other than what we are, say at a social event or on a rail journey. Assuming we are convincing enough, this allows us to compare the responses we get with those we normally receive. Categorization of people on the basis of small snippets of information is common in social life. One's outward appearance can often affect the treatment one receives in places like banks, garages or large stores. Most of us pay some heed to this, for example, when we go to an interview for a job. What is happening here is clearly not far removed from what social scientists do when they classify people in terms of social class. They are assuming that a single piece of information – typically occupation – is a good general predictor of a host of other factors such as income, education, style of life, attitudes, interests and beliefs, which together form their concept of social class. Their research is likely to be based on hypotheses (which can be seen as informed guesses, or hunches) rather similar to those used in face-to-face situations. Their categories are similarly crude and resilient as are our 'real-life' ones, but they are likely to be much more systematic in collecting data, and their judgements can thus be rationally appraised.

General interest in social differences is reflected in, and fuelled by, the mass media. News programmes make full play of people's occupation, age and gender (not to mention titles), even when these can be seen as irrelevant or marginal to a story. Social class as an issue in itself is newsworthy, almost to the same extent as sex and crime, and provides a fertile and constant theme, or subplot, for plays, films, novels and humour. There also appears a clear tendency to highlight the trivial at the expense of the fundamental and to indulge in rhetoric rather than review the evidence. So great play is made of such aspects as snobbery, political views, interests and opinions, with far less, if any, attention being paid to the underlying economic inequalities affecting not only life-styles but also life-chances. A further deflection from serious consideration is the regular claim that things have changed and become better: that we no longer live in a class society, since the classes have merged or become very similar; that equality has gone as far as necessary, or has almost been achieved. An added gloss to this sort of argument is that those who appear to be disadvantaged either actually enjoy their situation or do not want any change, and would not know what to do with it. Such views may sound to readers to be those of the advantaged in the situations, that is, the middle classes, since they represent those parties' interests in the maintenance of the status quo, or its minimal change. However, we need to remember that ideas and values do not necessarily have discrete boundaries and that the disadvantaged may also hold such views. Shared, general views of social reality, apparently supporting a particular group's interests, are common, especially in social situations where one party has control or influence over information, knowledge and ideas, or where power in its general sense is unequal between the parties. This is certainly true in respect to social class and indeed gender, where such views continue to be supported by those who have nothing to gain and, indeed, may be losing, by their continued acceptance.

The importance of entrenched values, beliefs or ideologies is almost impossible to overestimate, to the extent that they are not necessarily affected or changed through experience or exposure to facts. Hopes that people would realize the injustice or unfairness of social situations merely by being told 'the facts' have often been dashed because of resistance to their acceptance, caused mainly by participants' 'understandings' based on deeply rooted cultural assumptions. Despite, and because of, these cautions, it is valuable for society to have as many facts as possible readily available, to enable informed discussion and understanding, if not action.

Clearly, too, social class features in a whole range of academic disciplines – such as history, economics, politics, psychology, medicine, indeed all the social sciences and literature – and above all in sociology, where social class has to be seen as one of the central concepts and concerns, given the time, energy and space devoted to it. This is witnessed not only by the number of books on the subject and the impossibility of finding an introductory textbook, or syllabus, in the subject which does not include it, but also by its prominence in journal articles and research, demonstrating its acknowledged importance as a vital variable. This interest is to be found as well in a range of institutions concerned with human social behaviour and its possible prediction, notably the government, industry and commerce, which have long and considerable involvement. Many governmental agencies collect, record and publish a whole variety of material on social class. Its importance in marketing, advertising and selling commodities and services, in creating and servicing needs, has given rise to what amounts to an industry of market research.

This level of interest and involvement in social class differences has generated a considerable range of opinions about them. These range between the extremes, from denying that they matter to seeing them as the sole explanatory variable for a whole host of situations. For example, while some people dismiss social class completely, others believe that it is *the* vital factor that explains all spheres of social life, including relationships between the sexes and within families. The shades of opinion in between are too numerous and subtle to recount here. Discussions about class, both face-to-face and in the literature, take on many of the same characteristics as those about religion. Subtle differences of belief and emphasis and the interpretation of facts and events become the grounds of major division. The avid devotion and zeal of believers is equally matched by those who reject any possibility of its existence.

Such debates appear to change in popularity. Currently, gender and ethnicity are more popular concerns than class, which has enjoyed greater popularity in the past. Some people react to social differences and inequalities with lack of interest or even with delight, seeing them as adding to the richness and diversity of life. Certainly, class differences do not in themselves present society, or its members, with a problem. Perhaps few people would see the ideal world as one in which everybody was identical, while nearly all would reject one in which groups were denied their basic rights and the wherewithal to exist. Most are probably concerned by the fact that some groups in our society can be shown to be materially deprived through no fault of their own, and others disadvantaged in terms of length of life, health, and access to services like health and education (and the quality of what they receive when they get it), which are supposed to be provided fully and freely for all on the basis of need. In turn these issues are based on questions of social equality and justice. Here the prime concern appears to have been not so much with attempts to achieve general equality, as with changing the legitimate criteria for inequality and extending equality of opportunity rather than equality of treatment or outcome. In the field of education, for example, the grounds of the debate since the Second World War have shifted from social class to gender and ethnicity, and have been concerned mainly with attempts to remove barriers to the various types of schooling, education and achievement for members of those groups. The goal has been to extend the opportunities for children from different classes, sexes and ethnic groups to gain educational achievements – and hence be differentiated on educational rather than social grounds. For some the provision of equal opportunities is a sufficient end in itself; for others the end is equality of outcome, which is only achieved when the educational attainment of the classes, sexes and ethnic groups is identical. As can be seen in chapter 7, there is a considerable way to go to achieve either of these ends, though significant progress has been made in some respects in terms of gender.

Social class as strata

Social scientists have a somewhat different view of social class, seeing it, along with gender, ethnicity and age, as a form of social stratification. Put as simply as possible, social stratification is an arrangement of society into layers. In some ways the idea is similar to that of layers or strata of rock. However, social stratification usually also implies some form of differentiation between, or comparative evaluation of, the layers; reference is being made not only to different groups within society, but to a hierarchy or ranking of these groups. This implied evaluation and ranking can be seen in the definitions of social class outlined in appendix B. These classifications are ordinarily ranked by number or letter and listed from the 'highest' to the 'lowest'. The very common use of contrasting terms such as 'middle class' and 'working class' or 'non-manual class' and 'manual class' reveals the same evaluative connotations.

The number of criteria on which social stratification (or categorization) could be based is theoretically infinite. Any culturally recognizable difference – forms of skill, type and amount of knowledge, religious practice, strength, length of hair, beauty and so on – could be such a basis, depending on the social context. Some kind of social stratification seems almost universal, or even inevitable, in social life. Even among groups of peers certain hierarchies are likely to be perceived. In any group, whether of friends, colleagues or even a family, we are likely to categorize the members by some such differences. To some extent the recognition of such criteria affects people's behaviour towards each other and their behaviour and organization as a social group. In turn this may mean differences in people's use and control of resources, in their power and status within the group. The more visible the criteria of differentiation, the more strict the social stratification, and the more regulated the relationships between the strata. Extreme examples are the armed forces and hospitals, where the wearing of uniform ensures recognition of differences and hence regulates relationships and behaviour.

In society, social stratification is essentially about groups' relationships to social wealth, used here in the generic sense of anything in society which is both scarce and valued by society. Hence it includes not only wealth, income and the ownership of property, but also power and prestige, together with a large number of associated factors including style of life, education, values, beliefs, attitudes and patterns of behaviour. Since our society, like all Western societies, runs on a cash nexus, many of these differences can be seen to have an economic basis. This is not to say that the differences are necessarily economically determined, but rather that most aspects of social life are directly and/or indirectly affected by economic circumstances. Therefore most social analysts see social class, which has an economic basis, as the most important and fundamental form of social stratification.

Traditional sociological treatments of stratification often contrast social class with the comparative and historical examples of caste, such as that in traditional Indian society, and estate, which characterized medieval Europe. It is much more meaningful, however, to compare it with other forms of stratification in our society, such as the two almost universal forms of age and sex. To a great extent people of different ages, or different sex, are given, and expect, differential treatment; they have different rights, privileges and duties, they have differing levels of access to forms of social wealth, and they hold views of the world and of themselves which are related to such differences.

Our recognition and understanding of what are female and male characteristics come from our culture, what we have learned as members of society. In other words, we use what amount to generalized stereotypes, which involve inaccuracies and unwarranted assumptions. In reality, all the supposed social characteristics of each sex exist in both females and males, although their display and recognition are differently encouraged or discouraged. A whole series of social forces, ranging from the law, through custom and norms, institutions and the media, to humour, affect our understanding.

No new idea

A commonly expressed opinion about social class is that, if sociologists, political scientists and the like did not actually invent the term, then they are certainly active in maintaining and popularizing it. This contention demands some consideration since it is untrue. There are many clear historical indications that divisions in society which exhibit most of the characteristics associated with social class have long been recognized. Plato, some 300 years before the birth of Christ, wrote about gold, silver and tin people. The rights and privileges of these groups he saw as being based on inheritance, effort and worth to society. Aristotle wrote that the best-administered states had a large middle class – larger if possible than both the others – which is clearly a reference to the different degrees of political power enjoyed by the classes. Romans used the term *classis,* which was a division of people on the basis of property and taxation. According to the Roman historian Pliny, the classes were judged by wealth measured in asses of brass. In the twelfth century John Ball wrote in his text for a sermon on the Peasants' Revolt:

> When Adam delved and Eve span,
> Who was then the gentleman?

A clause in the 1844 Railway Act read: 'it is expedient to secure to the poorer class of travellers the means of travelling by railway at moderate fares ... Companies shall ... provide for the conveyance of third-class passengers.' Such historical allusions, and there are many more, suggest that all the usual concomitants of class – status, power, wealth and so on – have been recognized as a basis for dividing people into groups probably for as long as societies have existed. Ossowski (1963) has traced the ideas of class and class consciousness from what he calls biblical legends through to the 1960s.

However, Briggs (1960) has argued that in Britain the term 'social class', as we understand it, started to be used only after the Industrial Revolution. Previously, in the eighteenth century, society was perceived in terms of broad bands, reflecting the comparatively simple social structure of what was basically an agrarian society. Industrialization not only broke up the existing order of society, but replaced it with a greater division of labour. People became much more differentiated in their occupations, which varied in terms of skills and rewards. These differences, together with the great migration to the cities (urbanization), also brought about separation in residence, style of life and interests. Certainly the Victorian era was characterized by what might be termed 'class consciousness' or 'awareness'. It was perhaps not by chance that Marx chose England as the model on which to base the development of his ideas. However, the flames of class consciousness were probably fuelled not so much by Marx as by the lingering fears created by the French Revolution, and the reaction to those fears on the part of established power. Hence the established Church of England sang:

> The rich man in his castle,
> The poor man at his gate,
> God made them, high or lowly,
> And order'd their estate. (*Hymns Ancient and Modern*, 1950)

Marwick (1980; 1990) has comprehensively surveyed the use of the images of class through the recent history of our society to the present, and related these to the reality of inequalities. While certain classical sociologists, namely Marx and Weber, saw social class as a central concept in sociology, other sociologists did not. It was not so much sociologists who were initially involved in the systematic collection of social class data as medically inspired census workers (see Stevenson, 1928; and see the introduction to chapter 3), empirically minded social reformers such as Booth and Rowntree, and social statisticians (see Cullen, 1975). Subsequently, government and commercial market researchers have played a major role in empirical research using social class. They have helped in shaping research fashions, but more importantly they have sustained the use of the concept and provided much of the data in the field.

In much the same way, discussions about the reality and the utility of social class have a history. There are two different ways in which social class can be seen to exist. First, classifications in terms of social class are seen, to some extent, as comparable to those used by a scientist wishing to classify physical phenomena. Such a classification, for example of moths, needs only to fit the known instances of moths, and to be recognized as useful by other scientists. In this sense it has what can be described as 'objective existence'. It does not rely for its usefulness or legitimacy on whether or not the moths themselves agree with it! Social class too has objective existence, as is clearly witnessed by the data presented in this book: social class is accepted and used by social scientists and others as a classification of the population they investigate. The concerns of sociologists, however, are rarely as straightforward as those of other scientists. As has already been suggested, ideas of social class, or social differences, appear to exist, and to have existed, among the general population (see also 'How the Public Sees Social Class' in chapter 2). Indeed it could be argued that sociologists have only systematized pre-existing knowledge of divisions in human society. Here the second way of looking at the existence of social class comes in. To the extent to which people in society perceive, or accept, social class, it has a 'subjective existence'. Hence we can identify two long-standing concerns of sociologists about the classifications they construct. They are:

How well do they fit the social reality they are designed to explain or describe?

How meaningful are they to the people to whom they apply?

These concerns, which are interrelated, form the basis of much discussion about sociology, both inside and outside the discipline, and are far from new. Marx, who is recognized by many as being father to the present interest in, and use of, the idea of social class, clearly recognized them both (his ideas are complex and his writings extensive: for a most useful selection see Bottomore and Rubel, 1963). Marx's basic idea was that there were two social classes: the bourgeoisie, who owned the means of production, and the proletariat, who did not – as he saw it, the exploiters and the exploited. However, Marx recognized that in the social situation he was describing there were other groups which, while not owning the means of production, were evidently not being exploited to the same degree as the proletariat. He used the terms 'petty bourgeoisie' and 'middle class' to describe such groups. In a similar fashion Marx was concerned that the proletariat did not share his concept of their position in society. They failed to recognize their exploitation because, while they were a class 'in itself' (objective), they were not a class 'for itself' (subjective). To put it more forcibly, as Marx did (but only once), they were suffering from 'false consciousness', that is, they did not recognize their 'real' situation as he had defined it.

These sorts of concern continue, and would be seen by some to be of central importance for this book and for the researches from which it uses data. Some would argue that in the social as opposed to the physical world objective classifications have only limited utility. They argue that a proper understanding of social reality will be achieved only when social scientists use concepts which have real foundations in the consciousness of the people involved. Whether the efficacy of the concept of social class is dependent on the realization and acceptance by the general population that social class exists is open to debate. If it is so dependent, then the discussion of subjective views of class in chapter 2 ('How the Public Sees Social Class') is vitally related to the rest of the book. If the evidence there is found wanting – which would suggest that the concept does not exist in people's minds – then possibly the utility of the rest of the book could be held in doubt. Others would be more concerned with social class in the objective sense. They would judge its utility by how usefully the concept performed in research: does it, for example, reveal consistent and illuminating facts about society? This volume provides a review of the findings of empirical research upon which such a judgement might be made.

Social Class in Research

There is a good deal of discussion, or even confusion, in sociological and other literature about the nature, utility and meaning of social class (for a recent sociological review see Lee and Turner, 1996). Crisp definitions of social class rarely appear, and the concept is generally seen to be problematic. Such caution is well advised, since social class is a multidimensional concept, involving not only the identification of categories that are partly invisible in society, but also an understanding of the effects of these on the people involved. Fortunately, for the purposes of this book, we can afford to be bolder, and accept as a working definition that: social class is 'a grouping of people into categories on the basis of occupation'. This is not to suggest that social class is simply or only based on occupation, or for that matter any other single criterion such as income or education. It is to recognize that occupation has been seen and used as the best single indicator of a person's social standing and socio-economic circumstance, both in sociological treatments (see reviews by Duke and Edgell, 1987; Drudy, 1991) and by government, social and commercial research concerns (see classifications in appendix B).

The main reason why an occupational definition of class can be accepted here is that our exclusive concern is with empirical research. In British research occupation is almost the sole criterion of social class to have been used. While British researchers have expressed some reservations about the use of this single factor, it is accepted as a reasonable general-purpose tool for classifying people into social classes. There have been some multidimensional scales, using combinations of factors such as occupation, income and education, and a few that have included more unusual factors such as participation in the community, family prestige, and contents and condition of living rooms. However, most of these scales were developed for a particular study, and their general use has been very limited. This is because they are more expensive to use in time and money and also raise the potential problem of relating their findings to those of others and to existing knowledge based on occupational scales. Occupation, almost certainly because it is easily collected and simple to treat, has remained universally the most popular criterion. Moreover, occupation has been consistently shown to be highly related to most other factors associated with social class, particularly income and education.

Occupation, then, is recognized as an element of social class in all sociological and other treatments of the concept. The reasons for this are very simple and can be dealt with briefly. In all societies based on a cash nexus occupations are differentially rewarded. Income is obviously an important determinant of possessions, style of life and place of living. Since earned income is for the majority their main form of wealth, occupation is a good indicator of the economic situation of a person and a family. Furthermore, holding down an occupation takes up a considerable amount of people's time and life, and typically involves them in interaction with particular groups of people in particular ways. It would be surprising if the experience of work did not affect in some way a person's view of the world, attitudes and opinions. Broadly speaking, too, people are residentially segregated by occupation. People with similar incomes are likely to be able to afford similar housing, and will thus share many other aspects of life with each other. So doctors are likely to have more in common with other doctors than with unskilled manual workers.

The strengths of using occupation as the basis for class in empirical research are quite straightforward. Occupation is an easily collected piece of information, regularly required of people and freely given, which is easy to use and interpret. Occupational class has been used extensively for a long time, and is 'official' in that it is used by the government in the census and other research. As a consequence it enables researchers to compare their findings with those of others and for comparisons to be made over time.

At the same time the use of occupation has been seen as having a number of shortcomings. In concentrating on those in employment it excludes, or treats slightly, or differently, others: the unemployed, retired and students. It also ignores the major difference between those that own and do not own capital and wealth. Most existing classifications can be seen as having been established on male occupations, or as carrying assumptions based on these. Since women's employment is different from men's, questions can be asked about the suitability of such classifications, particularly as women have become an increasingly significant part of the paid workforce.

A number of reservations arise from the changing nature of employment in our society. These include the growth in part-time work and unemployment, increased and decreased skill levels of occupations, the balance between public sector and private workers, and shifts between non-manual and manual occupations (which has never been a very clear line). A particular concern arises in determining the social class of families or households with more than one employed person in different classes. While this can be resolved for research purposes by identifying a 'head' (see appendix C), arguably it does not take into proper account cross-class families/households, or the role of women. A considerable debate has arisen from the use of male occupation to identify the class of families, centred on Goldthorpe's (1983) statement 'the class position of the family is a unitary one which derives from that of its male head – in the sense of the family member who has the fullest commitment to labour-market participation'. Much of this debate has been little informed by empirical research, which is precisely where it can be resolved. For example, one study concluded 'married or cohabiting women aged 16–24 years analysed by their own social class show almost identical differences as when analysed by the social class of their partner' (*Morbidity Statistics from General Practice 1981–82*). Similar findings emerged from the General Household Survey (GHS) – see chapter 3 – and this issue is further discussed in chapter 2.

Even more fundamental are questions as to whether, or to what extent, occupational class is related to theoretical or conceptual understandings of class, and how it relates to other accounts of and research into class (such as historical and case studies). These issues, which have given rise to a considerable literature and protracted debate (well covered by Crompton, 1993), do not need to detain us long here. The material in this book clearly makes the assumption that class can be described by occupation. Hence we can agree with Crompton in her review of classifications 'through which the structure of employment . . . may be divided in order to produce statistical aggregates which are then labelled "social classes" ' and that 'Many . . . are largely descriptive in their intentions' providing 'a convenient measure of the broad contours of structured social inequality . . . an indication of "lifestyle" and social attitudes.' We can also accept her conclusion that arguments about which class scheme is correct are unlikely to be productive and that it is the task of sociologists to establish which is the best for a particular problem.

Dissatisfaction with occupational class has led some to use what amount to proxy measures for class, for example, access to cars, housing tenure and even height. These are either very easy to measure or readily available from, for example, the census, and have been used either on their own or in combination with occupational class. The former use may well have been chosen because these factors have fewer political connotations than class and appeal to those who would deny class. However, as can be seen in this book, they are also related to social class themselves. Hence on their own they do not answer any basic problem, and when used in combination they are likely to be simply measures of location within occupational classes, indicating that there are within-class as well as between-class differences.

As outlined above there is a wide range of criticisms of the use of occupation-based social class. Some of these criticisms can be seen as gratuitous in that they reject social class classifications because they do not fulfil criteria which the classifications do not claim for themselves, or that they fail to meet the theoretical, ideological or perceptual understandings of their critics. It is also true that few, if any, of the critics have done more than point up shortcomings of existing classifications, and no new operationalizations capable of comparable empirical use have been developed. This is not to suggest that the criticisms are sterile. In some cases they have led to useful modifications and adjusted applications. In general, criticism of existing classifications has pointed up the truism that all research tools have their limitations, that these need to be recognized and that the evidence produced using them needs to be viewed from within those limitations.

This latter caution clearly applies to the contents of this book, where limitations arise from several sources. First, in looking at differences, precisely these are emphasized, and similarities are overlooked or played down. Social class differences are rarely, if ever, total, since while the majority of one class may differ from the majority of others in a certain respect, some of both may well be alike. In turn this raises the question of within-class rather than between-class differences: why are some different to others? In some instances, the first type of difference may be of the same order and interest as the second. It is useful, then, to review the data in this book along such lines, though the explanation of similarity between and differences within groups is not treated in any detail. It may well be that explanation of differences within groups is more complex than differences between groups.

Second, limitations arise because many of the data presented were collected for purposes other than displaying or exploring social class differences. The result of using available, mainly 'official' data is that some interesting areas are left unexplored and criticisms can easily be raised about the data's collection, classification and presentation. These may be seen to incorporate particular values and assumptions. Since we live in a clearly stratified society, we must expect that the identification of problems and the conduct of research into them, let alone attempts to resolve them, will display at least elements of classist, sexist, racist or other forms of cultural assumption and imperialism. Sometimes these may be blatant, but more frequently they are subtle and implicit.

Third, and perhaps most serious, is that many of the data can be seen as theoretically inadequate. As Halsey (1972) argued in another context:

> A recurring problem is one which arises particularly in interpreting data relevant to social policy and the provision of welfare services. This is the difficulty of gaining from the statistics any idea of quality or adequacy. Obviously any analysis of health or welfare services or of housing should include some statement about how far the standard or amount of service supplied meets the need for it. But for the most part the figures are concerned with supply; independent measures of need which would be required to judge adequacy are virtually nonexistent.

Similarly, the data in this book often lack any clear or consistent conceptual framework of equality and/or justice within which to judge and interpret them. At present they do not match Halsey's call for a measure of need in order to make an evaluation. Ideally, the answer to theoretically inadequate data is for research to be explicitly related to theory. As yet such research is piecemeal, though there are developments in some areas. In any case, it is by no means apparent that adequate theories for research have yet been developed. This does not mean that this book and its approach are atheoretical except in the formal sense. Social classes are seen as cultural products within a societal and historical setting. Consequently, differences between them are clearly related to societal organization and capable of almost infinite form and change. Basically, then, the position of any strata in our society is constrained by, or the result of, their assumed role within the social structure. The fundamental assumption is that differences between classes and strata are caused by and persist because of their differing access to almost all social resources, to power positions and to opportunities that, in general, are to the decided advantage of some and the decided disadvantage of others.

Finally, it needs to be appreciated that the variety of ideas about, and involvement with, social differences are interrelated. For example, everyone, or so it seems, has their own ideas and theories about social class. A consequence of the popularity of class in our life and literature, therefore, is the difficulty in presenting a comprehensive and satisfactory account. As Giddens (1973) observed, immediate controversy awaits anyone with the temerity to write in the field, through what they choose to include and exclude. This book is no exception, despite being devoted exclusively to the presentation of contemporary empirical material. Hence the rest of this chapter outlines the particular approach and the criteria used for the selection of the material presented.

About This Book

Criteria for inclusion and presentation

In achieving the central aim of this book within a single volume it has been necessary to limit its scope. The obvious, intentional omission is any direct consideration of sociological and other theory about social class. Not only are theories in this field dynamic and extensive, but also, as we have seen, their relevance to the empirical investigation of class differences has been limited and indirect.

The empirical data in this book are sometimes directly limited by the nature of available sources. It is surprising, for example, that some areas of social differences, which one would judge from their treatment in the literature and media to be well catered for, turn out to be otherwise. Similarly, even where information is collected and recorded on a social class basis, it is not always published in that manner. This is particularly true recently of research by government agencies. Conversely, in some areas it has been possible to choose from a number of similar sources. It is therefore necessary to spell out the criteria upon which data have been selected and used.

Only British data have been used The vagaries of research and publication do not allow the consistent use of data for Britain as properly defined. For example, official statistics are often published for the UK, Great Britain, England, Wales, England and Wales, Northern Ireland and Scotland, and are not always identical in content. As a rule of thumb, it may be assumed that wherever a choice was available the data and studies chosen are those which covered the largest part of Britain.

Wherever possible the most up-to-date and large-scale research figures obtainable have been used A selection has been made from available sources up to spring 1997, in order to present, as far as possible, a picture of contemporary British class differences, though the vagaries of social research mean that for some topics the most recent, relevant studies are from the 1980s and 1970s. This is not to deny the importance of the historical/developmental perspective in the study of social class but merely to assert that the use, or particularly the overuse, of dated material without access to the contemporary is misleading and confusing. In any case, historical treatments of many of the areas dealt with in this present volume exist elsewhere (for example, Halsey, 1972/1988; 1978/1981/1986/1995; Marsh, 1965; Routh, 1965; 1980; Sampson, 1982).

At the same time some attention has been paid to the continuity, or its lack, in the results of empirical research into aspects of class differences and to significant changes in its results.

Large-scale studies have been used, since a wider spread of samples and data probably better reflects social class differences in Britain as a whole. At the same time it is true that some of these studies suffer, in comparison with smaller-scale research, from superficiality, and disguise some illuminating trends and variations. Smaller-scale and/or greater-depth studies have been used where large-scale studies do not exist or where smaller studies, in the author's opinion, make a significant contribution to the aim of the book.

Data have been presented in a straightforward way but without oversimplification Data have been recast into standard-format tables, with social class always as the top axis. As a general rule figures and percentages have been rounded to the nearest whole number for the sake of clarity. When available, an average of the percentages or figures for the whole sample has been provided to allow comparison. In very few cases have the class categories used in a piece of research or a publication been collapsed. In particular the common combination of the classes into manual/non-manual or middle-class/working-class categories has been avoided. Not only does such a dichotomy oversimplify differences, but it typically disguises variations and trends between social classes.

The text has been designed to be a commentary on the data Apart from necessary introductory and linking passages, there is little exposition of the topics under consideration. This has been done because it is assumed that readers will have access to other appropriate descriptive and explanatory sources, or that their immediate interest centres, like that of this book, on the phenomenon of social class, rather than on the nature of its context and the processes involved.

Data have been organized around topics commonly found in textbooks and syllabuses This strategy was adopted to make for cogent chapters, and also to facilitate references to, and from, the type of sources referred to above. At the same time a system of cross-referencing (appendix B, the subject index and text) enables readers to make comparisons between different approaches and social institutions, together with social class differences.

Areas with few available data have not been ignored Since one aim of this book is to illustrate the state of knowledge regarding social class differences, comprehensive coverage has been an objective. To some extent this implies not only reviewing available data but also asking what ought to be or might be available. The author has pointed out the lack or paucity of data at places where he felt it necessary or where readers might have expected evidence to exist.

Ways of using this book

At one level this book is a collection of some of the existing empirical knowledge concerning social class in contemporary Britain. At another it is a textbook, though not a traditional one, since it is a sourcebook – which complements and supplements existing books, knowledge, courses and teaching. This section describes in general terms the layout of the book, and some of the uses to which it can be put.

The bulk of the book, chapters 2 to 9, consists of data on British class differences grouped around typical syllabus topics such as work, health, family, education, leisure. These are supported by a running commentary on the data. Each chapter constitutes a useful source of information on specific topics. Used with introductory texts in sociology and texts on particular topics, the chapters provide a basis on which the reader may evaluate the evidence and arguments used both here and elsewhere.

Appendix B contains all the operational classifications of social class used in the studies reported in the book. These are coded so that reference can be made to the definition involved wherever social class is used in tables. This avoids the misunderstandings which can arise from the simultaneous presentation of sets of social class differences based on different class classifications.

Chapter 10 provides a brief overview of aspects of class differences and, more importantly, places these within the contemporary context in which claims are made that Britain is or is about to be a classless society.

It should be borne in mind that one of the virtues of the book's format, major axis and emphasis is that it should encourage the reader to move outwards from an initial interest in a particular topic. It is hoped that the structure and content of the book will encourage this. This book should generate in the minds of readers some interesting connections or correlations between data in different areas. Readers should be aware both of the value of this – in some ways it is the essence of sociology – and also of its dangers, since correlations are not necessarily causations. Indeed, in this area they rarely are since class differences, on their own, generally have no explanatory power. To produce data to show social class differences in children's performances at school is merely to present a statement. To evaluate that statement, one has to ask certain questions such as, 'What does social class mean in this context?', 'What were the criteria of achievement?', and 'How and where was the evidence obtained?' While this book attempts to provide answers to such questions, it does not attempt to explain the reasons why such results should be obtained. It does not approach questions which seek to identify the actual factors, or to describe the processes involved. For these the readers must turn to other literature.

It is also necessary to point out that categorizing knowledge in any field is problematic. That chapters 2 to 9 give cogent accounts of class differences observed in particular scenarios may give an impression of separateness. This would be false, since differences feed into and out of the different topics and should be viewed as a single phenomenon. Hopefully, readers will appreciate these interrelationships, and the cross-referencing in text and index will assist the exploration and understanding of this important point.

Exploring differences

Since in a book about class differences these are emphasized, similarities can be overlooked. A valuable exercise is to review the data, looking for similarities between the social classes. These similarities, or what might be called 'non-data', lead one to speculate why such 'deviance' exists. Does it reflect the crudeness of the social class classification used – or are other factors, specific to the topic under consideration, responsible?

Since this book is a commentary on data about class differences, it presents material in a relatively objective way – that is, independently of the observer's attitudes, values and beliefs. Though this is how many sociologists and others try to approach social reality, it is, generally speaking, a somewhat unusual approach. The author has avoided, at least consciously, presenting data from any particular political or philosophical standpoint, preferring that the reader brings their own to the material, and perhaps develops it while in contact with the book. This is not in any way to subscribe to the common fallacy that facts speak for themselves. That they do not is witnessed by the endless debates and controversies aroused by almost all facts, but particularly social ones. For most people, their beliefs, feelings and ways of understanding are as important as the facts themselves. It is a valuable exercise, therefore, to attempt to appreciate the variety of ways in which the class differences outlined in this volume can be interpreted. The extremes of these interpretations are marked, on the one hand, by the view that the individual is completely responsible for their situation and, on the other, by complete economic and/or social determinism; and there are countless shades in between.

No mention is made in this book of the statistical significance of the social differences reported. Briefly, statistical significance is a mathematical concept used to decide whether a difference which has been observed is likely to have happened by chance – or, to put it the other way around, it is the degree of confidence one can have that the difference is a real one and would therefore be found again in further research. Social scientists are usually happy if a test shows that the likelihood of their results having occurred by chance is only one in a hundred, and reasonably content if it is as high as one in twenty. The lack of reference to statistical significance in this text is, of course, intentional. First, the large size of the samples used in most of the research reported means that quite small differences are in fact statistically significant (sample sizes are given as notes to the tables; census data are based on a 10 per cent sample of census returns). Second, statistical significance does not tell one much about the importance of an observed difference in real terms. Very small differences in voting behaviour which are not statistically significant can, and indeed often do, have vitally important outcomes, while much larger differences elsewhere, say in choice of washing powder, may be totally irrelevant except to washing powder manufacturers and sellers. It is, then, in 'common-sense' terms that the social differences in this book ought to be viewed and considered.

The differences presented in the chapters which follow vary considerably in size, but their importance stems not from that but from interpretation. For example, small differences between classes are capable of being viewed as insignificant or as examples of advantage and/or disadvantage. Readers will undoubtedly interpret differences according to their own predisposition, values and beliefs. At the same time it is again a valuable experience to bear in mind the range of interpretations that may be used by others while viewing the data which follow and to review them in that light.

Few people will read this book without in some way identifying with its contents. Looking at the data relevant to oneself, to one's family, acquaintances and experiences, is likely to provoke agreement, amazement, disagreement or amusement. One interesting exercise for readers is to compare their own reactions with those of others. Do one's friends or colleagues have concepts of social class, and what are they? Are they willing to identify themselves as being members of a social class? Do their opinions, habits and actions fit their social class ascriptions?

2

The Social Classes in Britain

The first section of this chapter provides a view of the distribution of the social classes in our society, related to other social strata – gender, age and ethnic group – and to industry and geographical area. As such it provides a context within which to review the data on social differences contained in the following chapters. The first section makes exclusive use of the Registrar General's (RG) scale of social class: for details of this and its relationship with other scales see appendix B. The second section of this chapter views how the public itself sees social class and relates these subjective views to those incorporated in objective classifications.

The Distribution of Social Class in Britain

National

The only data base capable of relating social class to the entire population of Great Britain is the census. Theoretically it would be possible to allocate each person enumerated in the 1991 census, some 54,889,000, to a class. More meaningful is to view that part of the population who have or have had an occupation, that is those aged 16 years or over who are either economically active, that is in paid work (*the working population*), or unemployed or economically inactive (retired, permanently sick, students and others) (*the non-working population*). While not all of these persons are allocated to a class (for exclusions see note to table 2.1), in this part of the population some 30.5 million persons were allocated to a social class, 16.4 million men and 14.1

Table 2.1 Distribution of the population by social class,* Great Britain, 1991 (percentages)

	Social class RG						
	I	II	IIIN	IIIM	IV	V	All
All	4	27	24	21	17	7	Each
Males	7	28	11	33	16	6	row
Females	2	26	39	8	18	8	=100%
As % of each class							
Males	82	55	25	83	51	45	54
Females	18	45	75	17	49	55	46

* Of residents, aged 16 and over; for employees and self-employed, based on occupation in week prior to census; for unemployed and economically inactive, based on most recent paid job in the 10 years prior to census: excluding members of the armed forces, those whose occupations were inadequately described or not stated and those who had had no paid job in 10 years prior to census.

Calculated from tables 14 and 15, 1991 Census, Economic Activity (10 per cent), Great Britain, 1994

million women. Hence table 2.1 presents the most accurate picture available of the national distribution of social class. As can be seen, overall the largest single social class is II, which represents some 27 per cent of the population, followed by IIIN and IIIM with 24 and 21 per cent. Overall, 55 per cent are classified as non-manual (classes I, II and IIIN) and 45 per cent as manual (classes IIIM, IV and V). Comparison with similar figures from the 1981 census reveals that the occupational and class structure of Britain has changed. In 1981, 48 per cent were classified as non-manual and 52 per cent as manual; the largest class was IIIM at 26 per cent, followed by classes II and IIIN, both at 22 per cent (*Economic Activity, 1981 Census*, table 16A).

Gender

The difference between the social class distributions of the sexes is very marked, and clearly related to the fact that men and women follow different types of occupation. In class I the proportion of males is some three and a half times the proportion of females (7 compared with 2 per cent), a situation reversed in the case of class IIIN, where the proportion of females is about three and a half times the proportion of males (39 compared with 11 per cent). Although a much higher proportion of women are classified as non-manual than men (67 compared with 46 per cent), the majority are to be found in IIIN, the routine, lower-skilled end of the range of occupations (including secretaries and shop

Table 2.2 Distribution of the working population by social class,* Great Britain, 1991 (percentages)

	Social class RG						
	I	II	IIIN	IIIM	IV	V	All
All	5	29	24	21	16	6	Each
Males	7	29	11	32	15	5	row
Females	2	28	39	7	16	7	=100%
As % of each class							
Males	83	56	27	85	53	44	56
Females	17	44	73	15	47	56	44

* Of residents, aged 16 and over, employees and self-employed, based on occupation in week prior to census; excluding members of the armed forces and those whose occupations were inadequately described or not stated.

Calculated from table 14, Census 1991, Economic Activity (10 per cent), Great Britain, 1994

assistants; for further examples see appendix B). This pattern is interestingly reversed in the manual classes. Here the proportion of men is larger than that of women (55 and 34 per cent), but men are more often to be found in IIIM, that is skilled occupations (33 per cent of men, 8 per cent of women) and somewhat less often in partly skilled occupations (IV: 16 compared with 18 per cent) and among the unskilled (V: 6 compared with 8).

A parallel view of the same data is provided in the lower part of table 2.1, the sex composition of each social class. Note that because of the way in which the population has been defined the overall representation of the sexes is 54 per cent men, 46 per cent women. This allows for comparison with each class, the split almost being reproduced in class II. Basically the figures underline the fact that classes I and IIIM are predominantly male (more than eight in every ten people in them are men) and that only class IIIN is predominantly female (some three-quarters of its members are women).

The class distribution of the working population in table 2.2 displays the patterns outlined above, albeit somewhat more markedly, reflecting the changing structure between those currently and those previously employed. The non-manual classes include 58, 47 and 69 per cent respectively of the working population, of males and of females; the manual classes, 43, 52 and 30 per cent. There are some clear differences in the class distribution for the non-working population contained in table 2.3. Here the overall non-manual/manual split is 35 and 65 per cent and the largest proportion is in class IIIM. This split and the class distribution are very similar for both the unemployed (dealt with in

Table 2.3 Distribution of the non-working population by social class,* Great Britain, 1991 (percentages)

	Social class RG						
	I	II	IIIN	IIIM	IV	V	All
Unemployed	2	16	17	29	24	12	Each
Permanently sick	2	17	14	31	25	12	row
Retired	4	27	22	21	18	9	=100%
Students and other inactive	2	17	40	10	23	9	
All non-working population	2	16	17	29	24	12	

* Of residents, aged 16 and over, on basis of most recent paid job held during 10 years prior to census; excluding those who had no such job, members of the armed forces and those whose occupations were inadequately described or not stated.

Calculated from table 15, 1991 Census, Economic Activity (10 per cent), Great Britain, 1994

more detail in chapter 5) and the permanently sick. The proportion of the retired in the non-manual classes at 53 per cent is much higher, and that in class I is twice the overall percentage. Students and other inactive persons show an even more markedly different distribution than the overall, with 59 per cent in the non-manual classes and 40 per cent in class IIIN, reflecting both their average age and class background (see chapter 7).

Age

Because the occupational structure of our society changes over time and entry into and out of some jobs is age related, it is fairly obvious that age and social class are interrelated. This can be illustrated by looking either at the class compositions of age groups, or at the age structures of the classes. The figures for the population are in table 2.4. The top part of that table should be read horizontally: each row shows the percentage of an age group in each social class. The percentage of each age group in class IIIM is broadly the same. That for class V increases over the age groups: compare 16–24 and 25–44 with 45–64 and 65 and over. Between the 16–24 and 25–44 groups there is a sharp rise in the percentages in classes I and II (2 to 5 and 14 to 30) and a similar decline in classes IIIN and IV (32 to 24 and 28 to 15). The lower part of the table should be read vertically: each column displays the percentage of a social class in each age group. The figures in the right-hand column show the overall percentage for each age group, allowing comparisons

Table 2.4 Percentage of population in each age group by social class and each social class by age group,* Great Britain, 1991

	Social class RG						
	I	II	IIIN	IIIM	IV	V	All
16–24	2	14	32	19	28	6	Each
25–44	5	30	24	20	15	5	group
45–64	4	28	21	22	17	9	=100%
65 and over	5	26	20	22	18	10	
All	4	26	24	21	18	7	
16–24	8	9	23	16	26	14	17
25–44	55	51	45	44	38	36	45
45–64	30	33	27	33	29	39	31
65 and over	8	7	6	8	7	10	7
All	Each class = 100%						

* Of residents, aged 16 and over; for employees and self-employed, based on occupation in week prior to census; for unemployed and economically inactive, based on most recent paid job in the 10 years prior to census: excluding members of the armed forces, those whose occupations were inadequately described or not stated and those who had no paid job in 10 years prior to census.

Calculated from tables 14 and 15, 1991 Census, Economic Activity (10 per cent), Great Britain, 1994

to be made across the classes. Hence, 16–24 year olds (17 per cent of the population) make up a larger proportion of classes IIIN and IV (23 and 26 per cent) and a lower one of classes I and II (8 and 9 per cent). These latter differences are reversed among those aged 25–44 (45 per cent of the population), who are 55 and 51 per cent of classes I and II but 38 and 36 per cent of classes IV and V respectively. Those aged between 45 and 64 (31 per cent of the population) are 'over-represented' in class V and slightly so in classes II and IIIM. The percentage of those aged 65 and over in classes I to IV is very similar to the proportion they are of the population, 7 per cent, only class V being higher at 10 per cent. The data in table 2.5 (which should be read in the same way as table 2.4) are for the working population only and, with the exception of those aged 65 and over, show broadly similar patterns to those outlined above.

Fairly obviously, then, an immediate conclusion is that the social classes have different age structures. Such differences are crucial when comparing classes in terms of a whole set of factors, but particularly when those factors themselves are related to age – such as sickness and death (see chapter 3). Explanation of these differences is not straightforward because a number of complex, interrelated factors are involved. A major factor is obviously changes in the country's occupational structure over time. Some occupations can be entered only after

Table 2.5 Percentage of working population in each age group by social class and each social class by age group,* Great Britain, 1991

	Social class RG						
	I	II	IIIN	IIIM	IV	V	All
16–24	3	17	35	22	19	5	Each
25–44	6	32	22	21	14	5	group
45–64	5	30	20	22	16	8	=100%
65 and over	6	30	20	14	16	13	
All	5	29	25	21	16	6	
16–24	8	10	24	17	20	14	17
25–44	60	56	48	49	46	41	50
45–64	30	33	27	33	33	42	32
65 and over	2	2	1	1	2	4	2
All	Each class = 100%						

* Of residents, aged 16 and over, employees and self-employed, based on occupation in week prior to census; excluding members of the armed forces and those whose occupations were inadequately described or not stated.

Calculated from tables 14 and 15, 1991 Census, Economic Activity (10 per cent), Great Britain, 1994

gaining qualifications, for example, professional jobs in class I, while others like those in class II (mainly managerial) are likely to be dependent on age and experience: hence the jump in the proportion in these classes between the age groups 16–24 and 25–44. At the same time all the differences will reflect changes in occupation during working careers, some of which involve movement between the classes (see intra-generational social mobility in chapter 5). Some of this movement will be 'upwards' as suggested above and be related to career and to changing job, education and training opportunities. Other will be 'downwards' and related to redundancy and/or ability to cope with, or get, jobs of a comparable type. A large proportion of women break their employment for, or have it affected by, family reasons. The timing and extent of such interruptions almost certainly vary according to social class: see, for example, chapter 6, which illustrates class variation in age at marriage, age of motherhood and size of family. This results in many women changing to, or returning to, work in differently classified jobs. The nature and extent of these factors would be revealed only by longitudinal studies of people's careers, while here only a cross-sectional picture is presented.

Table 2.6 Working population by gender, ethnic group and social class,* Great Britain, 1991 (percentages)

	Social class RG						
	I	II	IIIN	IIIM	IV	V	All
Males							
White	7	29	11	33	15	5	Each
Black Caribbean	3	17	11	40	22	8	group
Black African	14	25	18	19	17	8	=100%
Black Other	5	26	17	29	18	5	
Indian	13	30	14	23	17	3	
Pakistani	7	23	13	29	22	5	
Bangladeshi	5	11	18	30	31	5	
Chinese	17	21	20	32	8	2	
Other Asian	14	38	16	16	13	3	
Other	15	34	16	19	12	4	
Born in Ireland	8	26	8	33	16	9	
Females							
White	2	28	39	7	16	7	Each
Black Caribbean	1	33	33	7	18	8	group
Black African	4	32	29	7	17	12	=100%
Black Other	2	31	40	8	15	4	
Indian	5	24	35	6	27	3	
Pakistani	4	27	34	7	26	2	
Bangladeshi	5	21	32	9	30	3	
Chinese	8	30	31	13	13	5	
Other Asian	5	31	33	8	16	7	
Other	5	35	37	6	13	4	
Born in Ireland	3	35	27	7	18	11	

* Of residents, aged 16 and over, employees and self-employed, based on occupation in week prior to census; excluding members of the armed forces and those whose occupations were inadequately described or not stated.

Calculated from table 16, 1991 Census, Ethnic Group and Country of Birth (10 per cent), Great Britain, 1993

Ethnic group

There are problems surrounding the definition and operationalization of ethnic groups, and these impose limitations to identifying their social class location and distribution. These need not entertain us much here to the extent that the data in table 2.6 are from the 1991 census, the first one to contain a question on ethnic group membership. This question asked respondents to tick the appropriate answer from the categories listed in the first ten rows on table 2.6 (White to Other). It is worth noting that these choices exclude some ethnic groups, for example Jews;

contain catch-all categories, for example White, Black Other, Other Asian; and imply a homogeneity that is questionable, for example that a range of differences in White, or differences of religion among Indians, are not of significance. A separate question asked respondents to indicate their country of birth, and those who recorded 'Irish Republic' or wrote simply 'Ireland' in the 'elsewhere' box were included as a category along with the other ethnic groups.

Since the data for White in table 2.6 are almost identical to those for the working population of Great Britain they provide the basis for comparison with other groups. As will be seen the variation is considerable. In the case of males, Black Caribbean and Bangladeshi stand out as having a much larger proportion in the manual classes (70 and 66 per cent) than White (53 per cent) and this is true to a lesser extent for those born in Ireland (58 per cent). On the other hand Black African, Indian, Chinese, Other Asian and Other have considerably larger percentages in the non-manual classes (57, 57, 58, 68 and 65 per cent) than White (47 per cent). These groups display marked differences in the percentage of professional workers (class I), it being twice or more than that for White; the percentage ranges from 17 for Chinese to 3 for Black Caribbean. A similar range is true at the other extreme around the White 5 per cent in class V, from a low of 2 for Chinese to highs of 9 for those Born in Ireland and 8 for Black Caribbean and Black African. The pattern of differences in respect to the non-manual/manual divide among women is rather similar to that of men, though less marked. However, the range in the proportion of those in class I around the White 2 per cent is greater, from 1 per cent Black Caribbean to 8 per cent for Chinese. The range in class V runs from 2 per cent for Pakistani to 11 and 12 per cent for those Born in Ireland and Black African, compared with White at 7 per cent. While earlier data are not directly comparable they suggest that there has been some convergence of the social class profiles of ethnic groups towards the overall since the 1970s (*Country of Birth, 1971 Census*; Lomas and Monck, 1977; Brown, 1984a; 1984b; all reviewed in Reid, 1989a).

Industry

The economic activities of a society can be seen as centred around particular production processes, trades or services, normally referred to as industries. Clearly those industries which are concerned with production as distinct from the provision of a service will differ from each other in structure and in the nature of the occupations involved. Since social class is based on occupation, industries will have different proportions of each class within them. As can be seen from the class profiles of the ten industry divisions listed in table 2.7, some industries are predominantly

Table 2.7 Social class profiles* of industry divisions, Great Britain, 1991 (percentages)

	Social class RG						
	I	II	IIIN	IIIM	IV	V	All
Agriculture, forestry and fishing	5	29	24	21	16	6	Each row =100%
Energy and water supply industries	0.4	46	3	4	45	1	
Extraction of minerals and ores, manufacture of metals/mineral products/chemicals	6	21	14	31	24	5	
Metal goods, engineering and vehicles industries	7	20	12	33	25	3	
Other manufacturing industries	1	18	12	40	24	4	
Construction	3	13	8	57	11	9	
Distribution, hotels and catering, repairs	1	28	36	16	14	5	
Transport and communication	2	17	16	43	16	5	
Banking, finance, insurance, business services and leasing	13	33	44	4	4	2	
Other services	6	41	22	7	14	9	
All divisions	5	29	24	21	16	6	

* Of residents, aged 16 and over, employees and self-employed, based on occupation in week prior to census; excluding members of the armed forces and those whose occupations were inadequately described or not stated.

Calculated from table 16, 1991 Census, Economic Activity (10 per cent), Great Britain, 1994

non-manual, others manual. In banking, finance, insurance, etc. 90 per cent of employees are in classes I, II and IIIN, while distribution, hotels and catering at 65 per cent and other services at 69 per cent are also well above the overall percentage of 58. In contrast 77 per cent of those employed in construction are in the manual classes, while extraction, other manufacturing, metal goods and engineering, and transport and communication industries have percentages of 60 or over, compared with the overall of 43. The table shows other interesting differences between industries with similar non-manual/manual profiles. For

Table 2.8 Social class profile of the working population* in each region of Great Britain, 1991 (percentages)

	Social class RG						% of
	I	II	IIIN	IIIM	IV	V	population
Scotland	5	27	23	22	16	7	9
Wales	4	28	22	22	17	7	5
North	4	25	23	24	17	8	5
Yorkshire and Humberside	4	27	22	23	18	7	9
North West	5	27	24	22	17	6	11
East Midlands	4	27	21	24	18	6	8
West Midlands	4	26	22	24	18	6	10
East Anglia	5	28	22	22	17	6	4
South East	6	33	26	18	13	5	33
South West	5	30	24	21	16	6	8
Great Britain/ England	5	29	24	21	16	6	100%

* Of residents, aged 16 and over, employees and self-employed, based on occupation in week prior to census; excluding members of the armed forces and those whose occupations were inadequately described or not stated.

Calculated from table 93, 1991 Census, Report for Great Britain, 1993

example, the percentage of class I in banking, finance, insurance, etc. is 13, while it is but 1 per cent in distribution, hotels and catering and 0.4 per cent in energy and water supply. Comparing the manual classes' distribution in construction with that in metal goods, engineering and vehicles industries reveals that in the first some three-quarters of those in manual occupations are skilled (IIIM) and 12 per cent unskilled (V) while in the second the proportions are just over a half and 5 per cent.

Geographical

The Registrar General divides Great Britain into ten regions, listed in table 2.8. These regions are not equal in size, or in terms of the proportion of the population of Great Britain living in them. In order to facilitate comparison between the regions, each row of the table gives the percentages of the working population from each social class within each region and the right-hand column the overall percentage.

As will be seen, the largest region in terms of population, the South East (which includes London), has the most distinctively different distribution of social classes. It had the highest percentage in each of the non-manual classes and the lowest in each of the manual classes. Overall it had 7 per cent more non-manual and 7 per cent fewer manual

Table 2.9 Percentage of the male working population in each social class* by region of Great Britain, 1991

	Social class RG						% of
	I	II	IIIN	IIIM	IV	V	population
Scotland	8.5	7.8	8.4	9.1	9.7	10.0	8.7
Wales	3.8	4.4	4.3	4.9	5.1	5.6	4.7
North	4.2	4.2	4.7	5.8	5.7	5.7	5.1
Yorkshire and Humberside	6.8	7.8	8.0	9.5	9.2	9.5	8.6
North West	10.0	10.0	11.0	11.3	11.2	11.2	10.8
East Midlands	6.6	7.1	6.5	8.3	8.1	7.3	7.5
West Midlands	8.3	8.7	8.5	10.7	10.7	8.9	9.6
East Anglia	3.8	3.8	3.5	3.9	4.2	3.8	3.9
South East	39.8	37.5	36.9	28.2	27.6	29.9	32.8
South West	8.3	8.7	8.2	8.3	8.6	8.0	8.4
	Each column = 100%						

* Of residents, aged 16 and over, employees and self-employed, based on occupation in week prior to census; excluding members of the armed forces and those whose occupations were inadequately described or not stated.

Calculated from table 17, 1991 Census, Economic Activity (10 per cent), Great Britain 1994

workers than the averages for Great Britain of 58 and 43 per cent respectively. A similar, though less marked, pattern applies to the South West. Conversely, the North region had a comparatively high percentage of manually occupied males (49 per cent, or 6 per cent higher than the average), and a correspondingly lower percentage of non-manual. There are also interesting differences between the countries involved. While England has the same class profile as Great Britain, Scotland and Wales are somewhat different, having non-manual/manual splits of 55/45.

Another detailed view of the regional distribution of the social classes in Great Britain is given in table 2.9, this time of the male working population. Here, the numbers in each social class in a region are expressed as a percentage of the total for each social class in Great Britain. For example, 8.5 per cent of all the male working population in social class I in Great Britain were in Scotland in 1991. The first column in the table discloses that the regional percentages of economically active social class I males range from almost 40 per cent in the South East to 3.8 per cent in East Anglia. The right-hand column of the table shows the percentage each region contains of the male working population of Great Britain. Approaching a third (32.8 per cent) of such males reside in the South East, and the figures range down to 3.9 per cent in East Anglia. If each social class was equally distributed throughout the regions, then the figures in the separate social class columns would correspond with the figure in the appropriate right-hand column. For example, one might expect to find about a third of the economically active males in each social class in the South East, since that proportion of all the male working population lives there. In fact there is considerable variation. In the South East region the percentages in the non-manual classes (I, II and IIIN) are consistently higher than the population and those for the manual classes are all lower. The opposite is true of Scotland, where the percentages for non-manual classes are all lower and those for manual all higher. Other regions display more complex patterns, as can be seen from the table.

Larger and more contrasting class composition differences are to be found in smaller geographical areas. Small Area Statistics, as they are referred to, for some census variables are published by county (*Ward and Civil Parish Monitor(s)*). Full census results for these areas are available on request and payment to the ONS. The smallest area for which they are available is the enumerator district (literally the area in which a single person collects the census forms), comprising around 250 houses. Data are also available for postcode sectors and at parish and electoral ward levels. Use is made of such data by local authorities and they feature in research which treats class on an areal rather than an individual level (for examples see chapters 3 and 7). As would be expected by anyone familiar with a town or city, the wards within them typically contain social class composition variations. While representatives of all classes are likely to be found in all wards, some can be characterized as middle or working class, others as more mixed. There is then an element of class residential segregation. For example, an analysis of the Bradford Metropolitan District (Reid, 1989a, figure 3.2) found that the twenty-three wards ranged in the percentage of economically active males in classes (RG) I and II from 8 to 55 and in IV and V from 13 to 54. In the north-east were five wards with 32 per cent or over of classes I and II and between 13 and 19 per cent of classes IV and V. In the centre to south-west were six wards with 37 per cent or more of classes I and II and between 8 and 13 per cent of classes IV and V.

How the Public Sees Social Class

Recognition and identification

There is ample evidence over the past four decades that, in answer to straightforward questions as to whether there are social classes in Britain and what class they would see themselves as a member of, over 90 per cent of the public will answer 'yes' and place themselves in a class. In the following selection of studies, the figure that follows each is

Table 2.10 Own and parental self-assigned social class* (percentages)

	Upper middle	Middle	Upper working	Working	Poor	Don't know
1983						
Own class	1	24	23	46	3	3
Parents' class	2	16	12	58	9	2
1991						
Own class	2	27	18	46	4	2
Parents' class	3	19	11	59	7	1

* Respondents were shown a card with the above titles and asked, 'Which would you say you belong to?' and 'Which did your parents belong to when you started primary school?'
N = 2918

Devised from table on p. 177, Young, 1992

the percentage that identified themselves as a member of a social class: Martin (1954), 96; Runciman (1964), 99; Rosser and Harris (1965), 93; Kahan et al. (1966), 96; NOP (1972), 91; Roberts et al. (1977), 96; Reid (1978), 97; Townsend (1979), 94; Airey (1984), 96; Abbott and Sapsford (1987), 93; Marshall et al. (1988), 92; Young (1992), 98; MORI (unpublished data 1996), 93. While the actual questions and samples involved in these studies varied, a reasonable conclusion is that the term 'social class' has a good deal of currency among the population at large and that they are prepared to use it of themselves. Such responses have continuity over time and appear little affected by social and political change. The British Social Attitudes survey has included a self-assignment question on social class every year between 1983 and 1991. In each year some 98 per cent of respondents have answered – around two-thirds classifying themselves as upper working or working class, and the rest, around a quarter, as middle class (see table 2.10). As can be seen, a similar proportion identified the social class of their parents when they themselves started school, giving an indication of perceived social mobility (see chapter 5). In 1983 the percentage seeing both themselves and their parents as working class was almost the same; in 1991 there was a difference of 6 per cent. Analysis reveals that some 82 per cent did not think they had crossed the boundary between working and middle classes; about one in ten believed that they had moved from working to middle class and 4 per cent that they had moved in the opposite direction. Young (1992) argues that a sense of class in Britain resembles an inherited characteristic and that the majority of respondents (58 per cent) profess feeling very or fairly close to other people of the same class background.

A further question asked the extent to which a person's class affects their opportunities in Britain today. Responses show some variation year on year, with between two-thirds and three-quarters claiming 'a great deal' or 'quite a lot'; the highest perception of class disadvantage were in 1991, with but 3 per cent claiming 'not at all' and 21 per cent 'not very much'. As Young comments: 'Despite great changes in the patterns of work and the continuing contraction of manual employment, the expectation that class divisions would thereby be eroded has yet to be fulfilled.'

Townsend (1979) reports that his respondents' replies to open-ended questions were mostly similarly worded and could be grouped without difficulty. Few used terms other than 'middle class' (42 per cent including 'upper middle' and 'lower middle') or 'working class' (48 per cent including 'upper working'); only four people claimed to be upper class, while 4 per cent, at least initially, rejected the idea of class and 1.5 per cent had no, or only a hazy, concept of it. (Other studies, for example Butler and Stokes (1969), found that, after prompting, nearly all respondents would use these terms; their 'refusers' were only 1 per cent.) Some of the studies listed above have also invited their subjects to respond to further questions aimed at gaining finer definitions of social class. Kahan et al. (1966), for example, asked their subjects whether they belonged to the upper or lower parts of the class they had chosen. Few chose to modify their identification; of those who 'were' middle class, 4 per cent changed – equally in both directions – while of the 67 per cent who said they were working class, 9 per cent modified this to upper and 4 per cent to lower. Townsend (1979) presented his sample with a list of class names, but three-fifths opted not to change and a further fifth merely to be more specific within their original choice. However, a smaller group changed fairly dramatically: 6 per cent from middle to working (half to upper working), and 2 per cent from working to middle. The first group of 'changers' tended to have lower incomes than those maintaining the middle-class choice and were similar in several other respects to those who originally chose working class. Those changing from working to middle class had two features distinguishing them from those who 'stayed' working class: a larger percentage had had eleven years or more education and owned their own homes.

Subjective and objective class

Of obvious interest is the extent to which the subjective social class (that which respondents gave themselves) related to researchers' objective scales based on occupation. A number of studies in viewing this relationship have found a high correspondence at the extremes, with around four-fifths of those in the variously defined 'highest' class seeing themselves as middle class and a similar proportion of the 'lowest' two classes seeing themselves as working class (Butler and Stokes, 1974; Roberts et al., 1977; Townsend, 1979; Abbott and Sapsford, 1987; Marshall et al., 1988). However, in each case sizeable minorities of respondents were at variance with the objective classifications, this being particularly pronounced in the intermediary classes (those in the middle of the scales). The changeover from a clear majority self-rating middle class to one self-rating working class generally occurred around the manual/non-manual divide in the objective scales, though in two studies a bare majority of the lower/routine non-manual classes rated themselves working class. Roberts et al. (1977) argue that non-conformers perhaps enhance the value of the manual/non-manual divide, since they deviate not only in self-rating, but also from their objective class in other ways. In their study there were differences in terms of political affiliation, trade union membership and so on. Butler and Stokes (1974) demonstrated that income was related to self-rating, especially among the working classes, those with higher incomes being more likely to choose the middle class. In all cases, a substantial majority of those in manual classes rated themselves working class, and similarly those in non-manual classes, especially the 'higher', saw themselves as middle class. It can therefore be argued that the public's use of the terms 'middle' and 'working' has a fairly strong relationship with social scientists' non-manual and manual classes.

Similarly patterned conceptions of social class have been found among young people aged between 15 and 21, suggesting that social class recognition occurs at an early age in Britain and, since most were classed according to their parents' or head of household's occupation, (for definition see appendix C), that class recognition is produced through association as well as by involvement (NOP, 1978). Abbott and Sapsford (1987) found on the basis of the non-manual/manual divide that female self-ratings were very similar in respect to objective class whether this was based on the occupation of the head of household or on their own, and that both matched male self-ratings well. In each case over three-quarters of those classed as 'middle' and about 70 per cent of those classed as 'working' rated themselves the same.

The criteria of class

The existence of some divergence between people's occupational level and their idea of which class they belong to can be taken to suggest that factors as well as, or other than, occupation count when people are classing themselves. Again a number of inquiries have been made into the criteria or bases used in the public's definition of social class. Kahan et al. (1966) asked their sample to describe the sort of people they regarded as belonging to the middle and to the working class. From the replies they identified the implicit frames of reference used. The major factor was occupation. A majority of respondents (61 per cent) chose this as the criterion for describing the middle class, and a larger one (74 per cent) chose it to describe the working class. These findings are very close to those of Martin (1954) a decade before this study, where about three-quarters of the subjects viewed the working class in terms of occupation. However, as the authors remark, occupation cannot be seen as the sole basis of perceived social class. Other factors such as income and education (which are obviously, but not exactly, related: see chapters 4 and 7), social graces and parentage were present. These factors were further emphasized by the respondents when they were asked what they saw as being important in relation to social mobility (that is, the movement of people between the social classes: see chapter 5). It would appear, however, that occupation was seen as the primary basis for social class judgements.

Much the same general picture emerges from the two studies whose data are in table 2.11, but with differing emphases due to different methodology. In the first, respondents were given a choice of class criteria, and their replies were categorized by the main one they used in replying (upper part of table 2.11). As can be seen the major overall factor was 'way of life' followed in almost equal proportions by 'family', 'job' and 'money'. There are gender differences, men having 'job' and women 'family' in second place to 'way of life'. Of course this last term has a very broad meaning, and probably, in people's minds, includes economic factors which, in turn, are likely to be related to occupation. Townsend (1979) argued that the fact that almost half the adults in his survey chose 'way of life' or 'family' as the criterion 'testifies to the public consciousness of what are the underlying and long-term or life-long determinants'.

This seems to tie up with Marshall et al.'s (1988) question, 'How is it that people come to belong to the class that they do?', to which three-quarters of the respondents said that it was birth: the authors concluded that class is commonly taken to be an ascribed rather than an achieved characteristic. Marshall et al. also explored aspects of their respondents' social identity and class awareness, and concluded that 'class is by far the most common and seemingly the most salient frame of reference employed in the construction of social identities'. Almost three-quarters of the respondents felt that class was an inevitable feature of society, and half that there were important issues causing conflict between the classes; the same proportion endorsed the view of gross class inequalities. When asked to suggest other groups that they identified with, 79 per cent could not think of any other.

Respondents in the Marshall et al. study were asked what sort of people they thought of in respect to upper, middle and working class

Table 2.11 Rank order of social class criteria in two studies

Based on answers to question 'What decides what class you are in? Is it mainly job, education, the family you are born into, your way of life, money or anything else?'
Rank order based on principal factor identified from those mentioned in the question.
Figures in brackets are the percentages of respondents using the factor.

Men		Women		Men and women	
Way of life	(29)	Way of life	(33)	Way of life	(31)
Job	(22)	Family	(21)	Family	(18)
Money	(17)	Money	(16)	Job	(17)
Family	(15)	Job	(12)	Money	(17)
Education	(10)	Education	(11)	Education	(10)

N = 3224

Devised from table 10.2, Townsend, 1979

Based on answers to question 'When you hear someone described as "upper", "middle", "working class", what sort of people do you think of?'
Responses generically categorized.
Figures in brackets are percentages of respondents using the category.

Upper class		Middle class		Working class	
Status*	(65)	Occupation	(74)	Occupation	(70)
Income	(43)	Status*	(45)	Market**	(35)
Occupation	(36)	Income	(25)	Status*	(32)
Market**	(27)	Market**	(22)	Income	(21)
Education	(13)	Education	(5)	Education	(3)
Political†	(8)	Political†	(1)	Political†	(0.4)

* Class as status, e.g. particular life-style, the aristocracy, home owners.
** Class as a relationship with system of production, e.g. owners of land, self-employed.
† Class as a political phenomenon, e.g. those voting for a given party.
N = 1170

Devised from table 6.3, Marshall et al., 1988

and their replies were placed in one of six categories (see lower part of table 2.11). Occupation was by far the most commonly used criterion for both the middle and working classes, with status and income preceding it for the upper class. Income and 'market' (relationship with the system of production) also feature, but education (as in Townsend's study) was little used and hardly any saw class as 'political'. As the figures suggest, most respondents used more than one item to describe the classes, an indication that class was seen as multi-faceted and complex. Abbott and Sapsford (1987) used a similar question – 'What sort of person do you mean when you talk about the middle/working class?' – and subsequently categorized the answers. For the middle class, 'style of life/attitude' was most frequently used, followed by 'income/standard of life' and 'occupation'; for the working class the order of the first two was reversed (and between them was 'all who work'). The three meaningful factors could be interpreted either as separate and different or as related aspects of occupation/economic situation.

Opinion polls have also explored this area. When respondents in a 1991 survey were shown a list of things people use to decide which social class a person belongs to, the overall most popular choices were the same in respect to both the middle and the working class, though the rank order was different. For the middle class the rank order was amount of education, the neighbourhood they live in, the job they do, and how much money they earn; for the working class it was the job they do, the neighbourhood they live in, how much money they earn, and amount of education. The survey also indicated that Britain is seen as a class society and that people are happy with their own class. When presented with a list of statements the majority (percentages in brackets) agreed strongly or tended to agree with the following: this country has too many barriers based on social class (76), you are more likely to get to the top in this country if you have been to a private school (69), if you want to get ahead it is important to talk with the right accent (59), there will never be a classless society in Britain (80). They disagreed that it was easy for people to move up from one class to another (56) and that they would be happier if they belonged to another class (80). The results of the survey also suggested that the public hold class stereotypes about a number of activities (from unpublished data supplied by MORI from a survey completed August 1991). In 1996 more than three-quarters of respondents disagreed that Britain was a classless society, with a larger percentage (84) of the middle than the working class (69) so doing. Over two-thirds of both did not see Britain's class system as healthy for the country, and overall 45 per cent thought the country more divided by class then than in 1979 – middle class 39 and working class 50. Just over half of the middle and working classes thought that if elected the Conservatives were more likely to make the class divide wider compared with one in five who thought that Labour would (unpublished data supplied by MORI from a survey conducted October 1996).

From all the studies mentioned and others in the field, it is reasonable to conclude that the public sees social class as an amalgam of factors, importantly including but not necessarily predominated by occupation. This is not, of course, contradictory to the way in which class is viewed by social scientists who classify classes on the single criterion of occupation (see also pp. 6–13, 43–4 and appendix B).

A question of questions

A good deal of debate about the sort of research described above, particularly about its meaning and reliability, is evident in the literature. This amounts almost to a suggestion that 'You asks your question, and you gets your answer' – in other words, that the question is the vital factor, different questions producing different responses. Webb (1973) contrasts the answers to two distinct questions: a straightforward request for a self-rating of social class, where middle-class respondents had a stronger class identification than working-class ones; and 'What type of person are you thinking of when you talk about people like yourself?' ('free self-alignment'), where working-class respondents were more likely to reply in terms of social class. In his conclusion, Webb restates a point basic to the whole enterprise of social science research: if (social) class is a meaningful term in their (the respondents') normal day-to-day existence – which the interview best taps – it is perhaps advisable to let the respondents themselves select the term rather than to have it thrust upon them.

It is possible to explore people's ideas and use of social class quite indirectly. For example, the author has interviewed teachers, asking them to talk about the pupils or students they teach, their objectives in teaching, the differences between the family they grew up in and the one they now belong to, and the people with whom they spend their spare time (Reid, 1980b). When tape recordings of the interviews were analysed, both direct and indirect references to social class or social class imagery were discerned. Obviously, though, this type of research, apart from being time-consuming, relies heavily on the understanding and interpretation of the researcher; different researchers might draw different conclusions about the same data. My impression was that the teachers had spontaneously used a general awareness of social group if not social class differences, with respect to both their professional and their personal lives. The extent of this awareness appeared related to their biography and professional experience, awareness being highest among those who had experienced contrasts. Professional experience appeared to colour their view and understanding in that many saw education, ability and interests as important elements in social differences. In response to a final, direct question, the general picture to emerge was of three social classes: a very large middle class (with which they identified themselves); a very small upper class, based on real money and power; and a lower class, based on poverty and ignorance.

Platt (1971), in reviewing some of the 'affluent worker' study material in this field, makes a parallel, if somewhat different, set of points. The research attempted to gain a view of respondents' 'image of class' with a number of open-ended questions, from which were identified three basic images:

1 a 'power' model, with two classes, based on power and authority
2 a 'prestige' model, with three or more classes, based on life-style, social background or acceptance
3 A 'money' model, with one large central class, and one or more small ones, based on wealth, income and consumption.

The 'money' model was found to predominate: 54 per cent subscribed to it, 4 per cent to model 1, and 8 per cent to model 2; the remaining 34 per cent used 'other' models – which is itself perhaps remarkable. Respondents were also asked to rank six occupations, presented together with their incomes on a card, in order of their 'standing in the community'. Their ranking was compared with an orthodox status order (i.e. objective ranking) and revealed considerable unorthodoxy. Moreover, in stark comparison with the findings above, in this second context 61 per cent of the affluent manual workers used a 'prestige' model and only 2 per cent a pure 'money' model. Platt suggests a number of alternative explanations for this incongruence:

1 Respondents distinguished between 'social class' and 'standing in the community'
2 Their responses were differently coded (analysed) by the researchers
3 The social range of the occupations presented was very narrow, and because of this respondents used criteria other than money in discriminating between them
4 Since the 'class' questions were general, and the 'standing in the community' question was specific, the respondents used different frames of reference in answering them
5 The financial information (income) given in the second question directed the respondents' attention away from money.

Clearly one has to agree with the author that 'questions which are intended to refer to the same general area of a subject-matter may in fact vary and consequently create difficulties of interpretation. In particular caution is necessary in comparing findings from questions of different kinds, and in generalizing from them.'

Townsend (1979) identified two models within his sample's images of class:

1 a status model in which the population is arranged in at least three ranks – upper, middle and lower class, or more finely defined with subdivisions
2 a power model in which there are two ranks – working class, and an employer, rich or prosperous class.

He argued that the two logically distinct models are crudely combined in public and scientific discussion and that the terms 'middle' and 'working' class are inconsistent. He suggests that people who ascribe themselves to the middle class are implying that there are three classes, and that they have advantage over one without superiority over the other. Those aligning themselves with the working class are resisting the acknowledgment of disadvantage of inferiority by using a term which carries the implication that other classes are non-working or non-productive and therefore inferior. He concludes that the illogical combination of terms from the two models produces a subjective distortion of reality in that very few people unreservedly believe they belong to the uppermost or lowest class in society.

Britten (1984) suggests that the sexes differ in their models of class. She found that working-class men saw two classes and themselves in the lower; middle-class men saw three classes and themselves in the middle. Women, irrespective of class, saw three classes and themselves in the middle. Abbott and Sapsford (1987) tentatively suggest that the majority of women in their study 'see society more in terms of a continuous hierarchy than in terms of bounded classes'. What is clear is that women's views on social class have in the past been either neglected or investigated in the same way as men's. This has been and is being questioned, as has the applicability of existing social class classifications (see for example Arber et al., 1986). Indeed, more fundamental issues have been raised concerning the extent to which a woman's class position is determined by that of her husband/partner, whether class or sex is the more important axis of social differentiation, and even whether gender can be seen as class. According to Goldthorpe (1983), married women's class is appropriately determined by husband's occupation, both because of the women's different involvement in the labour market and because their disadvantage in most areas of social life makes them dependent. Others claim women have dual class, as housewife and as paid worker (Walby, 1986), or that women can and should be separately classified (Stanworth, 1984). What does seem pretty obvious is that class and gender qualify one another: relationships between the sexes are different in the different classes, and being male or female in any class is also different. The debates on these topics are unresolved and on-going and as yet have not directly affected the type of research reported in this book.

There have been some developments in the operationalization of social class, which while they do not feature in the research reported in this book nevertheless are of interest. These are attempts to produce women's social class classifications, in response to the perceived shortcomings of classing households solely by their heads (typically male) and classing women on the basis of classes developed in respect of men's paid employment. The latter both ignores unpaid work and fails to discriminate accurately women's occupations and part-time employment. Some scales combine the class of spouses/domestic partners using existing classifications (for example Heath and Britten, 1984; Pahl and Wallace, 1985), as did that used in the NSHD (see chapter 6), or include some aspects other than occupation (Osborn and Morris, 1979). Others have constructed separate classifications for women, which cover in more detail women's occupations and both full-time and part-time work (for example Murgatroyd, 1982; Dale et al., 1985; Roberts, 1987). The problem of female social class and the inadequacies of existing scales in describing and explaining inequalities between women are fully explored in Carr-Hill and Pritchard (1992). They do not however offer a new scale.

The ranking of occupations

A second type of evidence on the existence of social class in the subjective sense arises from the interest of researchers in whether their social class definitions, based on occupation, have any commonly accepted basis. The most famous British study was that connected with the development of the Hall–Jones scale. Respondents were asked, 'We should like to know in what order as to their social standing you would grade the occupations in the list given to you' (Hall and Jones, 1950; details of the scale are in appendix B). The question was basically that which Stevenson claimed to have answered, but presumably without the fieldwork, with reference to the Registrar General's social classification of 1921 (Stevenson, 1928). The list contained thirty occupations and the respondents apparently had no difficulty in ranking them according to the criterion supplied. A close correspondence between the standard (objective) classification of the authors and the undirected (subjective) judgement of the sample was found. Hall and Jones concluded that there were no major differences of opinion among those tested, and that the consensus was greater than they had expected.

A somewhat similar, though more sophisticated, approach was adopted by the Oxford Social Mobility Project. Part of this study was concerned with the construction of a grading scale for all male occupations on the basis of popular assessment (see Goldthorpe and Hope, 1974). In the initial inquiry respondents were asked to rank a list of forty occupations according to four criteria: standard of living, power and influence over other people, level of qualifications and value to society. Once again the people involved had little difficulty, in general, in performing the task. The main findings were as follows. The four criteria were not treated as the same by respondents and the distinctions made between them were shared to an extent by all. The degree of agreement in ranking on the basis of the four criteria was very high indeed. Separate analysis of ranking by the sexes, three age groups and four occupational categories confirmed overall agreement with some minor differences. In repeating the exercise after two or three months, respondents displayed stability in their ranking. In the light of these findings the conventional criterion of 'social standing' was seen as the most useful. Hence, in the main study respondents were asked to rank representative occupational titles according to their social standing. From these rankings was produced the Hope–Goldthorpe scale, further details of which are in appendix B.

Such evidence suggests that the public can and will rank occupations with a fair degree of ease and similarity. This facility is not limited to British samples, being evident in other Western societies; there is also a similarity in rankings by people in different societies (see for example a review of studies in twenty-four countries: Hodge et al., 1966; Trieman, 1977). However, nearly all these researches have involved 'non-conforming' respondents whose ranking has been at variance with the majority's. In the past there has been a tendency to dismiss such divergent views as being idiosyncratic, rather than socially or sociologically important. One might expect such differing views of the overall structure to arise from the fact that the respondents were occupying different positions in that structure. However, some studies have revealed these differences within the same occupational level.

Some research has explored how different concepts of the occupational structure differ in socially significant ways. For example, Coxon and Jones (1974), reporting on a preliminary analysis of just such a study, suggest that 'it seems ... that people with similar occupational histories, rather than current occupational membership, make rather similar judgements'. Coxon and Jones have also questioned the meaning of the ranking of occupations. The fact that the public agree in evaluating occupations does not, they suggest, allow one to assume that people share the same perception (view) of, or cognition of (way of thinking about), the occupations involved. Or, as they illustrate:

> In discussing 'images of society' there is a danger of jumping from the fact that people talk about society in a particular way (say as a polarized dichotomy) to inferring that they *perceive* it that way. But this is by no means inconsistent with the hypothesis that such people *are just* as aware of social differentiations and gradations, and can equally make as fine discriminations around those positions, as a person who tends to talk in terms of graded hierarchies.

Coxon and Jones (1978), influenced by cognitive psychology, have criticized the sociological use of occupational images and the ranking of occupations on the criterion of their general desirability. They contend that these are based on unwarranted assumptions and oversimplifications, and have argued that what is necessary is a thorough examination of the cognition involved in ranking and a full exploration of the social meaning of occupations; this they have undertaken (Coxon and Jones, 1979; Coxon et al., 1986; for a similar exploration see Davis, 1979). This type of research certainly reveals some of the thinking and values implicit in people's ranking of occupations and their use and concept of social class. Quite how this knowledge, with its depth and subtlety – long recognized by many social scientists – might be incorporated into an instrument for research on any scale has yet to be displayed.

Some conclusions about the public's view of class

This review together with chapter 1 has pointed to the complexity of the idea of social class. It has also outlined a variety of approaches to its understanding. Several general conclusions can be drawn. It cannot be, nor has it been, claimed that, simply because the public, when invited, is willing to recognize and identify with social class, therefore class is a fundamental and meaningful factor in their everyday life. To make such a claim empirically would require extensive observation of behaviour and exploration of language and thought. This clearly lies outside the scope of empirical research on any large scale and presents severe methodological problems in collection, classification and presentation. In any case it is very far from clear how such knowledge (some of which exists now) could be operationalized into a social class classification capable of being used for survey purposes.

It is hardly surprising that deeper or indirect questions elicit increasingly complex or even conflicting shades of recognition and understanding of social class. This can be expected in any involved and emotional subject. Numerous examples might be used. People happily answer direct questions about the existence of God (interestingly enough, fewer agree here than about class: see tables 8.4 and 8.5). However, if you probe people's ideas of God or deduce them from indirect questions or conversation, let alone behaviour, considerable differences will be observed. Not only is there a tremendous range of ideas, witnessed by differences in religions and denominations, but you would be led to consider whether some who claimed there was not a God in fact shared a great deal in common with those who believed. Without delving into psychology, it is obvious that what people declare is some sort of combination of what they think and feel in response to a given question or stimulus in a particular social context. Social survey techniques cannot be expected to go much further than to collect and classify these. Therefore, while it is not being suggested that social class classifications used in empirical research encompass the whole of people's subjective awareness, it can be claimed that they contain sufficient for their purpose. Social class is used in research to identify large, general groups in society. These groups are recognized by users as relatively broad and heterogeneous. Given this level of generality, the evidence on the public's responses to questions about social class in the early part of this review may be accepted as adequate support. Clearly a two-way process is at work here. While social scientists pay attention and perhaps respond to the public's subjective awareness, the public, in turn, responds to what it sees and understands of social science classifications. That the two are more than coincidental is, then, hardly surprising. In any case, as was pointed out in chapter 1, social class classifications do not necessarily stand or fall by research into their subjective existence but do so according to their utility in research. The weight of the views expressed here is neatly summarized in the following:

> Many of the theoretical concepts which sociologists use – social class ... [etc.] – are complex, intricate and rich in meaning. They do not lend themselves easily to being reduced to their elements, specified in terms of indicators and measured; yet if social scientists are to exploit the explanatory potential of large-scale survey research, using representative sampling and quantitative techniques to investigate causal relationships, this is a necessary step along the way. (Bulmer, 1977/1984)

This review should prevent readers from assuming that sociology's treatment of social class is as naive as some popular writings might suggest. Even though only empirical research was taken into account, the discipline was seen to have a continuing, active and deep concern with the notion of social class. While this has as yet borne little fruit in terms of new research methods, and new scales of social class have yet to be used in any extensive research, this may be a matter of time. The continuing abundance in this field of theoretical and descriptive works, which have not been discussed here, reflects an imbalance between theory and research in British sociology. Further, readers have been enabled to compare the simplicity of the operationalization of social class with the complexity of its concept and understanding.

Finally, this discussion has also emphasized the discontent about social class shared by sociologists and the general public. Both groups, it would appear, subscribe to the existence of social class in broad general terms, while disagreeing to some extent about its nature, structure and meaning. Both groups share the basic idea that occupation is a factor in social class, but not the only one. They are therefore equally likely to be relatively dissatisfied with the use of occupation as the sole criterion of social class, social standing or status in society. But neither party, apparently, can put forward any simple or complex alternative definition, and both are likely to resort to occupation as the best, the only or the most convenient 'shorthand' reference point in terms of which to pin down this extensively used, complex concept.

3

Life-Chances

For many people social class is mainly or only about differing life-styles and they overlook that it is also concerned with the fundamental, vital aspects of birth, health and death. This chapter traces how social class in our society affects, and is related to, life-chances from before birth, through birth and life, to death. It also reviews something of the roles of the health service, life-styles and social institutions in affecting these life-chances.

There is a long history to the class analysis of life-chances. The relationship between wealth and health was well established and recognized by the turn of this century, partly as a result of the work of those pioneers of the social survey, Booth and Rowntree (for a short account of their work see Abrams, 1951). Stevenson (1928), the 'inventor' of the Registrar General's social class classification of 1921, which is the basis of the present one, was particularly interested in the influence of wealth and culture on mortality (death rates), natality (birth rates) and disease. Prior to his interest, surveys had been made of whole districts chosen to represent wealth and poverty: hence he argued that there had been a neglect of culture as opposed to wealth. The criterion of wealth placed publicans, well known for their high death rate (they lived less long), above clergymen who had low death rates. Stevenson argued that this conflict showed that culture – in this case, habits of diet and hygiene – was also important in relation to health. Similarly, he recognized that wealthy districts also contained relatively poor people – servants and the like – while poor districts contained relatively wealthy ones, such as pawnbrokers and publicans. For these reasons he saw the need for a 'scale of social position' (largely but by no means exclusively a matter of wealth or poverty, culture also having been taken into account) based on occupation. This allowed for the classification of the whole population in terms of individual, as opposed to area, criteria. Indeed, he went on to argue that his social classes were meaningful because the mortality statistics fitted them: that is, the 'highest' social class had the lowest mortality, and there was a fairly regular increase class-by-class so that the 'lowest' class had the highest mortality. This type of distribution is commonly referred to as a gradient. As will be seen below, it remains a common and accurate characteristic of mortality and ill-health.

Similarly, and more obviously, sex and age have long been seen as important factors related to health and death. However, the complex interplay between all the forms of social stratification has not received as much attention as might be expected, at least in the manner which fits the concerns of this book. Hence what follows is neither as comprehensive nor as systematic as is desirable. It presents, however, some of the currently available evidence from the main viewpoint of social class data, with relevant reference to sex and age.

Many of the data in the topics which follow are taken from official sources and statistics. While the purpose and manner in which such data were collected do not always coincide with our objectives, they are comprehensive in scope and in providing both the national and a historical picture. As we have recognized earlier, all data have limitations and have to be viewed from within these limits. These considerations, not rehearsed here, must be borne in mind when reading this chapter, along with some particular concerns. Most medical data come from the analyses of people seeking or receiving treatment or care and so obviously tell us little directly about the health of others. Left unrecorded are those health incidents and conditions that remain untreated, or self-treated via the chemist, or otherwise. Self-reported levels of health and ill-health are clearly subjective and cannot be categorized in a way which would allow direct comparison with medical data. The categories used in medical research are often discrete entities in which aspects of the public's health concern may be lost or disguised. For example, menstrual-cycle problems and forms of back pain are not recorded in single categories and do not appear in the list of the ten most frequent reasons for women consulting a doctor. If they were treated as single categories they would be among the five most frequent reasons (Wells, 1987). Again, official statistics have been accused of being male-biased and therefore relatively uninformative about women (see for example Macfarlane, 1980). Even where social data, including class, are collected in respect to health, they are not always analysed or published. This situation is probably because the condition, rather than the patient and their culture, has traditionally been the centre of focus for much medical and governmental research. Some of these considerations are specifically illustrated below, but are raised here as a general issue.

Birth, Infancy and Childhood

It is perhaps surprising that social class variation can be found in natural and physiological events. For example a survey of all children born in Britain during a single week found differences in length of pregnancy (gestation) (Butler and Bonham, 1963; for earlier similar findings see Douglas, 1948). While birth is obvious and easily recorded, conception is not necessarily so, and length of pregnancy is not a precise measure – though this study was reliable to the extent of being based on medical reports. Normal or mature gestation is recognized as being 38–41 weeks, curtailed as 37 or fewer weeks, prolonged as 42 or more weeks. The percentage of normal gestation declined across the classes (RG) from 80 for mothers with husbands in class I to 66 for those in class V – overall 71. Length of gestation is importantly related to birth weight and to survival at birth. In particular, the mortality rate from curtailed gestation (the percentage of which rose from 7 to 10 per cent between classes I and V) was almost ten times higher than that for mature. The importance of this study was that it followed the children into adulthood (see also chapter 6) and therefore traced the effect of length of gestation on their subsequent development. Davie et al. (1972) showed it was related to such factors as school performance (reading and social adjustment), clumsiness, handicaps and ability to copy designs. While such relationships are not straightforward in that there are also social class differences in these variables as well as in length of gestation, the authors wrote of reading ability at age 7:

> the effect of length of pregnancy is relatively small, but nevertheless important ... After allowing for all other factors except birth weight the best readers were those born at the expected time, and the worst were those born more than two weeks early, the difference being equivalent to about three months of reading age.

The weight of babies at birth is a powerful predictor of survival during infancy and is related to subsequent health (Alberman, 1994). Some 44 per cent of babies born in England and Wales 1989–91 with a weight of under 1000 grams died within 28 days compared with but 2 in every 1000 of those of 3000 grams or more (*Mortality Statistics 1991*). There is a clear social class gradient to the percentage of babies with low birth weights (under 2500 grams or 5 lb $8\frac{1}{2}$ oz), rising from 4.8 in class I to 7.7 in class V (see first row of table 3.1).

Infant mortality refers to deaths between birth and the age of 1 year and is normally recorded under three headings:

Stillbirths Babies which display no life at birth.
Neonatal deaths Those which occur within the first month.
Postneonatal deaths Those which happen between 1 month and 1 year.

Table 3.1 Percentage of low birth weight babies, and stillbirths, neonatal, postneonatal and infant death rates*

	Social class RG						
	I	II	IIIN	IIIM	IV	V	All
% of babies <2500 g	4.8	5.1	5.9	6.4	6.8	7.7	6.5
Stillbirths**	3.4	3.4	4.0	4.4	4.9	6.9	4.3
Neonatal deaths†	3.3	3.6	4.3	3.9	4.3	4.5	4.0
Postneonatal deaths†	1.8	1.7	1.8	2.2	2.8	3.7	2.3
Infant deaths†	5.1	5.3	6.1	6.2	7.1	8.2	6.3

* For definitions see text; for births within marriage only; social class is of fathers; England and Wales.

** Rate per 1000 total births.

† Rate per 1000 live births.

Devised from table 4.2, The Health of our Children, 1995; table 7a, Mortality Statistics, Perinatal and Infant: Social and Biological Factors, England and Wales 1991, 1993

Infant deaths are those occurring between a live birth and the age of 1 year (i.e. neonatal and postneonatal deaths). As can be seen in table 3.1 (lower four rows) the rates for each of these, with the exception of neonatal deaths for class IIIN, rise across the social classes, with a particularly marked gradient for stillbirths – where the rate for class V is double that of class I. In respect to infant deaths the classes divide, with IIIN and IIIM being near the overall rate, I and II below it and IV and V above it.

One particular example of postneonatal mortality is sudden deaths or 'cot deaths', which occur most commonly between the ages of 1 and 3 months. These deaths have been found to be more common among males than females and lower for the non-manual classes, at around 1 per 1000 live births, than for the manual social classes, at more than 2 per 1000 (*Studies in Sudden Infant Deaths*, 1982). Since these differences remain when mother's age and number of previous births are held constant, it is concluded that other factors associated with class have an effect on postneonatal mortality, probably including: the availability and use of medical services, housing and living conditions, and other factors associated with income and education.

As in the case of infant deaths those among children aged 1 to 15 years are higher for males than females and rates rise across the social classes. Table 3.2 illustrates that the class gradient is most marked for deaths between the ages of 1 and 4, where the male rate for class V is more than three times that for class I and the female rate is two and a half times higher. For deaths between 1 and 15 years the class gradient

Table 3.2 Mortality rates per 100,000 for children aged under 16*

	Social class RG						Ratio
	I	II	IIIN	IIIM	IV	V	I to V
Age 1–4 years							
Males	33.0	34.2	41.3	52.7	63.8	111.5	3.4
Females	33.1	31.2	35.8	42.0	52.2	85.6	2.6
Age 1–15 years							
Males	25.2	24.1	26.3	32.5	38.3	56.8	2.3
Females	20.2	18.7	20.1	23.5	26.6	39.6	2.0

* Data for England and Wales 1979–80 and 1982–3 combined, rates rounded to one decimal place.

Devised from table 2.6, Occupational Mortality, Childhood Supplement, 1988

is somewhat less sharp, though the class V male and female rates are around twice those of class I. In both cases notice the very large difference between classes IV and V. As might be expected, mortality rates fall sharply with age through childhood. For example, in two surveyed years there were 16,000 stillbirths, 28,000 infant deaths and 12,000 deaths between 1 and 15 years (*Occupational Mortality, Childhood Supplement*, 1988).

A further view of deaths in childhood is provided by the male standardized mortality ratios (SMRs) in table 3.3 (these effectively hold social class age differences constant: see note to table). For 'all causes' of death the class gradient is easy to see, as are the marked differences both between classes I and II combined and classes IV and V combined and between the manual and non-manual classes. Such a rise was also true for females and in each age group. Most deaths at these ages are caused by neoplasms, infections, congenital anomalies and accidents. With the exception of neoplasms, death by these causes rises across the classes and all causes exhibit a clear divide between non-manual and manual which is most marked in respect to fire accidents. In general childhood is then less hazardous for girls than boys and for both sexes for those born of middle-class parents.

Health

There are two main types of data on the distribution of sickness, disease and conditions of ill-health – normally referred to as morbidity – which indirectly provide evidence concerning the state of health in our society.

Table 3.3 Standardized mortality ratios* of male children aged 1 to 15 for all and selected causes**

	Social class RG				
	I and II	IIIN	IIIM	IV and V	All
All causes	71	77	95	126	Each
Neoplasms	96	90	106	105	cause
Infectious/parasitic diseases	52	86	118	134	=100
Respiratory system diseases	77	82	99	133	
Congenital anomalies	72	88	102	134	
Accidents, fire and flame	24	18	93	171	
Motor vehicle traffic accidents	61	59	90	122	

* SMRs are computed by the formula (observed deaths)/(expected deaths) × 100, where expected deaths are those which would be found in a social class if the age-specific death rate for the whole population was replicated in the class in question. The SMR for any given population is 100; the figures relating to any group within it are expressed as a ratio: hence a ratio of 200 is twice and of 50 is half the overall rate.

** Data refer to years 1979–80 and 1982–3, for England and Wales.

Devised from table 2.12, Occupational Mortality, Childhood Supplement, 1988

One is surveys of self-reported health and sickness, together with surveys of particular conditions, which is viewed here. The other is analyses of the causes of death – normally referred to as mortality – which is viewed later in this chapter (section 'Mortality').

Two aspects of health can be identified, which while related do not always coincide. The subjective, that is how people feel about, and react to, their health or its lack; and what might be seen as the objective, that is the diagnosis made, and treatment given, by doctors when consulted. In the next three sections of this chapter we are mainly concerned with views of health, health behaviour and the use of health services gained from the general public and analysed in terms of social class.

Self-reported health

The General Household Survey (GHS), the research for which is continuous, provides a rich source of self-reported health and associated behaviours. Some of the topics covered are published for each year, while others feature, and are treated in greater depth, only from time to time. Hence the data here are not necessarily the most up to date, but have been chosen to provide a general idea of the health of the social classes in our society. Since no efforts were made to define medically or diagnose either conditions or their severity, what we view are subjective attitudes. In a real sense this enhances our understanding, in that people's attitudes to their health can be as important as clinical symptoms in terms of their behaviour, including use of health services, and consequently the effects of their health upon their lives.

Perhaps surprisingly most views of health in our society focus on ill rather than good health and this has to be reflected in its treatment here. The GHS draws a distinction between two types of sickness:

Chronic Long-standing illness, disability or infirmity and, as a measure of its severity, whether it limits normal activities.

Acute That occurring in the fourteen days prior to interview and which restricted normal activities.

The incidence of self-reported chronic sickness increases across the social classes, from 27 per cent of males in class 1 to 38 per cent in class 6 and from 24 to 45 per cent for females (table 3.4) (RG SEG classes, see appendix B). Put positively the proportion of those seeing themselves free of chronic sickness declines across the classes. The proportion of sufferers who saw chronic sickness as limiting their activities in any way rises even more steeply, with that of class 6 being twice or more that of class 1 (males, 24 and 12; females, 29 and 12 per cent). Overall sex differences are small, 33 per cent of women compared with 31 per cent of men reporting chronic sickness, with a similar percentage difference (19 and 17) reporting such sickness as limiting their normal activities. The percentage of those reporting chronic sickness who do *not* see it as limiting was slightly higher for males at 45 compared with 42 for females, though there were class differences. In the non-manual classes (1–3) a higher proportion of males than females did not see their chronic sickness as limiting, whereas in the manual classes the reverse was true in classes 4 and 6, with identical proportions in class 6.

Obviously, age is a significant factor in health and sickness. For example, the percentage of people reporting long-standing illness consistently increases over the age groups from 24 per cent of those aged 16–44 years to 66 per cent of those 75 or over. This age pattern is true for both sexes and for each of the social classes. However, in comparing the sexes some interesting differences can be observed. In childhood males have higher rates of long-standing illness than females, between the ages of 16 and 74 the rates are similar, but females have markedly higher rates at age 75 or over (70 compared with 61 per cent). This difference is at least partly due to longer life expectancy for females, so that elderly women are, on average, older than men in the same age group (see pp. 76–7). Social class differences however are still clearly apparent when the age differences are taken into account. Table 3.5 shows that the incidence of long-standing illness with the age effect removed rises across the social classes for both sexes, with non-manual classes (1–4) having a lower prevalence than would be expected (less than 100) and the manual classes (5–7) higher prevalence.

Table 3.4 Self-reported health and health behaviour by social class and gender*

	Social class RG						
	1	2	3	4	5	6	All**
Chronic sickness (%)							
Males	27	29	29	33	34	38	31
Females	24	28	33	32	39	45	33
Limiting chronic sickness (%)							
Males	12	13	13	19	21	24	17
Females	12	14	19	18	23	29	19
Acute sickness in past 14 days (%)							
Males	9	10	10	12	12	13	11
Females	12	14	16	15	16	19	15
Average restricted activity days in previous year (no.)							
Males	14	19	17	24	25	30	22
Females	20	26	30	29	25	41	30
GP consultations in past 14 days (%)							
Males	9	11	11	12	13	16	12
Females	12	16	17	18	19	20	17
GP consultations per year (no.)							
Males	3	3	4	4	4	5	4
Females	4	5	5	6	6	6	6

* Married women whose husbands were in the household classified according to husband's occupation; children under 16 classified by father's occupation.
** Includes unclassified.
N = 13,030

Devised from tables 4.16, 4.17, 4.27 and 4.31, General Household Survey 1989, 1991

Table 3.5 Age-standardized long-standing illness ratios*

	Social class RG SEG							
	1	2	3	4	5	6	7	All
Men	84	93	97	94	103	109	117	100
Women	87	90	95	99	102	109	115	100

* Data for 1988 and 1989 combined. Age groups used for standardization were 16–44, 45–64, 65–74 and 75 and over. Excludes members of the armed forces, persons who have never worked and those whose occupations were inadequately described.
N = 34,859

Devised from table 4.2, General Household Survey 1989, 1991

The GHS 1989 used two social class measures for women. The first was life-style, in which married women were classified by their husband's, and other women by their own current or last, occupation. This reflects the material circumstances of married women who do not work, and where the husband is the main breadwinner, but fails to take into account the effect of a woman's own job on her material circumstances and own health. The second was personal, in which their own occupation was used and which had several shortcomings. Women not currently in paid occupations were classified by their last, which may have been a number of years prior to interview. It has also been argued that the occupations of married women may not adequately reflect their current life-style (Arber, 1990). Neither can the personal classification assign class to women who have never worked – of whom there is a higher proportion than of men. As has been seen (table 3.5), using the life-style classification in respect to female long-standing illness produced both a class pattern of incidence and a clear distinction between middle-class and working-class women. The personal classification produced a less clearly defined pattern among married working women, with class 1 having the lowest, but class 4 having the highest rather than class 7. The GHS concluded: 'The stronger class gradient shown by lifestyle classification suggests that household circumstances, as measured by her husband's occupation, are more strongly associated with health status than is her own occupation. This is consistent with other research in the area' (Arber, 1989). The life-style classification was therefore used.

GHS respondents in 1994 were asked about the nature of their long-standing illness and this was coded into the broad categories shown in table 3.6. For each of the six most common condition groups the manual classes had higher rates than the non-manual – a pattern true for most age and sex groups. The largest differences were found in musculoskeletal, heart and circulatory and digestive complaints where the rate for class 6 was over twice that for class 1. Age-standardized ratios for long-standing illness in the GHS 1989 also revealed clear class relationships with the prevalence of musculoskeletal, heart and circulatory and respiratory systems complaints.

There is no clear social class pattern in self-reported acute sickness (fifth and sixth rows, table 3.4), though there is a marked difference between classes 1 and 6 for both sexes. No such class differences were found in the *Health Survey for England 1994.* Acute sickness is more common among females than males, both overall (15 compared with 11 per cent) and in each of the classes – the difference ranging from 3 to 6 per cent. This gender difference was also found by the *Health Survey for England 1994* and *The Health and Lifestyle Survey* (1987). The latter asked its respondents to identify which of thirteen common symptoms they had experienced in the previous month. Some 28 per cent of

Table 3.6 Rate per 1000 reporting selected long-standing condition groups*

	Social class RG SEG						
	1	2	3	4	5	6	All**
Musculoskeletal system	94	122	160	157	179	196	151
Heart and circulatory system	63	73	93	99	116	130	93
Respiratory system	67	65	63	72	82	79	71
Endocrine and metabolic system	26	31	28	34	40	45	33
Digestive system	17	26	34	33	41	43	32
Nervous system	23	22	27	27	32	39	28

* Coded from respondent's description of symptoms; persons aged 16 and over; social class of head of household.

** Includes unclassified.

N = 18,008

Devised from tables 3.17, General Household Survey 1994, 1996

women, compared with 16 per cent of men, reported having suffered from four or more symptoms, the biggest differences occurring in the ages 40 to 59 years. The number of days in which health restricted activity shows a steeply rising gradient across the classes, the number more than doubling for both males (from 14 to 30) and females (from 20 to 41) (seventh and eighth rows, table 3.4), and being markedly higher for females than males.

There are examples of more general inquiries into the public's perception of their health. *The Health and Lifestyle Survey* (1987) asked for self-assessment as excellent, good, fair or poor 'compared with someone of your own age' and found such assessments to be very strongly related to socio-economic circumstance. For example, of men over the age of 50, three times as many in the lowest as in the highest income group saw their health as fair or poor. The *Health Survey for England 1994* asked its respondents to rate their health on a five-point scale, very good to very bad. There were no gender differences for bad and very bad, but men were more likely to report good or very good. Using age-standardized data the study found both sexes in the middle classes to be more likely to see their health as good than those in the working classes – males 85 compared with 71 per cent. Reports of good health declined through the age groups for both groups of classes, but the decline was far more marked in the manual. Explanation of these differences is not simply a question of the incidence of health problems. Apart from the possible variation in the seriousness of conditions, it seems probable that the variation also reflects differences in attitudes

Table 3.7 Sight, hearing and teeth* (percentages)

	Social class RG SEG						
	1	2	3	4	5	6	All
Sight							
Wears glasses/ lenses**	66	63	59	47	50	54	56
Has difficulty with sight†	10	12	13	14	18	19	14
Had sight test in year prior to interview**	40	37	37	28	30	31	34
Hearing							
Wears hearing aid or has difficulty hearing	7	12	11	13	16	21	13
Teeth							
No natural teeth	3	11	12	19	23	33	16
Regular dental check-up††	64	62	55	44	41	38	51

* Persons aged 16 and over.
** Economically active, own social class.
† Includes those who wore and did not wear glasses.
†† Of those with some natural teeth.
N = 10,816; 16,629; 18,454

Devised from tables 3.36, 3.39, General Household Survey 1994, 1996; tables 6.40 and 6.43, General Household Survey 1993, 1995; tables 7.19 and 7.20, General Household Survey 1979, 1981

towards health between the social strata: for example, that there are different concepts of good health; that some strata may be less and others more willing to admit problems, or to be concerned about them; that occupational and social demands for and on health vary; together with interrelationships between these and the provision of health services.

Sight, hearing and teeth

Table 3.7 summarizes data on self-reported aspects of sight, hearing and dental health of persons aged over 16 years. The GHS 1994 found that overall some 65 per cent of their sample wore glasses or contact lenses, just over a third of those aged 16–34 and nearly all (97 per cent) of those aged 65 and over. Nearly seven in ten of all women and just over six in ten men wore them, while among the economically active the percentages were 59 and 52 per cent respectively. Overall there is no precise pattern to the class distribution of the wearing of glasses among the economically active, though classes 1 to 3 have higher rates than the overall average and that for classes 4 to 6 (top row, table 3.7). The most pronounced difference occurred among economically active men, with two-thirds of class 1 wearing glasses compared with two-fifths of class 6. Reported difficulty with sight among wearers and non-wearers of glasses or lenses rises across the classes, the percentage in class 1 being just over half that for class 6 (10 compared with 19 per cent), and is more frequent among women than men (16 and 12 per cent). A higher percentage of middle-class than working-class respondents reported having had a sight test in the year prior to interview.

The wearing of hearing aids or having difficulty with hearing rises across the social classes, with a very marked difference, three times greater, at the extremes – the two together being reported by 7 per cent of class 1 and 21 per cent of class 6. In contrast to sight, more men than women have difficulty with their hearing: 15 compared with 12 per cent. A fairly common form of hearing problem is tinnitus – the subjective sensation of noise (typically ringing, hissing or booming) in the ears or head without any relevant auditory stimulus – the severity and duration of which vary very widely. The GHS 1981 found that 15 per cent of those interviewed had experienced it, and there were clear class and age gradients: from 10 per cent in class 1 to 19 in class 6; and from 12 per cent of those aged 16–44 to 20 per cent aged 65 and over. In each age group and social class more women than men had experienced it.

The percentage of those without any natural teeth rises from 3 in class 1 to 33 in class 6, with the rate in the manual classes being more than twice that in the non-manual: 22 compared with 10 per cent, a difference seen in all age groups above 35 years. Between 1985 and 1993 the percentage of those without natural teeth fell from 23 to 16, the proportionally largest decline being in the non-manual classes: for example, that of class 1 halved while that of class 6 fell by but 6 per cent. Social class figures for total tooth loss in 1968 ranged from 15 per cent in class I (RG) to 47 per cent in class V (Gray et al., 1970). While not directly comparable with the data here, these suggest a drop of the order of 80 per cent in total tooth loss in class I, but of only 30 per cent in class V. Such class differences may well reflect differing and changing attitudes towards dental health and use of dental services.

Mental health

The prevalence of psychiatric disorders in Great Britain has been investigated (*The Prevalence of Psychiatric Morbidity among Adults Living in Private Households*, 1995). About one in six of the adults surveyed had suffered a neurotic disorder – such as depression, phobia, obsessive-compulsive disorder, panic, generalized anxiety, mixed anxiety and depressive disorder – in the week prior to interview. Women had higher rates than men and there were some class differences. Among women (overall rate 195 per 1000), classes (RG, based on head of household) I and II had the lowest rates at 155 and 154; classes IV and V the highest at 235 and 247. The pattern for men (overall rate 123 per 1000) was less marked, with class I the lowest, their rate being very much lower at 60 per 1000 (1995, table 6.7). The incidence of schizophrenia, manic depressive psychosis and schizo-affective disorder was the same for both sexes, with only class V having a markedly higher rate. Men were twice as likely to be drug dependent and three times more likely to have alcohol dependency than women. Overall class V again had markedly the highest and class I the lowest rates for both disorders, though this pattern was much less pronounced for women than for men.

Life-Style and Health

There is substantial evidence that certain social habits are related to health, or are hazards to health. In other words, life-style may well be a key to health and morbidity patterns. Being overweight, cigarette smoking, high alcohol consumption, unhealthy diet and lack of exercise have been so associated and display evidence of variation along social class lines. However, health, or its lack, is the result of the interplay of many factors, the complexity of which is not as yet fully understood, rather than of one in isolation.

Height and weight

The heights and weights of adults have been shown to vary according to social class. Table 3.8 shows that on average men in classes I and II combined are just over 3 centimetres taller than those in classes IV and V combined, with the difference for women similar at just under 3 centimetres. Such differences are to be found in almost every age group and indicate a class effect on height independent of age and sex (Knight and Eldridge, 1984). Interestingly enough, adult height has been identified as an objective physical measurement, the product of heredity and earlier environment, which is related to previous and future health, together with mortality (for a review see Power et al., 1991).

Since there is a relationship between the two, height and weight are used to produce a body mass index (BMI) from which a measure of obesity, separately formulated for each sex, can be derived (for definition see note to table 3.8). The percentage of obese adults rises

Table 3.8 Average height and obesity of adults

Average height of adults (cm)

	Social class RG			
	I and II	IIIN	IIIM	IV and V
Men	175.5	174.9	173.4	172.3
Women	162.5	161.6	160.2	159.6

*Obese adults** (%)

	Social class RG SEG						
	1	2	3	4	5	6	All**
Men	5	10	6	9	7	13	8
Women	6	13	12	18	17	19	15

* Based on body mass index (BMI) derived from weight (kg) over height (m) squared; obesity is defined for men as BMI = 30.0 and over, and for women as BMI = 28.6 and over.
N = 7939; 9003

Calculated from table 2.2, Knight and Eldridge, 1984; table 4.7, The Health and Lifestyle Survey, 1987

unevenly across the social classes – from 5 in class 1 to 13 in class 6 for men and from 6 to 19 for women. The percentage of obese females is higher in each class and about twice that of males, both overall – 15 compared with 8 per cent – and in classes 3, 4 and 5. The *Health Survey for England 1994* found that BMI and obesity had an inverse association with class for both men and women, and that they were independent of behavioural factors – smoking, alcohol consumption and physical activity. In addition, for women only they were inversely related to educational level. This study also used the waist–hip ratio (WHR), a measure of the deposition of abdominal fat, shown to be associated with heart disease, diabetes and hypertension. This is simply calculated: waist girth divided by hip girth. Social class was significantly associated with WHR for both sexes: for women it rose steadily across the classes I to V, for men it rose from class I to IIIM and then was constant for IV and V. These relationships were found to be independent of both BMI and behavioural factors. WHR was also found to be related to educational level, men and women without formal qualifications having higher WHRs than those with A level GCE or higher qualifications.

The Health and Lifestyle Survey (1987) showed that while the consumption of fruit and salads declined across the classes (especially for men), the consumption of fried food and chips increased. However, food is not the only factor in obesity. Current healthy eating advice includes that to eat more starchy foods rich in fibre and less fatty, salty and sugary foods. Findings based on self-report show that members of the non-manual social classes are more likely to use cooking oil than solid fat, and to usually eat wholemeal bread and breakfast cereals, and less likely to use whole fat milk. Those in classes I and II (RG) compared with IV and V ate more fruit, vegetables and salads and added less salt during cooking and at the table (*Health Survey for England 1993*). A British Social Attitudes survey looked at both the eating habits and the attitudes towards food, diet and health of its respondents (Sheiham et al., 1988). There were considerable social class differences between classes (RG) I and II and IV and V, the respective percentages of these defined as healthy eaters with positive attitudes being 44 and 21, of unhealthy eaters with negative attitudes 16 and 35.

Exercise

While regular, energetic physical leisure activity is a minority pursuit, there is clear evidence that those who undertake it have lower resting pulse rates and blood pressures, better respiratory functioning and fewer weight problems than those who do not (Fenner, 1987). In addition, exercise is associated with protection from, and prevention of, a variety of forms of ill-health, including mental, and with independence in old age (Wells, 1987; Fenner, 1987). Participation in sports, games and physical activities declines across the social classes (see table 9.9). The critical factors in exercise are its frequency, length and intensity. *The Health and Lifestyle Survey* (1987) measured these factors in respect to active leisure pursuits and divided the reported activity of its respondents in the two preceding weeks into three groups – none, some, a lot. The percentage in 'a lot' was higher among the employed in non-manual than manual classes and that in 'none' lower. This might be expected because of assumed differences in levels of physical activity involved in work. However, Fenner reports that respondents' perceptions of the amount of physical effort in their work suggest such assumptions are inaccurate.

Data from a further, more detailed study are in table 3.9. This study used sophisticated measures and a distinction was made between types of activity and its intensity, measured by energy cost in kilocalories per minute: vigorous being 7.5 or over, moderate at least 5. As can be seen the age-standardized class variation in types of activity is not consistent. As would be expected occupational activity was much higher for those in manual than in non-manual jobs – much higher for men, though for women only markedly so in comparison with class IIIN. There was little variation in levels of home activity, though that of men in classes I and II combined was slightly higher than in IV and V combined. Walking at the specified level was more common among those in the middle

Table 3.9 Age-standardized percentages of persons undertaking moderate or vigorous physical activity*

	Social class RG				
	I and II	IIIN	IIIM	IV and V	All**
Men					
Occupation	9	13	31	32	20
Home	66	64	65	62	64
Walking	39	34	25	27	32
Sports†	47	46	37	36	42
Women					
Occupation	13	5	16	18	11
Home	69	71	69	72	70
Walking	26	21	19	17	22
Sports†	42	35	31	26	35

* Respondent's own class. Vigorous and moderate are defined in text. Based on activity in 4 weeks prior to interview.
** Includes unclassified.
† 20 or more minutes.
N = 13,772

Devised from table 6.11, Health Survey for England 1994, 1996

classes, but this arises from different self-reported assessments of walking pace. Working-class respondents actually walked more often but were less likely to define their pace as brisk or fast. In sports the middle classes were again the most active, a difference most marked among women.

Smoking

Cigarette smoking is probably the best-recognized health hazard and is regularly surveyed in the GHS. This self-reporting is suspected of understating cigarette consumption and to a lesser extent prevalence, owing to young respondents not admitting to smoking and smokers rounding down their consumption to the nearest ten (GHS 1994). As will be seen on table 3.10, the percentage of smokers rises sharply across the social classes. For men the percentage of smokers more than doubles from 18 to 39 per cent from class 1 to 6, while that of heavy smokers (twenty or more cigarettes a day) almost trebles from 6 to 17 per cent. For women the class differences are somewhat more marked, the percentage of smokers rising from class 1 to classes 5 and 6 from 13 to 32, and heavy smokers rising fourfold from 3 per cent in class 1 to 13 in class 6. The table also shows that the percentage who never or only

Table 3.10 Cigarette smoking* (percentages)

	Social class RG SEG						
	1	2	3	4	5	6	All**
Males							
Current smokers	18	21	24	32	26	39	28
Heavy smokers†	6	9	9	14	14	17	12
Never/occasional smokers	54	44	44	36	34	33	40
Females							
Current smokers	13	20	24	28	32	32	26
Heavy smokers†	3	6	5	9	11	13	8
Never/occasional smokers	62	58	54	51	50	47	54

* Persons age 16 and over; social class of head of household.
** Includes unclassified.
† 20 or more cigarettes per day.
N = 16,750

Devised from table 4.8, General Household Survey 1994, 1996

occasionally smoke is higher for women than men and for the middle than the working classes. A higher percentage of middle-class smokers use low tar cigarettes, men at 35 and women at 48, than do the manual classes at 16 and 28 respectively (GHS 1994, table 4.20).

Cigarette smoking declined quite sharply between 1974 and 1994; proportionally the decline was more marked for men than for women and for the middle than the working class. The percentage of men smoking fell from 51 to 28 per cent, middle class 45 to 21 and working class 56 to 35, while that of women fell from 41 to 26, middle class 38 to 21 and working class 45 to 31 (GHS 1994, table 4.9). A further study showed that a higher proportion of middle-class smokers said they were very or fairly likely to give up smoking – 71 per cent of classes (RG) I and II compared with 49 per cent of classes IV and V (Ben-Shlomo et al., 1991).

Drinking

The recommended 'sensible' weekly alcohol consumption for men is 21 units (for definition see note to table 3.11) and for women 14 units. Excessive consumption when sustained increases the risk of raised blood pressure and stroke, is associated with other medical conditions such as heart disease, cancers and liver cirrhosis, and is linked with

Table 3.11 Weekly alcohol consumption* by persons aged 16 and over (percentages)

	Social class RG SEG						
	1	2	3	4	5	6	All**
Males							
Non-drinkers	3	5	7	8	9	11	7
Up to 10 units	44	42	47	45	47	47	44
11–21 units	26	23	22	21	22	21	22
22 or more units	27	30	24	26	22	21	27
Mean weekly units	15.5	16.5	14.1	15.8	13.6	13.6	15.4
Females							
Non-drinkers	8	10	12	14	17	22	14
Up to 7 units	53	53	60	59	63	62	58
8–14 units	19	19	17	14	11	9	15
15 or more units	19	18	11	12	8	8	13
Mean weekly units	7.2	7.0	5.2	5.3	4.0	3.2	5.4

* A unit is half a pint of beer, lager or cider; a measure of spirits; a glass of wine; a small glass of port, sherry or fortified wine.
** Includes unclassified.
N = 16,740

Calculated from table 5.9, General Household Survey 1994, 1995

alcohol-related social problems and criminal behaviour. The Royal College of Psychiatrists (1986) estimated that alcohol is responsible for some 4000 deaths and 5000 first admissions to psychiatric hospitals each year. While in the past the major concern has been with men, who have higher levels of consumption than women, evidence is growing which suggests that women may be at higher risk of physical harm than men from given a quantity of alcohol. Accurate data on the population's drinking are, of course, very difficult to collect: reported drinking has been consistently lower than would be expected from alcohol sales figures (GHS 1994)! Drinking at home, which has become much more common, is likely to lead to under-reporting of consumption, since the quantities are not accurately measured. Sample household surveys may well miss interviewing some heavy drinkers.

The GHS asks respondents how often and what quantity of five types of drink they have drunk in the previous year, from which an estimate is made of their weekly consumption level. Table 3.11 shows that the proportion of women non-drinkers is twice that of men – 14 compared with 7 per cent – and for both sexes the incidence rises steadily across the classes, in the case of women from 8 for class 1 to 22 per cent for class 6, and for men from 3 to 11 per cent. The proportion of women exceeding the recommended sensible level of consumption is just less than half that of men – 13 compared with 27 per cent. While the percentage of such female drinkers declines across the classes, from almost one in five for class 1 to around one in twelve for classes 5 and 6, no such pattern is found among males, though class 2 is the highest and the only one higher than the overall figure. The proportion of males exceeding the sensible level remained stable between 1986 and 1994, while that for females rose from 9 per cent in 1984 to 13 in 1994.

A further view of consumption is provided by the mean number of units consumed (fifth and tenth rows of the table). Again there is no clear pattern for males, while for females the number declines across the classes from 7.2 to 3.2. The relationship between male and female consumption increases across the classes: class 1 male consumption is a little more than twice that of female, whereas in class 6 it is more than four times higher.

Use of Health Services

At a straightforward level, the use of health services would be expected to vary according to an individual's or group's health. The GHS data in table 3.4 show a considerably higher percentage of females than males – 17 compared with 12 – had consulted a GP in the two weeks prior to interview. This is partly accounted for by aspects of childbirth and family planning, which accounted for 12 per cent of consultations by that group in 1981 (GHS 1981), although, as we have seen, acute sickness is more prevalent among women than men. For both sexes the class gradient in GP consultations rises sharply between classes 1 and 2, males from 9 to 11, females from 12 to 16 per cent. For women the gradient then rises by 1 per cent per class to 20 for class 6, while for men the gradient is less marked but rises sharply from 13 to 16 per cent between classes 5 and 6. Differences at the extremes are wide: for men GP consultations in class 6 are 78 per cent higher than those in class 1, while the comparable figure for women is 67. Less dramatic but similar patterns are found in respect to the average number of GP consultations in the previous year. There were slight differences in whether a prescription was obtained at consultation: 69 per cent of non-manual patients compared with 72 per cent of the manual (GHS 1994, unpublished table GP24).

A further view of the use of GPs is provided by the age-standardized data from a survey of NHS general practices in table 3.12. These show that consultations, home visits and the number of new episodes for both sexes rise across the social classes. In general the overall average divides the non-manual, which are lower, from the manual classes, which are higher than it. Again there are very marked differences

Table 3.12 Standardized ratios* for GP consultations, home visits and new episodes

	Social class RG				
	I and II	IIIN	IIIM	IV and V	All
Number of consultations					
Males	87	101	104	112	100
Females	90	94	106	112	100
Number of home visits					
Males	93	93	104	109	100
Females	90	83	109	116	100
Number of new episodes					
Males	90	102	104	108	100
Females	91	96	106	111	100

* The result of comparing the actual for each social class with that expected if the age structure were the same as for the population.
N = 25 general practices

Devised from tables 3.11, 3.12 and 3.13, Morbidity Statistics from General Practice 1981–82, 1990

between classes I and II combined and IV and V combined. Such variation is not just a straightforward reflection of the need for GP consultation due to prevalence of chronic sickness. Apart from need, together with the willingness and necessity to make use of the services, also involved are differences in the physical health demands made by types of occupation. As is discussed below (pp. 69–70) there is some evidence which suggests that when standardized for age and sex the middle classes, on the basis of self-reported need, receive proportionately more of NHS expenditure and make greater use of some health services than do the working classes.

The use of dentists provides an example of where the working classes make relatively less use of a health service. Table 3.7 shows that only 51 per cent of those with some natural teeth had regular dental check-ups – the percentage falling from 64 to 38 across the social classes 1 to 6. A survey found no class variation in having been to a dentist among children aged over 12. The percentage of those aged 5 who had never been to a dentist rose from 7 for classes (RG) I, II, IIIN to 10 for IIIM and 15 for IV and V, and at age 8 the percentages were 2, 3 and 6 (*Children's Dental Health in the United Kingdom 1993*, table 6.1).

The *Health Survey for England 1994* using age-standardized data found that taking prescription medicines rose across the classes, from 33 per cent of men and 47 per cent of women in classes I and II (RG) to 37 and 52 per cent in classes IV and V. Table 3.7 shows that a third of

GHS respondents had had a sight test in the year prior to interview, ranging from 40 per cent of class 1 to 30 and 31 per cent for classes 5 and 6. Some 71 per cent of class 1 paid for their tests, with the NHS paying for 12 per cent, and the comparable percentages for class 6 were 49 and 37 – the remainder in both cases being paid by employer or insurance company or provided free by an optician (GHS 1994).

Admission into hospital can be taken as a general indicator of more serious ill-health than those viewed so far. Hospital admission covers a wide range of conditions and is subject to variation on factors such as availability of beds, referral practices, circumstances of the would-be patient and, indeed, choice.

In the past *Scottish Hospital In-Patients Statistics* collected occupational data, which enabled social class analysis of all NHS patients (excluding maternity and mental cases) using two age-standardized measures related to use and length of use of hospital beds (discharge and mean stay ratios). For both measures and sexes there was a steady rise across the classes (RG) I to V, with the rates for classes IV and V much higher than for I to III (Carstairs, 1966). Of course, differences in admission to, and length of stay in, hospital reflected not only differences in rates of illness and disease, in the classes and sexes, but also differences in physical and social environment. For example, poor housing, lack of amenities or privacy and overcrowding are likely to limit the possibility of home care and treatment. This could well lead to more frequent admission and longer stays in hospital, particularly for those in class V, where such provisions are most limited (see chapter 6). Similarly there are likely to be gender differences in respect to the role demands made upon, and home care available to, discharged patients, probably in general balanced in favour of men. The *Hospital In-Patient Inquiry 1983* found admission rates for all causes other than maternities were highest, and markedly so, for ages 0 to 4 and 65 years and over, for both sexes. Males had higher rates than females in childhood (0–14 years), lower rates between the ages of 15 and 54, and higher rates from 55 years and upwards. The average length of stay in hospital also displayed a sex difference – nine days for males and twelve for females. Sex differences in length of stay were pronounced at ages 65 and over. Women's average stay rose from three days longer than men at ages 65 to 69, to eight days longer at 75 to 79 and eleven days at 85 to 89; with 69 per cent of female beds and 53 per cent of male beds being occupied by those over the age of 65. Length of stay was very similar for both sexes among children up to the age of 15, while between the ages of 16 and 64 the average male stay was slightly longer than the female.

The percentages of GHS respondents reporting in-patient hospital stays in the year prior to interview across the classes (RG SEG) 1 to 6 were: 7.1, 8.5, 8.5, 8.7, 9.8 and 9.6 (GHS 1994, unpublished table IP2IF). The percentages for out-patient attendance in the 3 months prior to

Table 3.13 Private medical insurance and hospital use* (percentages)

	Social class RG SEG						
	1	2	3	4	5	6	All
Private medical insurance							
Males	21	23	9	3	2	2	8**
Females	24	21	7	2	1	1	7**
Private hospital use							
In-patient stays	13	16	7	2	1	0	5
Out-patient visits	5	4	2	1	2	(–)	2

* Persons aged over 16, during previous 12 months.
** Includes unclassified.
(–) less than 0.5 per cent.
N = 19,056; 2743 (in-patients); 6343 (out-patients)

Devised from table 7.33, Social Trends no. 17, 1987; tables 9.21 and 9.24, General Household Survey 1983, 1985

interview were: 12.6, 13.4, 14.3, 14.8, 14.6 and 16 (GHS 1994, unpublished table OP2).

Private medicine

Like private schooling, private medicine has coexisted with the welfare state provision since its establishment. The growth of occupation-based health insurance schemes, with 'free' or discounted premiums for employees, together with perceived and actual concerns over NHS provision, have led to substantial growth in the private health services sector in recent years. Apart from the question of choice, the ability to pay for and/or the opportunity to participate in schemes of private health services are likely to be limited to some parts of society. Table 3.13 illustrates how the incidence of private medical insurance is strongly related to social class and gender (see also table 4.8). For both sexes it is common only in classes 1 and 2 (over 20 per cent) and it is rare in classes 5 and 6 (2 per cent of males, 1 per cent of females). Overall, slightly more males than females are covered – 8 compared with 7 per cent. People of 65 years and over are less likely to be covered than those between 16 and 64. This is likely to reflect the changes and opportunities outlined above, as well as the fact that the elderly can be excluded from such schemes or be charged very high subscriptions. The lower section of the table shows that some 5 per cent of hospital in-patient stays and 2 per cent of out-patient visits were private, again with a sharply marked class pattern.

The role of the NHS

Our considerations so far have shown something of the very real social inequalities in health and these are further and dramatically illustrated in respect of mortality (see next section). Such inequalities raise a number of questions about the use and role of the NHS in this situation. The government's intentions at the inception of the NHS were very clear: it wanted

> to ensure that in future every man and woman and child can rely on getting all the advice and treatment and care which they may need in matters of personal health, that what they get shall be the best medical and other facilities available: that their getting these shall not depend on whether they can pay for them, or on any other factor irrelevant to the real need. (*A National Health Service,* 1944)

The essential elements, then, were that need should be the sole criterion of use and quality of service and that the service should be free at point of use. Since there has been no formal reformulation of the NHS it is appropriate to ask the question whether or not it functions in the way it was designed. We concentrate on the first two criteria, need and quality, though in passing it should be noted that some charges were introduced early on and that their scope and level have increased since, particularly over the last decades. The deterrent effect of charges on the use of health services, balanced as they are to an extent by exemptions, is extremely difficult to assess.

At a straightforward level, the use of health services would be expected to vary directly according to the ill-health or needs of an individual or group. As we have seen, there is evidence that the working classes (especially the semi-skilled and unskilled) make greater use of the health service than the others, and this is also true of women in comparison with men. The question now is the extent to which that use accurately reflects the differences in need based on the incidence of ill-health or, put differently, whether other factors intervene. Obviously, measuring the need for, let alone the quality received of, health services is a difficult area to research.

In some ways sex differences in the use of health services are more straightforward than social class ones. Quite apart from the differing age structures of the sexes, a major factor is the conditions surrounding, and related to, reproduction. The exclusion of pregnancy and childbirth together with associated complications removes much of the reported higher female usage (Reid, 1989b). What cannot be discovered, as yet, is the extent to which the long-term effects of childbearing and, indeed, contraception (particularly the 'pill') affect the health of women and hence their use of health services. For a discussion of the need for a new definition of reproductive mortality, see Beral (1979). Nor, for that matter, can we tell the difference between that and the effects of particular occupations on men, and for many women the combination of the two. Beral (1985) analysed the causes of death of 1.2 million women aged between 45 and 74 years and found that those who had given birth were more likely to have died from diabetes mellitus and gall bladder disease and certain circulatory diseases than those who had not. However, as yet, the available data do not allow for the identification of which aspects of pregnancy are most strongly related (Wells, 1987). For a review of some of the various issues which surround the health of women, including reproduction and the training of medical personnel, see Roberts (1981; 1990). Given the differences in the sexes' use of the health services, it is not surprising that the average annual cost to the NHS per female is higher than that per male – £272 compared with £234 in 1984 *(Social Trends no. 17)*. This difference was almost completely accounted for by the much greater cost per female aged 75 years and over (£1159 compared with £945), since from ages 0 to 24 and 45 to 74 the average male costs were higher, and for ages 25 to 44 the female cost amounted to only £6 more.

In respect to social class use of health services, there is the added factor of private medicine, which is mainly the prerogative of the middle classes, especially 1 and 2 (see table 3.13). This situation might be seen as enhancing the health care opportunities of the working classes, since it relieves the NHS of certain of its patients. That this is not demonstrated adds an extra dimension to inequalities in health care and the functioning of the NHS. A further point of note is that, perhaps surprisingly given its importance, research in the area of the social aspects of health care provision and use tends to be somewhat piecemeal, and well removed from the consistent monitoring of overall aspects of the NHS. In his now classic survey of welfare in our society, Titmuss (1968) wrote:

> We have learnt ... that the higher-income groups know how to make better use of the service (i.e. NHS); they tend to receive more specialist attention; occupy more of the beds in better equipped hospitals; receive more elective surgery; have better maternal care; and are more likely to get psychiatric help and psychotherapy than the low-income groups – especially the unskilled.

Hart (1971) claimed that there existed 'massive but mostly non-statistical evidence in favour of Titmuss's generalizations'. Brotherston (1976) has accurately pointed out that the NHS is a 'self-help' system, which reacts to individual demands rather than seeking out those in most need. Consequently, it is likely that knowledge of the system and ability to use it – which he saw as related to intelligence and education (and which can be suspected of social class distribution) – affect the dispensation of both preventive and curative services.

In an extremely interesting analysis of GHS data, Le Grand (1978;

1982) produced evidence of social class differences in NHS expenditure related to need. Having computed the unit cost of GP consultation, hospital in-patient stay and out-patient visit (dividing total costing by total numbers for the NHS) he was able to show what proportion of NHS expenditure was received by each grouped social class (RG SEG 1 and 2; 3; 4; 5 and 6). This showed no consistent pattern. However, when the calculation was done on the age-standardized class profile of self-reported long-standing and acute sickness, differences were found. If expenditure were simply on the basis of need, he argued, the percentages for each class of self-reported ill-health and NHS expenditure should match. These figures were closest for classes 3 and 4; expenditure was higher in classes 1 and 2 and lower in classes 5 and 6. Estimating the ratio of expenditure per sick person in each class to that for classes 5 and 6 revealed that sick persons in classes 1 and 2 received something in the order of 40 per cent more expenditure than those in classes 4, 5 and 6, while those in class 3 received 17 per cent more.

In fact, it is quite possible that these figures underestimated the differential expenditure to the extent that it has been assumed that each unit of use had equal cost. Some studies have shown that GPs tend to spend more time in consultations with middle-class than with working-class patients – from an average of over six minutes for class I to four and a half for class V (Buchan and Richardson, 1973; Cartwright and O'Brien, 1976). The latter study found:

> General practitioners knew more about the domestic situation of their middle-class patients, although working-class patients had been with them longer. Middle-class patients discussed more problems and spent longer in conversation with the doctor. They may also ask more questions and get more information.

Using unpublished GHS data, Le Grand concluded that the incidence of type of complaint did not vary much within the classes – in contrast to the rates. Hence he saw the differences between them as caused by class variation in the rate at which those reporting a condition use the health service – a conclusion reached in a similar study by Forster (1976). In reviewing the evidence, Le Grand identifies three further factors affecting the lower use of health services by classes 5 and 6. First, they have a greater need for sickness absence certificates, which does not necessarily lead to subsequent contact and may artificially 'inflate' their use. Second, the costs involved in use – for example, travelling and time off work – are relatively higher for the working classes, who also appear to have less favourable perceptions of the benefits from health care. Third, the GHS 1981 showed that these groups made fewer consultations on the basis of indicators of need.

Other aspects of the NHS – including mass radiography, cervical screening, pregnancy and infant care, dental treatment, breast operations and hospital referrals – have been shown, in relation to need, to be used most by classes (RG) I and II and least by IV and V (see also table 6.13). Alderson (1971) concluded that classes I and II were 'a group ... who are aware of the provisions of the health service and who also attain a higher proportion of the resources ... than would be expected by chance, and a much higher proportion in relation to their needs when compared with others'. This conclusion was supported by Cartwright and O'Brien (1976), who added, 'There is also evidence to suggest that the middle class may, in relation to a number of services, receive better care.'

While recognizing the limitations of the research and the absence of later evidence to the contrary, the conclusions of the Working Party on Inequalities in Health submitted to the Secretary of State in 1980, the Black Report (Black, 1980; see Townsend and Davidson, 1982), commented:

> The lack of improvement, and in some respects deterioration, of the health experience of ... [classes IV and V] relative to class I ... is striking. Inequalities exist also in the utilization of health services, particularly and most worryingly of the preventive services. Here, severe under-utilization by the working classes is a complex result of under-provision in working-class areas and of costs (financial and psychological) of attendance which are not, in this case, outweighed by disruption of normal activities by sickness.

Mortality

Perhaps surprisingly, much of our knowledge about the incidence of particular diseases and medical conditions among the British population (morbidity) stems from our knowledge of the causes of death (mortality). This is partly because the registration of death, as required by law, includes cause of death and the deceased's last occupation and therefore provides a ready, on-going data base. While there are many small-scale clinical studies of particular conditions, and the careful analysis of GP consultations *(Morbidity Statistics from General Practice 1981–82*) and hospital admissions *(Hospital In-Patient Inquiry 1983*), the latter are limited in social stratification analysis to sex and age (for a review see Reid, 1989b).

The most comprehensive view of class differences of the causes of death is via the Registrar General's *Decennial Supplements* which combine death data with population data from the census to produce mortality tables. These have been produced since 1911. At the time of writing the last published was based on deaths over four years around the 1981 census (*Occupational Mortality*, 1986), though the figures for males have been published (Drever, et al. 1996).

Problems arise in compiling data of this nature. For example, the simple recording of the incidence of death by cause and by social class would be rather meaningless, mainly because age is an obvious factor in death and, as has been seen in chapter 2, the age structures of the classes, and indeed the sexes, vary. In order to make comparisons more meaningful standardized mortality ratios (SMRs) and rates are used, which effectively remove any age differences between the classes (for definition see note to table 3.3). It is also fairly obvious that while death rates have traditionally been used as indicators of levels of health, they do not tell us very much directly about the living members in society. Social change and medical advance can, and do, affect the life-chances of succeeding generations. As the Registrar General pointed out in 1971, many of the then currently registered deaths 'reflect damage caused by infections in the pre-antibiotic era, and mirror the social class differences known to exist in those decades' *(Occupational Mortality,* 1971).

A further cause for debate has been that *Decennial Supplements* use information about occupation from two separate sources – death registration and a census. At the first the information as to 'last occupation' comes from a person other than the deceased and can be suspected of inaccuracy; at the census it comes in respect to 'occupation in the last week'. In addition there was considerable debate about the contribution of selective health-related mobility between the classes to the differences in class mortality. For example, subjects experiencing poor health may move down the social classes, resulting in fewer deaths in the higher and more deaths in the lower classes. This debate has now been resolved through the OPCS Longitudinal Study (LS) which avoids these pitfalls by tracing a 1 per cent sample of the population from the 1971 census to their deaths. A major finding of LS is that the assumed selective health-related mobility between the classes does not contribute to differentials in mortality and that its data confirm earlier estimates from the *Decennial Supplement.*

Our first view is of current patterns and trends in male mortality, shown in table 3.14. As can be seen the SMRs for all causes progressively increase across the classes from 66 for class I to 189 for class V, mortality in the latter being almost three times higher than in the former. Classes IIIM and IV have nearly double the mortality of class I, class IIIN more than 50 per cent higher and class II 9 per cent higher mortality than class I. The gradient across the classes is not even, being steepest between classes II and IIIN and between classes IV and V. Similar but varying gradients can be observed for the selected causes included in the table. There is a nearly fivefold increase in mortality from lung cancer and a fourfold increase in that from suicide and undetermined injury between classes I and V. For stroke, lung cancer and suicide there is a marked difference in class V mortality compared with

Table 3.14 Male standardized mortality ratios for selected causes and age*

	Social class RG						
	I	II	IIIN	IIIM	IV	V	All
All causes	66	72	100	117	116	189	Each
Stroke	70	67	96	118	125	219	row
Ischaemic heart disease	63	73	107	125	121	182	=100
Lung cancer**	45	61	87	138	132	206	
Suicide[†]	55	63	87	96	107	215	
20–24	40	56	64	89	79	150	
25–34	42	62	87	90	104	203	
35–44	60	66	104	105	116	227	
45–54	67	69	104	113	120	201	
55–64	71	74	103	124	120	184	

* England and Wales, 1991–3, men aged 20–64. For definition of SMR see note to table 3.3.
** Includes malignant neoplasms of bronchus, trachea and lung.
† Includes suicide and injury undetermined as to whether accidental or purposely inflicted.

Devised from tables 1 and 2, Drever et al., 1996

the other classes. With the exception of suicide there is a pronounced gap in mortality between the middle and working classes. The second part of table 3.14 displays clear class gradients in each of the age groups, though with some variation. The sharpest gradients are for 25 to 34 year olds with a fivefold increase between classes I and V, and 35 to 44 year olds with an almost fourfold increase. Among those aged 20 to 24 years only class V shows an excess mortality compared with the overall 100, whereas in the age groups from 35 upwards all classes other than I and II display an excess.

Perhaps surprisingly given social changes, the introduction of the NHS and medical advances, class mortality gradients have been consistently recorded since 1921–3 (for data up to 1970–2 see Brotherston, 1976). So, while all classes are healthier now than in the past, class inequalities in health have remained. Table 3.15 shows the trends in male mortality between 1970–2 and 1991–3. The first part of the table shows that the standardized rates per 100,000 men aged 20–64 for all causes have decreased overall by some 26 per cent, from 573 to 424. With the exception of class V there has been a decline in the rates for all social classes, markedly so for classes I and II – of 36 and 35 per cent respectively. The rate for class V rose between the 1970s and 1980s from 798 to 912 and then fell to 816 in the 1990s, when it was some 2 per cent higher than in the 1970s. While the differential between classes I and II has remained close over the twenty year period, the gap between these classes and the rest has grown. In the 1970s there was a

Table 3.15 Male standardized mortality rates* and ratios (all causes) in three time periods

	Social class RG						
	I	II	IIIN	IIIM	IV	V	All
Mortality rates							
1970–2	438	461	564	613	649	798	573
1979–80/1982–3	370	417	522	578	640	912	547
1991–3	282	302	432	496	500	816	424
Mortality ratios							
1970–2	77	81	99	106	114	137	100
1979–80/1982–3	66	74	93	103	114	159	100
1991–3	66	72	100	117	116	189	100

* Rates per 100,000 per year, men aged 20–64 (in 1970–2 age group was 15–64), England and Wales.

Devised from tables 3 and 4, Drever et al., 1996

twofold difference between classes I and V; by the 1990s it was almost threefold. Over the same period the ratio of class IIIN to class I mortality rose from 1.3 to 1.5, that of class IIIM from 1.4 to 1.8 and that of class IV from 1.5 to 1.8. This widening differential between classes I and II and the others, particularly pronounced for class V, can also be seen in the relevant SMRs in the second half of the table.

The data viewed so far have been for men aged 20 to 64 years. The LS allows an extension of the above patterns beyond retirement. Although social class mortality differentials narrow somewhat with age a clear class gradient remains. For example, among men dying at 75 years and over SMRs rise from 75 for class I, that is 25 per cent lower than for all men, to 111 for class V, 11 per cent higher (Harding, 1995). Since the majority of such men in this study would have been retired at the time of the 1971 census it is hardly feasible to argue that the observed gradient was caused by downward mobility through ill-health. The cumulative effects of socio-economic environment and health-related behaviour are much more probable explanations.

The LS produced data indicating that unemployed men and their wives in the period 1971–81 had higher mortality than all men. Whereas SMRs for all men rose across the classes I to V from 73 to 120 (all 100), those for men seeking work rose from 98 to 150 (all 137) (Moser et al., 1990). A further analysis in the early 1980s found that while unemployment had risen – 87 per cent of men were employed at the 1971 census, compared with 81 in the 1981 census – a higher proportion reported themselves as retired or permanently sick rather than seeking work.

Table 3.16 Women's standardized mortality* ratios and death rates per 100,000 for all causes

	Social class RG						
	I	II	IIIN	IIIM	IV	V	All**
Standardized mortality ratios	69	78	87	100	110	134	100
Death rates							
Married women	140	122	143	196	188	221	143
Single women	162	180	201	240	270	350	223

* Women aged 20–59, married women classified by husband's occupation, based on deaths in 1979–80, 1982–3 and population in 1981. For definition of SMR see note to table 3.3.
** Includes unclassified.

Devised from tables GD34, GD20 and GD24, Occupational Mortality, 1986

This was perhaps due to financial incentives of moving from unemployment to invalidity benefit and while this resulted in a healthier group, excess mortality was again found among those seeking work (Moser et al., 1987).

As can be seen in table 3.16 the SMRs for women display a similar pattern to those of men. Since the data for women are from the 1980s any comparison with the figures for men needs to be made via the second row in the two parts to table 3.15. Women's SMRs rise between classes I and V from 69 to 134 and there are marked differences between classes I and II and IV and V, the first pair being consistently considerably lower than the second. The same is true of mean annual death rates, and here it is clear that the male rate is both higher overall than the female rates and rises more steeply over the classes. Although some of this difference is due to the difference in the age groups used for the sexes (males 20 to 64, females 20 to 59), males do have higher death rates and on average live less long than females, and average length of life declines through the classes from I to V (see next section). The table shows that married women have lower death rates than do single women, both overall and in each class (note that the married are classified by husband's occupation).

Examination of both selected grouped causes and the definitive list of causes reveals very few instances of other class patterns for either sex – such as negative gradients, and irregular relationships with, or independence from, social class. The figures relating to infant and child deaths are at tables 3.1, 3.2 and 3.3.

The social class mortality data viewed so far have been based on individuals, but class differences can also be seen area by area. Hence table 3.17 shows the SMRs for English and Welsh local authorities grouped

Table 3.17 Standardized mortality ratios* for local authorities in England and Wales

	% private households with head in social class I or II RG					
	Under 15%	15–19%	20–24%	25–29%	30% and over	All
Males	150	106	99	93	90	100
Females	110	104	99	95	95	100
No. of local authorities	38	71	107	80	107	403

* For definition see note to table 3.3.

Devised from table 6.1, Mortality and Geography, 1990

by the percentage of households in classes I or II at the time of the 1981 census. The male SMRs decline from 150 for authorities with less than 15 per cent of households in classes I or II to 90 for those with 30 or more per cent. The pattern for female SMRs is similar though less extreme. The expected gradient occurred in each of the regions. This areal approach to social class differences – see also chapter 7 – illustrates something of the geography of class and its attendant inequalities.

While SMRs are the most common measure used in analysing class mortality, there is an alternative: to view them in terms of years of potential life lost. The advantage of this method is that it gives more weight to deaths occurring at early ages. Blane et al. (1990) so analysed deaths by all causes in 1971 and 1981 and revealed wider class differences during working life than those found using SMRs, together with an increase in class inequality in years lost between the two dates.

The interpretation of these strong general patterns of relationship between social class and mortality rates is far from straightforward. It has been argued that there are two major aspects of class involved:

1 life-style – wealth, personal habits, diet, home environment, physical exercise and mental stress (the last two are partly general occupational factors)
2 specific occupational hazards.

Obviously these are not the only factors, nor are they really separable. In the past it has been argued that occupational hazards might be isolated by comparing the death rates of men and married women (classified by husband's occupation), since the women would share only the first aspect. However, the usefulness of such comparisons has always been limited by our lack of knowledge concerning the proportion of married women at work and their own occupation; in contemporary times, with a large and growing proportion of women in the workforce, it is probably of even less utility. In any case there are further substantive factors. Mortality differences may well indicate differences in the availability, quality and/or use of medical care. In addition, there are questions concerning the diagnoses of cause of death – not always a straightforward affair – and as to whether these may have a class bias, as well as a gender one.

Life Expectancy

It is evident from the differences in the age structure and death rates of the social classes and sexes that they also enjoy different average lengths of life. The Registrar General, using the actual deaths and the estimated population, periodically computes life expectancy figures as displayed in table 3.18. While the life expectancies given here do not refer directly to the lives of the current population – being based on previously recorded lives and deaths which have been affected by conditions that may now be changed – they remain as accurate a view of life expectancy as is available. Apart from their use in considerations of the extent and persistence of social inequalities in health, life expectancy tables are also used in the pricing of life insurance and in the setting up of valuation bases for occupational pension schemes (Haberman and Bloomfield, 1988).

As can be seen in the top part of table 3.18 male expectation of life at birth and through life decreases across the social classes. At birth males in classes I and II combined have a life expectancy almost 5 years longer than those from classes IV and V combined – 72.5 compared with 67.7 years. Such differences are apparent at each of the ages shown, though their size diminishes, to exactly 4 years at age 25, 3.3 at age 45 and 1.6 at age 65. Note that the given age should be added to the life expectancy: at age 25 males from classes I and II would, on average, be expected to live until aged 73.8, those from IV and V until aged 69.8.

Although the figures in table 3.18 are not directly comparable with the last set from the RG (*Occupational Mortality,* 1978) they do indicate a widening of class differences: for example, at age 15, classes I and II combined have moved from 57 to 58.5 expected years, while classes IV and V combined have moved from 55 and 53.5 respectively to 54.3 together. It can be anticipated that this trend will be present in the next RG's *Decennial Supplement* to contain life expectancy by class.

The lower part of table 3.18 shows that girls at birth have an expectancy of life some 5.3 years longer than boys, 79.1 compared with

Table 3.18 Life expectancy tables by social class for men and by gender (years)
*For men**

		Social class RG	
	I and II	IIIN and IIIM	IV and V
At birth	72.5	70.6	67.7
At age: 15	58.5	56.7	54.3
25	48.8	47.1	44.8
45	29.6	28.2	26.3
65	13.2	12.7	11.6

*By gender***

	Males	Females
At birth	73.8	79.1
At age: 5	69.4	74.6
20	54.7	59.8
60	18.0	22.1
80	6.5	8.4

* Figures for males are for Great Britain around 1981 and have been rounded from the original to first place of decimal.
** Figures for males and females are for the United Kingdom and are for 1993, based on a three year period, with population estimates updated from 1991 census.

Devised from table 5, Bloomfield and Haberman, 1992; table 12, Population Trends No. 86, 1996

73.8 years. This difference remains at around 5 years until the age of 60 when it is 4, and it closes markedly at 80 to a shade under 2. During the present century there has been a fairly dramatic increase in life expectancy, though with marked sex differences, women benefiting more than men. Between 1910–12 and 1980–2 expectation at birth increased by 19.5 years for boys and 22 years for girls. Much of this change is due to the reduction of infant mortality, though at the age of 20 years life expectancy over the period has increased by just over 7 years for men and just over 10 for women. At older ages the proportional improvement in expectation is even greater for women, whose expectation at age 60 displayed an increase over the period of 5.5 years compared with only 2.3 years for men.

Overview

This chapter has been concerned with social differences and inequalities in the vital aspects of life – birth, health and death. In broad terms we have seen that the middle in comparison with the working classes are more likely to survive birth and childhood, enjoy better health and a longer life and receive, on the basis of need, more health care. These class differences are particularly stark at the extremes of the professional and unskilled manual classes. Not only have such class differences in health a considerable history, but they have persisted through five decades of NHS provision and continue to pose a social and political challenge. As the Working Party on Inequalities in Health reported to the Secretary of State, 'Present social inequalities in health in a country with substantial resources like Britain are unacceptable and deserve to be so declared by every section of public opinion' (Black, 1980).

We have also reviewed something of the life-chance differences between the sexes, where despite their higher rates of ill-health females have better survival rates and longer average life expectancy than males. The illustration of social differences in life-chances, at least within the limitations of the data, has been relatively straightforward. Their explanation is much more problematic, as are their implications. Explanations for social differences in health and survival are, and have been, sought across a broad spectrum. In respect to sex, at one end are biological factors, such as reproduction, constitutional and hormonal differences, and at the other social factors, such as differences in social environment, roles and behaviour. Many of these provide evidence of association rather than causal relationship. What remains clear, then, is that health and its lack are affected by a complex interrelationship of factors which are also dynamic. Recently attention has been focused on life-style and behavioural habits as key factors in health and morbidity (Wells, 1987). Hence it is still appropriate to conclude with Morris (1975) that there is a continuing debate over how much is biological and how much social, and with *The Health of the Nation* (1992) that the differences are by no means fully understood. As the latter points out the differences are a complex interplay of genetic and social, environmental, cultural and behavioural factors. Barker (1990; 1991) and colleagues have drawn attention to the long-term influence of class on health, that for example contemporary patterns of health and death are influenced by foetal and infant processes that in turn may have been affected by mother's nutrition when a girl. A reasonable conclusion is that of Macintyre (1994) who sees social classifications as 'markers of specific material, environmental or psycho-social processes or conditions which may, in measurable ways, be health promoting or damaging'.

4

Income, Wealth, Poverty and Expenditure

A large proportion of the social class differences dealt with in this book can be seen to have an economic basis. Many reflect existing economic inequalities, others are the results of long-term or past inequality. At a straightforward level the ownership of goods and the use of services to some extent depend on the ability to pay for them. Of course, the relationship is not simple or direct, for motivation or desire to own or use something is important and can be overriding. Clearly, though, choice and even motivation are affected by economic circumstance.

In our society earnings, and particularly accumulated wealth, are very much private affairs. The census, unlike those in some other countries, contains no questions about them. While a question about gross income, banded up to £25,000 or more a year, has been included in the 1997 census test on 100,000 households, its inclusion in the test does not mean that it will appear in the census of 2001 (*Census News*, 1996). Industrial disputes over pay are often characterized by a lack, or confusion, of information about scales and earnings. In social research, as in real life, it is almost impossible to obtain an accurate and comprehensive picture of people's access to and possession of wealth in its variety of forms. What is available are some limited, separate views of aspects of income and wealth. The most common and important form of wealth for most adults in our society is earnings from an occupation, and it is here we begin.

Table 4.1 Average gross weekly earnings, hourly earnings and weekly hours for non-manual and manual employees*

	Social class RG/A			
	Full-time males		Full-time females	
	Non-manual	Manual	Non-manual	Manual
*Average gross weekly earnings***	465	301	302	195
Average hourly earnings†				
Including overtime	11.83	6.70	8.16	4.81
Excluding overtime	11.87	6.51	8.14	4.72
Average weekly hours				
Normal basic	37.9	39.6	36.4	38.3
Overtime	1.3	5.3	0.6	1.9
Total	39.1	44.8	37.1	40.2

* On adult rates and whose pay was not affected by absence, April 1996.
** In £ rounded.
† In £ and p rounded.
N = 119,468

Devised from tables 86 and 87, New Earnings Survey 1996, part D, 1996

Income

Earnings

The government regularly publishes very detailed statistics concerning the earnings of people in employment in Great Britain, based on a random survey of employees 'in all categories, in all occupations, in all types and sizes of business, in all industries'. Unfortunately, for our purpose, these data are only published by industry group and for manual and non-manual workers.

As might be expected, non-manual workers' average gross weekly earnings were higher than manual workers' (table 4.1). Both men and women non-manual workers earned 55 per cent more than manual workers (their pay being 155 per cent of the manual average): for men this difference amounted to £164, for women £107. These non-manual/manual earnings differences have grown considerably since 1979 when the comparable percentages were 20 and 22, and from 1987 when they were 43 and 37. Men in both non-manual and manual occupations earned just over half as much again (54 per cent) as women in 1996. This difference has closed in the past two decades: in 1973 men earned nearly twice as much as women and in 1987 around two-thirds more (*New Earnings Survey*, 1979; 1987).

Table 4.2 Men's average pay in each social class as a percentage of the average for all men, and the range of men's weekly earnings

	Social class RG/B								
	1A	1B	2	3	4	5	6	7	All
Average pay as % of all men	159	104	154	71	90	83	73	65	100
*Weekly earnings**									
Median**	109	96	98	68	86	79	73	66	82
Lowest 10%	73	64	60	50	62	57	50	47	55
Highest 10%	167	142	172	97	124	144	107	97	129
Highest 1%	256	211	324	140	182	168	154	143	220

* In £ rounded.
** For definition see text.

Devised from tables 2.28 and 2.30 Routh, 1980; table 6.8, Royal Commission on the Distribution of Income and Wealth, Report No. 8, 1979

It is also clear from the table that the differences in the actual rates of pay for manual and non-manual workers are greater, since normal hours worked and overtime are both higher for the former (third part of table 4.1). In terms of earnings per hour (second part of table), male non-manual workers earned 177 per cent of the male manual rate with overtime included and 182 per cent with overtime excluded. For women the differences were slightly smaller, at 170 and 173 per cent respectively. On an hourly basis, partly because women in full-time employment work fewer hours than men, the earnings differences are somewhat smaller than for weekly earnings. Excluding overtime non-manual male workers earned 146 per cent of the hourly rate for non-manual women and manual males 138 per cent of the manual females. Working hours are examined in more detail in chapter 5, 'Hours at work', tables 5.2 and 5.3.

A more detailed, though dated, social class analysis is provided in table 4.2. While inflation has affected the 'reality' of the figures, there are few grounds on which to suspect the pattern displayed has changed. For men in general, average pay declined across the classes as a percentage of all earnings, but the eightfold classification (see appendix B for details) reveals some interesting variation among the non-manual workers. Managers and administrators (2) earned more than lower professionals (1B), and clerical workers (3) earned less than all others, save for the unskilled (7). The same study revealed that overall, women in 1978 earned some 68 per cent of men's earnings, ranging from 52 per cent in the case of skilled manual workers to 81 per cent for higher professionals. This last figure reflects the need for higher educational qualifications for such occupations and the fact that the relationship between educational qualifications and income is more marked with respect to women than to men (see table 7.3).

Of course, average earnings cover a wide range, as is illustrated in the lower part of table 4.2. This range is illustrated by the averages for the lowest and highest 10 per cent of earners in each class and by the highest 1 per cent. For comparison the median weekly earnings are also shown: this is not the average but the figure in the middle of the earnings range, exactly half the earnings for each class being above the figure shown and half below it. The table clearly demonstrates not only the expected income differences between the classes, but also considerable variation within them. Each of the measures also displays a difference between non-manual and manual workers. The former, with the exception of class 3 (clerical workers), earned above the overall figure and the latter below. With this same exception there is a decline in earnings across the classes from 1A to 7. Differences in earnings between the sexes (not shown) were marked on all the measures and in all classes. The median weekly earnings of all women were below those earned by the lowest decile of all men, and differences were found even among higher professionals. The method of the payment of earnings also varies. Two-thirds of non-manual workers are paid monthly and over half have their wages paid directly into an account, whereas three-quarters of manual workers are paid weekly and just over half are paid in cash (*Social Trends no. 16*, table 6.17).

There are frequent claims and discussion about the closing of differentials of incomes between social groups – sometimes amounting to the suggestion that we shall all soon earn the same! The Royal Commission on the Distribution of Income and Wealth (1979) surveyed the dispersion of earnings over time and concluded:

> The evidence, therefore, suggests that changes in occupational structure have tended to widen the dispersion of earnings. This may seem surprising given the apparent contraction in the differences in earnings between occupational classes. However, the summary figures show that although the dispersion of earnings for the higher paid occupational classes has declined over time it is still greater than that for the lower paid occupational groups. Hence the movement from lower to higher paid occupations has widened the overall dispersion of earnings. (para. G.25)

The Royal Commission on the Distribution of Income and Wealth was disbanded by the incoming Conservative government in 1979, but in 1992 the Joseph Rowntree Foundation established a somewhat similar programme of research (reported in Hills, 1996). This research found not only growing economic inequality in Britain but also a widening gap between the wealthy and the poor, and in contrasting Britain with other countries concluded that such increasing inequality has not been universal (Atkinson, 1996).

Viewing the wages of men between 1966 and 1992 Gosling et al. (1996) found that the dispersion of real hourly wages was fairly flat up to 1972, became more compressed between 1972 and 1977, and sharply rose in the period to 1992 – the lowest 10 per cent of earners showing zero growth, the overall median rising by 35 per cent and the highest 10 per cent of earners rising by over 50 per cent. There can be no doubt that the gap between lowest and highest earners has grown in the last two decades. Between 1971 and 1993 the earnings of the lowest-paid tenth of men increased in real terms by 27 per cent, that of the highest tenth by 69 per cent; a similar trend with lower earnings is true for women (*Social Trends no. 24*).

Earnings are, of course, subject to taxation and this in turn affects distribution of income. The net effect of changes in income tax and national insurance contributions between 1979 and 1985 was to widen weekly real take-home pay, as is illustrated in a governmental reply to a parliamentary question *(Hansard,* 17 July 1986, quoted in Townsend et al., 1987). The take-home pay of the bottom fifth of earners decreased by £2.33 or 2.9 per cent, that of middle earners increased by £2.61 or 2.3 per cent and that of the top fifth of earners increased by £20.41 or 11.6 per cent. Taking into account increases in indirect taxation and rates together with further cuts in income tax meant that over the period 1978–9 to 1988–9 the proportion of earnings paid in taxes by married men with children *increased* for those on or below average earnings and *decreased* for those above. The tax paid by a married man with two children on average earnings (estimated at £254 per week in 1988–9) increased from 35.1 to 37.3 per cent of his gross earnings, while for one on half the average the increase was from 2.5 to 7.1 per cent, over the period. On the other hand the tax paid by a married man with two children earning five times the average earnings decreased from 48.8 to 34.2 per cent of his gross earnings, and that for one on twenty times the average (just over £5000 per week) from 74.3 to 38.5 per cent (Treasury answer to parliamentary question, *Hansard*, 10 January 1989, quoted in *The Guardian*, 16 January 1989).

There are two further aspects, tax avoidance and fringe benefits from employment, which are largely unrevealed in official data. Opportunities for the first exist at most levels, though they vary widely according to source of income, being greatest in the case of self-employment (Playford and Pond, 1983). Fringe benefits are largest and most common among the better paid and their full value is not taxed. Hence they represent a further dimension of earnings differentials. Among directors surveyed in 1981 by the British Institute of Management almost 98 per cent had company cars (one in eight additionally had prime use of a chauffeur-driven company car), over 80 per cent had

Table 4.3 Weekly household income and percentage of income from different sources*

	Social class RG SEG						
	1	2	3	4	5	6	7
Disposable income**	519.6	503.4	388.7	295.8	307.8	252.4	213.6
Gross income**	685.4	673.2	499.8	365.8	380.5	304.7	250.7
Sources of income (%)							
Wages and salaries	87.4	89.3	88.2	85.1	87.6	84.3	77.4
Self-employment	2.5	1.7	1.6	0.6	1.2	1.0	–
Investments	4.3	3.8	3.3	2.8	1.4	1.2	1.3
Annuities and pensions[†]	2.1	1.8	1.7	2.1	0.9	1.9	2.1
Social security benefits	2.7	2.8	3.5	7.0	8.1	10.2	17.7
Other sources	0.9	0.6	1.8	2.3	0.7	1.4	1.5
			Each column = 100%				

* Social class is of head of household.
** In £ rounded to nearest 10p.
† Other than social security benefits.
N = 5190

Devised from table 8.6, Family Spending 1993, 1994

travel accident and life insurance, over half had private medical insurance and more than one in five had free telephone or allowance and low-interest loans. Further benefits, such as profit-sharing, share deals and private school fees, were part of the reward for smaller proportions.

Household income

Since the majority of people live with others in households (for definition see appendix C) individual income is only part of the picture. The data from the Family Expenditure Survey in table 4.3 show that weekly household income by head's social class declines across the classes 1 to 7, though that of the skilled manual (5) was slightly higher than that of the junior non-manual (4). The difference in disposable income between classes 1 and 7 was £306, the first being more than two and a quarter times higher. The second part of the table reveals class differences in the sources of income. The most dramatic of these is social security benefits which rise from less than 3 per cent for classes 1 and 2, to 10 and almost 18 per cent for classes 6 and 7. The percentage of income from investments declines over the non-manual classes 1 to 4, with that for the manual classes being half or less than that for class 4. Those in class 1 have a much higher percentage of income from self-employment than other classes.

Table 4.4 Feelings about total household income*

	Social class MR				
	AB	C1	C2	DE	All
Can live comfortably on	52	32	25	10	27
Are coping on	33	42	52	39	42
Fairly difficult to live on	9	16	15	28	18
Very difficult to live on	2	6	7	19	10
Other/don't know	3	4	2	3	3

* Respondents were shown a card with four phrases and invited to choose the one which came closest to how they felt.

N = 1034

Devised from table 1 in appendix to Townsend et al., 1996; fieldwork by MORI

As in the case of male earnings discussed above, recent changes in the dispersion of household incomes have led to growing economic inequality in Britain, with the gap between the wealthy and the poor widening. Data from the DSS (*Households below Average Income*, 1994) show that between 1979 and 1991–2 the income of the poorest 10 per cent of households fell by 17 per cent in real terms (after allowing for housing costs) compared with an overall rise of 36 per cent and a rise of 62 per cent for the richest 10 per cent. These figures have been disputed on the grounds of doubt over the accuracy of incomes of the self-employed; however, excluding these still showed a drop of 9 per cent in real income for the poorest (Hills, 1996).

Not only is income related to standard of life and expenditure (see last section to this chapter) but there is also a subjective aspect: people vary in their expectations and contentment. Townsend et al. (1996) asked their sample which of certain phrases (see table 4.4) came closest to their feelings about their total household income. Some 28 per cent felt it was fairly or very difficult to live on, ranging from 11 per cent of class AB to 47 of class DE. Over half of class AB felt they could live comfortably on it, compared with one in ten of DE.

The data considered so far identify neither the composition of households nor the number of incomes in them. Households with more than one working member are clearly likely to have a higher per capita income than those with one or none. The two main situations of this kind are families in which both spouses/partners and/or children are working, and non-family households. Table 4.5 demonstrates the social class variation in the distribution of households with economically active and retired heads having given numbers of economically active members. There is no clear class pattern, but some distinct differences. Social class I has the lowest proportion of households with none and with three or more, while class V has the highest without any and with

Table 4.5 Percentage of households* in each class with given number of economically active members, Great Britain, 1991

	Social class RG						
	I	II	IIIN	IIIM	IV	V	All
All households							
None	8	9	12	9	12	14	10
One	36	35	38	31	36	40	35
Two	46	44	39	43	38	32	42
Three or more	10	12	10	17	14	14	13
Households with economically active member(s)							
One	40	38	44	34	40	46	39
Two	50	49	45	47	43	38	47
Three or more	11	13	12	19	16	16	15

* Of classified heads of households with economically active and retired heads.

Calculated from table 9, 1991 Census, Household and Family Composition, Great Britain, 1994

one, while class IIIM has the lowest with one and the highest with three or more. Overall 55 per cent of all the households had two or more economically active members. Since most of those without economically active members are retired person households, more useful figures in respect to income can be gained by omitting them (see second part to table). Just over three in five households with economically active member(s) have two or more, 15 per cent three or more. In the latter case there is a clear class pattern, with the middle classes below and working classes above the overall figure. In the case of households with a single economically active member, only class IIIM is markedly below the average, and classes IIIN and V above. The use of head of household to identify the social class of a household obviously gives no indication of the class of other members. The valuable, complete picture of each member together with that of the head is not available, though that of the social class of married/cohabiting couples in which the partners are in paid employment can be found in table 6.5.

Wealth

Income and wealth are not easily separated. For our purposes, the latter can be identified as assets which have a marketable value and which belong to an individual or a household, both physical – property and land, consumer durables, and other possessions – and financial – money, rent and investments (accounts, stocks and shares). Obviously, many forms of wealth provide income, in the form of interest or divi-

Table 4.6 Distribution of wealth* in the UK, 1992

	Marketable wealth	Marketable wealth, less value of dwellings**
Percentage owned by†		
Most wealthy 1% of population	18	29
Most wealthy 5% of population	37	53
Most wealthy 10% of population	49	65
Most wealthy 25% of population	72	82
Most wealthy 50% of population	92	94

* Based on estates notified for probate 1992–3.
** Net of mortgage debt.
† Percentage of adult population, age 18 and over.

Devised from table 5.23, Social Trends no. 25, 1995

dends, but the importance of wealth is very wide-reaching. As Atkinson (1980) pointed out, it also provides 'security, freedom of manoeuvre and economic and political power. Moreover, wealth is very much more concentrated than income and has a major influence on the overall degree of inequality.'

Unlike social class differences in the ownership of wealth, for which there are no data, the concentration of personal wealth is readily illustrated (see table 4.6). The data are arrived at by combining the distribution of wealth disclosed by deceased persons' estates notified for probate with estimates by the Central Statistical Office based on personal sector balance sheets. As can be seen, 1 per cent of the adult population (around 430,000 people) owned 18 per cent of marketable wealth in 1992, 10 per cent owned very nearly half, and the most wealthy half of the population owned 92 per cent, leaving the other half of society to share only 8 per cent of the wealth. In fact, 1 per cent owned two and a quarter times the wealth owned by half the population. Removing the value of dwellings from marketable wealth produces an even more dramatic picture of the concentration of wealth (see right-hand column of table 4.6). The wealthiest 1, 10 and 50 per cent owned 29, 65 and 94 per cent respectively of the wealth, leaving but 6 per cent of the wealth for half of the population. Inequality in wealth is then extremely marked and blatant: indeed, it may be difficult to appreciate. Pond (1983) provided a useful illustration based on the figures for 1979. If wealth at that time had been equally shared, each adult would have had £12,000; in reality the lower half had on average £1200, the higher £23,000 (almost twenty times higher), and the top 1 per cent had almost a third of a million pounds. Of course, there is also a considerable range of wealth to be found within each grouping.

There are two further aspects of wealth to be considered. First, its concentration has a history (see for example Royal Commission on the Distribution of Income and Wealth, 1979; Atkinson and Harrison, 1978). Wealth has remained similarly distributed throughout this century, and appears not seriously affected by changes in government. During the Conservative period 1970–4 the richest group's share of wealth fell somewhat, mainly owing to the fall in stock market prices of 1970; hence, there was no comparable gain for the poor. During the Labour government of 1974–9, committed to 'a redistribution of wealth and power in favour of working people', the earlier loss was partly regained (Pond, 1983). It is difficult to see that dramatic reductions in the top rates of income tax, changes in other forms of taxation and changes in the economic climate by the Conservative governments of the 1980s and 1990s have not been to the benefit of the already rich. Indeed, the proportion of wealth (less value of dwellings) owned by the wealthiest half of the population grew from 88 to 94 per cent between 1976 and 1992. Second, inheritance plays a substantial role in both its accumulation and its continued concentration. For example, Harbury and McMahon (1980) found that two-thirds of those who left £100,000 or more in 1965 had had fathers who had left at least £25,000. They comment, 'This illustrates the importance of having a moderately wealthy father. If there were no connection between wealth of fathers and sons, one would expect less than 1 per cent of the population of sons to have had fathers with this size fortune.'

While it is not possible to demonstrate by data a relationship between personal wealth and social class, one may be safely assumed. Such wealth is the result of inheritance, creation, saving or accumulation, the legal opportunities for which are clearly related to class. Some relatively minor aspects of wealth are dealt with elsewhere: home ownership and consumer durables at tables 6.18 and 6.22, motor cars at table 9.8. As table 4.7 shows, the proportion of households with members owning shares declines across the classes from more than half of classes 1 and 2 to less than one in ten of class 6 – and this despite governmental efforts to democratize or widen share ownership through privatization. If shares were held equally by the classes then the sample's class profile would match those of the different types of shareholders in the second part of the table. As will be seen, classes 1 and 2 are markedly over-represented as shareholders, classes 5 and 6 under-represented. Of course, these figures do not indicate differences in the quantity of shares and consequent wealth, though these are very large. In 1992 classes (MR) A and B, some 18 per cent of the population, held a third of all shares in private ownership, while classes D and E, almost a third of the population, held 15 per cent (*Social Trends no. 24*, chart 5.24).

A similar view is provided in table 4.8, together with the use of a range of financial services. Of those surveyed some 22 per cent claimed

Table 4.7 Percentage of households* with a shareholder and the social class profiles of owners of types of shares

	Social class RG SEG						
	1	2	3	4	5	6	All
% households with shareholder	55	51	31	24	15	9	30**
Profiles of shareholders							
Privatized companies	13	32	24	21	8	2	Each
Owned as employee	8	43	17	24	7	1	row
PEPs†	13	39	22	20	4	1	=100%
All shares	12	34	22	22	8	1	
Sample	6	20	22	31	16	5	

* By social class of head of household.
** Includes unclassified.
† Personal equity plans.
N = 9067; 18,155

Devised from tables 8.7 and 8.18, General Household Survey 1988, 1990

ownership of stocks and shares, the percentage in class AB approaching twice the overall value and being more than four times higher than that of class E. The figures for unit trusts are much lower and have a sharper class pattern. As might be expected, the rest of the table shows that in general the use of various financial services is greater in the middle classes than the working classes and declines across the classes. Obviously many of these can be seen to reflect differences in income and wealth, which are related either to the need for a bank or building society account, or to the ease with which credit can be obtained or the service purchased. Notice that hire purchase, the more expensive form of credit, is slightly more common in the working than the middle classes. Other items, like private health (see also table 3.13) and belonging to a pension scheme, are likely to be related also to occupation. Notice that in the case of private health the gradient across the classes is sharper for that paid for by an employer than overall: from 8 to 0.2 per cent compared with 29 to 5 per cent. Car and house insurance, like mortgages, obviously also reflect class differences in ownership and home tenure (see tables 9.8 and 6.18). The high comparative percentage of class E who have made a will and have death-only life assurance almost certainly reflects age rather than class, since state pensioners form a major part of this class.

While it does not disturb the overall picture, it should be appreciated that relatively small quantities of wealth may make for dramatic

Table 4.8 Percentage using various financial services

	Social class MR					
	AB	C1	C2	D	E	All
Bank account	90	86	80	73	56	80
Life assurance						
Death only	44	41	49	48	39	44
Policy maturity/death	46	43	45	36	20	39
Insurance						
House/flat	68	59	52	39	26	51
Home contents	70	64	60	51	40	59
Comprehensive car	79	61	52	35	19	52
Any car	89	76	77	62	36	70
Private health	29	18	14	10	5	17
Private health paid by employer	8	5	2	2	0.2	4
Savings						
Building societies	74	68	61	52	39	61
Unit trusts	13	7	4	3	2	6
Stocks and shares	37	26	18	14	8	22
Premium Bonds	36	29	22	17	17	25
Credit						
Credit card	66	52	38	25	16	43
Hire purchase	6	8	9	9	4	7
Bank overdraft	7	7	5	5	2	6
Mortgage	36	33	32	22	9	29
Have made will	49	35	25	21	26	32
Belong to pension scheme	34	30	26	21	5	25

N = 25,296

Devised from data supplied by BMRB International from Target Group Index, 1994

differences between units of similar income – for example, the inheritance of a home or the availability of assets at time of crisis. The effect of these may be proportionately most pronounced among the less well-off. Obviously again, not all middle-class people can be seen as wealthy.

Our consideration of wealth has been neatly summed up by Pond (1983):

> Britain is a deeply divided society, and the deepest division of all is the equality in the ownership of wealth. That the inequalities have persisted for so long helps in itself to legitimate them, to make them more acceptable ... And the extremities of wealth inequalities somehow deprive the

statistics of credibility or meaning. Yet the truth is that inequality feeds on itself. Wealth begets income and opportunity, status and power; and from each of these springs wealth. The inequalities are circular and self-perpetuating.

Poverty

A good deal of debate surrounds the definition of poverty, in both real life and social research. Broadly speaking there are two approaches: the absolute, in which a minimal level of income is defined as the poverty line; and the relative, in which reference is made to a standard of living, rather than survival or subsistence. At least for most people the concept of abject poverty has given way to those which involve some measure of standard of living relative to that enjoyed by the majority of members in society. However, it is not difficult to find those who see poverty in very basic terms. Sir Keith Joseph, who became the Conservative Secretary of State for Education, wrote:

> An absolute standard means one defined by reference to the actual needs of the poor and not by reference to the expenditure of those who are not poor. A family is poor if it cannot afford to eat. It is not poor if it cannot afford endless smokes and it does not become poor by the mere fact that other people can afford them. A person who enjoys a standard of living equal to that of a medieval baron cannot be described as poor for the sole reason that he has chanced to be born into a society where the great majority can live like medieval kings. (Joseph and Sumption, 1979)

More recently the Commission of the European Communities (1991) defined the poor in a broad manner as 'persons whose resources (material, cultural and social) are so limited as to exclude them from the minimum acceptable way of life in the member State in which they live'. And relative deprivation and poverty are neatly summed up by Townsend's (1993) statement: 'People are relatively deprived if they cannot obtain at all, or sufficiently, the conditions of life – that is, the diets, amenities, standards and services – which allow them to play the roles, participate in the relationships and follow customary behaviour which is expected of them by virtue of their membership of society. If they lack or are denied resources to obtain access to these conditions of life and so fulfil membership of society they may be said to be in poverty.'

Undoubtedly the most extensive and best-known study of poverty is that of Townsend (1979) which identified an 'official' level of poverty as that income at which state supplementary benefit (since 1988 called income support) was payable together with the cost of housing (for a definition, see note to table 4.9). By this standard, poverty was shown to be more widespread and frequent than might be expected. Townsend

Table 4.9 Percentage of each class in households with net disposable incomes in previous year of given percentages of supplementary benefit plus housing costs*

	Social class HJ/A								
	1	2	3	4	5	6	7	8	All
Less than 100	3	1	4	7	1	6	5	15	6
100–139	6	9	10	18	22	25	29	32	22
140–199	15	24	33	35	35	37	34	32	33
200 and over	76	67	52	40	42	31	32	20	39

* Income at which state supplementary benefit was payable, plus rent including rates or mortgage and insurance but not repairs; less than 100 per cent of this income defined as poverty, 100–139 defined as on margins of poverty.
N = 5060

Devised from table 7.13, Townsend, 1979

calculated that some 6 per cent of the population (3.3 out of 55.5 million persons) was in poverty and a further 22 per cent (11.9 million persons) on its margins. These figures increased to 9 and 30 per cent in respect to a relative income standard – a net disposable income of less than 50 per cent, or between 50 and 79 per cent, of mean of household income for its type.

As can be seen in table 4.9 poverty was much more frequent in class 8 (at 15 per cent) than in the other classes, though its incidence is uneven across the classes. The percentage on the margin of poverty increases steadily over the classes from 6 per cent in class 1 to 32 per cent in class 8. Taken together, the two measures display a similar pattern, rising from just less than one in ten in class 1 to approaching half in class 8. When viewing these figures, bear in mind that the classification includes the retired and dependants of working people. Townsend comments, 'The correlation between occupational class and poverty is more striking if the retired are excluded.' At the same time the table also shows that the percentage of those enjoying an income 200 per cent or more above the supplementary standard, plus housing cost, declined sharply across the classes from 76 of class 1 to 20 of class 8.

Proportionately more children and elderly than young and middle-aged people were found in, or on the margin of, poverty. The percentage of women in poverty was higher than men at all ages over 15, and also in respect to being on the margin, save for those aged 30 to 44. The survey showed that the factors associated with poverty were unskilled manual occupation, old age, disability, childhood, one-parent families, lack of education and unemployment. The social groupings running the highest 'risk' of poverty were: households composed of a man, a woman and three or more children, with unskilled manual status (89 per cent in, or on the margin of, poverty); those aged 80 or over (86 per cent); those retired, living alone, aged 60 or over (82 per cent); those aged 0 to 14, with parents of unskilled manual status (76 per cent); those with appreciable or severe disability and of retirement age (73 per cent). The only group of households to escape risk completely was those of professional or managerial status living alone or with spouse only, aged under 60.

As Townsend (1996) has forcibly pointed out, not only have recent governments avoided using the term 'poverty', but there is a range of shortcomings in the collection, processing and presentation of data in respect to it and low incomes. Such criticism has even come from a past member of the Cabinet of the early 1980s who pointed out that measuring poverty at that time was 'difficult because of the inadequacy, and sometimes deliberate obfuscation of government statistics. Just as a government will only find it necessary to fiddle the unemployment figures when unemployment is rising fast, it will only fudge and conceal the figures on poverty when it knows that poverty is spreading' (Gilmour, 1992).

A survey of what the public in the 1980s regarded as necessities provides a further view of poverty (Mack and Lansley, 1985). It revealed that most people saw a wide range of goods and activities as necessities and that the concept of a minimum standard of living is based on social rather than survival or subsistence criteria. Respondents were presented with a list of thirty-five items and asked to choose (a) those that they thought necessary and which all adults should be able to afford and which they should not have to do without, (b) those that may be desirable but are not necessary. More than nine people in every ten placed the following in (a): heating, indoor toilet (not shared), damp-free home, a bath (not shared), and beds for everyone. More than two-thirds also included: enough money for public transport, warm waterproof coat, three meals a day for children, self-contained accommodation, two pairs of all-weather shoes, a bedroom for every child over 10 of different sex, a refrigerator, toys for children, carpets, celebrations on special occasions such as Christmas, roast joint or equivalent once a week, and a washing machine. There was considerable agreement across the different social groups in the sample about the concept of 'socially perceived necessities'. The authors argued that poverty amounts to the enforced lack of three or more necessities (caused by low pay, rather than choice). Multiplying the number in their sample by the population led them to suggest that one person in every seven was in poverty – some 5 million adults and 2.5 million children. They identified five particular groups, which to some extent overlap: the unemployed, single parents, the sick and disabled, pensioners and the low-paid.

A similar, comprehensive approach was adopted by Townsend et al. (1987) who developed an 'objective' index of seventy-seven indicators of deprivation, based on indicators of conditions, relationships and behaviour, covering both material and social aspects and grouped as follows:

Material deprivation Dietary, clothing, housing, home facilities, environment, location, work (paid and unpaid).

Social deprivation Rights to employment, family activities, integration into community, formal participation in social institutions, recreation, education.

Townsend et al. (1996) found that a large proportion of their respondents chose consumption and social items as well as bare necessities of subsistence in defining poverty. Around half included: food for activities as well as survival (no class differences), personal health costs (percentage declined from 58 to 42 between MR classes AB and DE) and transport and work costs (percentage declined from 64 to 36 between classes AB and DE). Just under a third included education or training costs (percentage declined from 41 to 22 between classes AB and DE) and 28 per cent the cost of keeping in touch with family and friends (percentage declined from 32 to 25 between classes AB and DE).

The same study provides a view of what income people thought their household needs to keep out of poverty (see table 4.10). As would be expected there is class variation from the mean income deemed necessary: while all classes used all the income ranges, around three in ten of AB chose £299 or more per week and DE up to £144. The latter also had the most marked difference from the overall mean of £211 at £177 (see fifth row, upper part of table 4.10). Of course, these estimates are related to household composition. Townsend et al. remark that most households' estimated income needs were far higher than income support rates and fairly similar to the estimates of modest but adequate household budgets made by Bradshaw (1993). They also point out that while individuals may differ extremely in their opinions of income needs the majority are close to the mean. Perhaps more revealing are the percentages seeing their household income as above or below the necessary income they had chosen (lower part of table 4.10). The percentages seeing their income a lot above, a little above and above in class AB were, 40, 38 and 78, in class DE 5, 17 and 22; those seeing it as a lot below, a little below and below in AB were 6, 5 and 11, in DE 30, 25 and 55.

Table 4.11 provides an interesting view of people's attitudes towards state benefits and anti-poverty measures. An overall majority saw pensions and supplementary benefit (now income support) as being too low, the percentage rising only slightly across the social classes, in contrast to the steep rises for unemployment benefit (now job seeker's allowance) (which doubles from AB to D and E) and child benefit (almost three times greater for E than AB). Men were somewhat more inclined than women to agree that benefits were too low. A fairly high

Table 4.10 Income per week, after tax, thought necessary to keep household like their own out of poverty and how far above or below that level they think their household is (percentages)*

	Social class MR				
	AB	C1	C2	DE	All
Up to £144	17	16	19	29	22
£145–£221	39	42	40	48	43
£222–£298	13	14	19	13	15
£299 or more	30	27	21	10	21
Mean (£)	236	235	216	177	211
A lot above	40	16	12	5	16
A little above	38	33	38	17	30
About the same	10	20	25	23	20
A little below	5	18	16	25	18
A lot below	6	11	10	30	16

* Excluding those who did not know.
N = 1034

Calculated from unpublished tables 3 and 5, supplied by MORI from a survey conducted September 1996

degree of overall consensus about, and support for, anti-poverty measures, with the percentages rising across the classes, can be seen. The least popular and that which shows the greatest class variation is increased taxes for the rich: only 40 per cent of class AB compared with 70 per cent of D and E agreed.

Expenditure

As we have seen, there is substantial evidence of differences in income and wealth between the social classes: in general the 'higher' the class, the higher the income and wealth. Obviously a similar relationship would be expected in the case of expenditure. The most comprehensive figures available are provided by the Family Expenditure Survey which regularly surveys the expenditure of a sample of households in the UK (*Family Spending 1993*). The data in tables 4.12 and 4.13 are for households, many of which have more than one earner (see table 4.5). There is some variation by class in the average number of persons in households, class IIIN having 2.5 and IIIM 3.1, all the others 2.8. It would then be possible to compute the per person expenditure item by item, though 'person' here includes children, and no allowance can be made for class variation in the number or age of children in households even

Table 4.11 Attitudes towards benefits and anti-poverty measures (percentages)

	Social class MR					
	AB	C1	C2	D	E	All
Agree too low						
State pension	53	58	59	62	60	59
Unemployment benefit	26	27	40	53	52	40
Child benefit	12	16	29	26	34	24
Supplementary benefit*	52	54	67	54	62	59
Agree						
Differences in pay between highest and lowest too great	59	65	83	83	81	76
Government should increase taxes for rich	40	56	69	71	70	63
Gap between rich and poor today is too great	51	64	83	81	83	74
Government should introduce minimum wage for all workers	58	65	66	75	66	66

* Respondents were told that those not working received £59.20 a week excluding rent, for a family with two young children.
N = 1174

Devised from tables 7.7, 9.6 and 9.7, Mack and Lansley, 1985

though this affects expenditure. In any case, such an analysis provides a very similar pattern to that presented here: the overall expenditure per person is shown in the last row of table 4.12.

Table 4.12 shows that the items with the highest expenditure for all classes were housing and food. The middle classes spent more on housing than food, the working classes more on food than housing. The bottom two rows show that expenditure, both per household and per person, declines across the classes I to V, the expenditure in class I being around two and a quarter times that in class V in both cases. This pattern is repeated in respect to each type of expenditure listed, with the exceptions of tobacco, which rises threefold across the classes, and fuel and power, food and alcoholic drink where the general pattern is disrupted. Class IIIM expenditure is higher than class IIIN on each of these items; for fuel and power the expenditure in classes IV and V is also higher, while for alcoholic drink the expenditure in class IV is also

Table 4.12 Average weekly itemized household expenditure*

	Social class RG						
	I	II	IIIN	IIIM	IV	V	All**
Housing (net)	85.07	75.63	54.04	48.71	40.68	32.81	44.85
Fuel and power	15.79	14.90	12.70	13.78	12.90	12.77	13.24
Food	73.61	65.50	50.95	57.49	49.55	46.00	49.96
Alcoholic drink	17.32	17.71	12.02	15.02	13.41	12.01	11.95
Tobacco	3.30	4.66	5.00	8.18	8.45	9.90	5.59
Clothing and footwear	30.01	27.75	20.25	19.12	16.65	13.07	17.40
Household goods and services	70.70	56.33	43.89	41.45	30.29	26.81	38.49
Personal goods and services	16.65	19.06	11.56	11.26	9.06	8.05	11.04
Motoring	72.58	53.51	45.98	43.62	36.54	24.09	36.28
Fares and other travel costs	11.70	11.50	7.98	7.34	5.93	4.27	6.95
Leisure goods and services	89.50	64.56	39.05	35.82	27.36	23.44	38.82
Miscellaneous	3.92	3.77	2.55	2.44	1.86	1.63	2.10
Total expenditure	490.20	415.00	306.00	304.30	252.70	214.80	276.20
Expenditure per person	172.70	146.70	121.20	99.50	89.90	77.50	111.70

* In £ and p. Total and per person expenditure rounded to nearest 10p. Social class is of head of household.

** Includes retired, unoccupied and unclassified.

N = 6979

Devised from table 3.5, Family Spending 1993, 1995

higher and that in V is almost identical. The range of expenditure at the extremes shows variation. While some items are close to the overall, class I households spend almost four times more than class V on leisure goods and services, three times more on motoring, and over twice as much on clothing and footwear. The differences are closer in respect to fuel and power, food and alcohol. Tobacco is the only exception where class V expenditure is higher than class I – some three times more.

A further view is provided in table 4.13 where data have been recast and expressed as a percentage of each class's overall expenditure. The percentages of expenditure directed to the necessities of fuel and power and food both rise across the classes; taken together they account for some 27 per cent of class V households' expenditure, but only 18 per cent of that of class I. Alcohol and tobacco expenditure also rise across the classes, accounting for some 4 per cent of class I and 10 per cent of

Table 4.13 Average weekly itemized expenditure as a percentage of total household expenditure*

	Social class RG						
	I	II	IIIN	IIIM	IV	V	All**
Housing (net)	17.3	18.2	17.7	16.0	16.1	15.3	16.2
Fuel and power	3.2	3.6	4.2	4.5	5.1	5.9	4.8
Food	15.0	15.8	16.7	18.9	19.6	21.4	18.0
Alcoholic drink	3.5	4.3	3.9	4.9	5.3	5.6	4.3
Tobacco	0.7	1.1	1.6	2.7	3.3	4.6	2.0
Clothing and footwear	6.1	6.7	6.6	6.3	6.6	6.1	6.3
Household goods and services	14.4	13.6	14.3	14.2	12.0	12.5	13.9
Personal goods and services	3.4	4.6	3.8	3.7	3.6	3.7	4.0
Motoring	14.8	12.9	15.0	14.3	14.5	11.2	13.1
Fares and other travel costs	2.4	2.8	2.6	2.4	2.3	2.0	2.5
Leisure goods and services	18.3	15.6	12.8	11.8	10.8	10.9	14.0
Miscellaneous	0.8	0.9	0.8	0.8	0.7	0.8	0.8

* Social class is of head of household.
** Includes retired, unoccupied and unclassified.
N = 6979

Calculated from table 3.5, Family Spending 1993, 1995

class V's expenditure. Other items display less marked differences, with net housing costs falling by only 2 per cent from class I to V and clothing and footwear together with personal goods and services being very similar for all classes. Leisure goods and services have the largest decline in percentage expenditure across the classes, 18 to 11 per cent.

Most forms of household expenditure are subject to indirect taxation – VAT, car tax, etc. – and while such taxes are obviously related to expenditure, there are large proportional differences related to household disposable income. In 1991, among households with heads below retirement age, those with incomes in the bottom fifth of the distribution found that indirect taxes accounted for 29 per cent of their income, those in the top fifth 14 per cent (*Social Trends no. 24*, chart 5.16).

This chapter has demonstrated the extent and strength of the relationship of inequalities of wealth and poverty with social class in Britain. Such differences may have been anticipated by readers, but are still likely to have an impact when straightforwardly presented. Severe divisions of economic well-being are not those terms in which many choose to see our society. Indeed, it may be argued that it is such a disinclination that limits not only discussion but also the extent and nature of research in the field. Certainly, as we have seen, knowledge is limited and somewhat piecemeal. In particular, and perhaps not surprisingly, the very rich and their circumstances are well shielded from public gaze and better protected from, and by, economic change. We have also seen that despite some apparent efforts towards redistribution, the realities of income and wealth differentials in our society not only appear stubbornly tied to those of our history, but also display clear signs of having increased in the last two decades. As Tawney (1931) observed: 'What thoughtful rich people call the problem of poverty, thoughtful poor people call with equal justice the problem of riches.'

5

Work, Unemployment and Social Mobility

Work

Work covers a wide range of activities and has a number of connotations. Our concern here is almost exclusively with paid work, since most of the data reviewed apply to those in full-time employment. This is not, of course, to deny the importance of unpaid work, the bulk of which is undertaken by women. Likewise it is important to appreciate that there are differences between the sexes in terms of their involvement in the labour market (for a review see Webb, 1989). In comparison with men, women are less likely to be economically active or self-employed and more likely to work part-time. It can be estimated that in 1991 some 82 per cent of the population of Great Britain aged 20 to 59 was economically active, 92 per cent of men, 74 per cent of married women and 72 per cent of non-married women (calculated from *Labour Force Survey 1990 and 1991*, tables 6.1 and 6.6). Women are more likely than men to work part-time. Of those aged 16 and over in employment, 94 per cent of men worked full-time compared with 71 per cent of non-married women and 50 per cent of married women. More than twice as many men as women in employment were self-employed (17 compared with 7 per cent, overall 13 per cent) (*Labour Force Survey 1990 and 1991*, tables 6.9 and 6.10). The aspects of work which follow need to be viewed within this context.

Table 5.1 Percentage of women aged 16 to 59 working full-time and part-time by own social class and age of youngest dependent child*

	Social class RG SEG					
	1 and 2	3	4	5	6	All
Youngest child aged 0–4						
Full-time	33	16	15	6	2	15
Part-time	28	34	40	27	44	33
Youngest child aged 5–9						
Full-time	53	22	28	10	3	21
Part-time	27	47	39	44	61	45
Youngest child aged 10 or over						
Full-time	61	33	40	22	6	32
Part-time	23	47	37	46	67	45
No dependent child						
Full-time	77	57	49	40	11	53
Part-time	10	21	24	24	50	22

* Of women whose hours of work were known, not including those on YT and ET; data for 1992–4 combined.
N = 18,754

Devised from table 7.11, General Household Survey 1994, 1996

Women and paid work

Women's employment is clearly affected by their role in mothering and child care. A GHS survey found overall that the percentage of women working full-time was 38 and part-time 30; of those without dependent children the percentages were 53 and 22, and of those with 22 and 40; all three groups had 6 per cent unemployed. As can be seen in table 5.1 the percentage of women with dependent children in paid employment increases with the age of the child, from 48 for those aged 0 to 4 to 77 for those aged 10 or over, which more than matches the proportion of women working without a dependent child. The percentage working full-time more than doubles, that for part-time increases by just over a third. The middle classes have higher proportions working and working full-time and a lower one working part-time than classes 5 and 6, regardless of having a dependent child(ren) or of the age of the youngest.

Table 5.2 Percentage of non-manual and manual employees* with certain normal basic working hours**

	Social class RG/A			
	Full-time males		Full-time females	
	Non-manual	Manual	Non-manual	Manual
Up to 36 hours	25	7	12	10
36–38	43	27	28	10
38–40	23	54	43	26
40–42	3	3	13	46
42 and over	6	9	4	7

* In April 1996, of full-time employees on adult rates whose normal basic hours were more than 30 (25 for teachers and academics) per week.
** For example, 36–38 means over 36 not over 38.
N = 120,766

Calculated from tables 149 and 150, New Earnings Survey 1996, part F, 1996

Hours at work

There are two continuous surveys which provide a view of the time spent at work, one in terms of employee's normal basic hours as identified by employers (New Earnings Survey) and the other of hours worked identified by respondents (Labour Force Survey). Table 5.2 shows the normal basic hours of full-time non-manual and manual employees (for definition of full-time see note to table) by sex. In the case of males it is clear that non-manual employees had shorter working weeks than the manual: for example, just over two-thirds of the former had basic hours of up to 38, while two-thirds of the latter had more than 38 hours. The extremes are more marked: the percentage of male non-manual employees with up to 36 hours is around three and a half times higher and that with 42 or more hours is appreciably lower than manual employees (25 compared with 7 per cent and 6 compared with 9). This pattern is the same as the overall view seen in the previous chapter (table 4.1). For females the pattern is similar, though the hours were longer than for males: for example, 17 per cent of non-manual and 53 per cent of manual employees had hours of 40 or over.

The LFS asks respondents: 'How many hours per week do you usually work excluding meal breaks in your main job/business?' The data in table 5.3, which is limited to full-time employees, presents a different picture of hours worked from table 5.2, with almost half the males claiming to work over 45 hours a week. There is no clear pattern across the classes. Classes I, II and IIIM have similar higher percentages working 41 or more hours (66 to 69) than the others (50 to 59). For

Table 5.3 Percentage of full-time employees claiming total usual hours worked in a week

	Social class RG						
	I	II	IIIN	IIIM	IV	V	All*
Male							
Up to 34	1	2	2	2	2	2	2
35 to 40	33	30	47	32	40	45	35
41 to 45	18	14	18	18	18	17	16
45+	48	55	32	48	41	35	48
Female							
Up to 34	3	5	5	13	14	29	7
35 to 40	38	48	74	53	56	47	58
41 to 45	18	16	11	16	12	8	14
45+	42	30	10	19	18	15	21
All							
Up to 34	1	2	4	3	7	9	3
35 to 40	34	37	64	35	45	45	43
41 to 45	18	15	14	17	16	15	16
45+	47	46	18	44	32	31	38

* Includes unclassified.
N = 148,426

Calculated from data supplied by Quantime Ltd from Labour Force Survey, Spring 1996

females the percentage working that number of hours declines across the classes from 60 to 23, with the exception of IIIN (21 per cent). The table also shows that overall women worked somewhat shorter hours than men: 65 per cent worked up to 40 hours compared with 64 per cent of men who worked 41 or more, and this difference can be seen in each social class.

Holidays

A further aspect of hours at work, and consequently of hourly pay, is the number of weeks worked in a year. Quite apart from such considerations, holiday entitlement is an important condition and attraction of employment. The latest published data on the range of holiday entitlements, not including the eight Bank Holidays, of full-time manual and non-manual employees by sex are in table 5.4. As can be seen, overall non-manual employees enjoyed the longest holidays, and men fared somewhat better than women – though this difference may be affected

Table 5.4 Percentage of full-time employees* with given number of weeks holiday**

	Weeks						
	2 or less	2+ to 3	3+ to 4	4+ to 5	5+ to 6	6+ to 8	8 or more
Males	3	4	20	24	39	8	3
Manual	3	5	19	28	40	5	0.3
Non-manual	4	3	20	19	38	10	5
Females	4	4	25	25	31	4	6
Manual	5	6	22	31	30	7	0.6
Non-manual	4	4	26	24	31	4	8

* On adult rates of pay.

** For example, 2+ to 3 means more than 2 and no more than 3. Not including eight Bank Holidays.

Devised from tables 193 and 194, New Earnings Survey 1987, part F, 1987

by differences in extra holidays given for long service, which are included but not identifiable.

In terms of overall male holiday entitlement, five weeks equally divides the range: half receive up to five weeks, half receive five weeks or more; and this provides a measure for comparison with other groups. Hence the percentage of employees entitled to five or more weeks ranged: male non-manual 53 per cent (15 per cent had six or more); male manual 45 per cent; female non-manual 43 per cent (12 per cent six or more); female manual 38 per cent. The higher proportion of female than male non-manual employees with eight or more weeks' holiday (eight compared with five) is accounted for by the sexual imbalance in such occupations as teaching.

Occupational pension schemes

Until 1988 there were two main forms of pension provision, that of the national insurance scheme (NIS) and the pensions provided by some employers, many of which were mandatory and involved opting out of the earnings-related part of NIS. Presently, employees may choose to opt out of both these forms of pension into private personal schemes, and can, of course, choose to have both employers' and personal pensions. Table 5.5 shows that the participation of full-time employees in employers' schemes for both sexes decreases across the classes from 1 to 6, somewhat more sharply for females than males (67 to 27 per cent compared with 74 to 43). In each class it is higher for men than women,

Table 5.5 Percentage of employees* who are members of their current employer's or personal pension schemes

	Social class RG SEG						
	1	2	3	4	5	6	All
Employer's scheme							
Males, full-time	74	70	68	50	47	43	60
Females, full-time	67	60	60	39	30	27	54
Females, part-time	44	39	27	15	11	9	19
Personal scheme							
Males, full-time	29	33	22	34	27	22	29
Females, full-time	28	28	20	25	19	13	22
Females, part-time	28	21	15	16	10	7	12

* Employees aged 16 and over, excluding YT and ET. Data for 1992–4 combined.
N = 25,210; 24,475

Devised from tables 8.8 and 8.9, General Household Survey 1994, 1996

and overall it is 60 compared with 54 per cent. These class differences are mainly explained by differences in employers' provision of a scheme. In 1991 the percentage of full-time employees who reported that their employer had no pension scheme rose across the classes 1 to 6, from 11 to 32 of men, and 7 to 26 of women (GHS 1991, table 6.9). The pattern for personal pensions is similar, though with much lower percentages and proportionally higher participation by class 4 than 3. The table suggests that a very small number of respondents had pensions of both types, and they appear to be limited to males in classes 1 and 2. Female part-time workers are clearly the least likely to be in a pension scheme of either type: both types display a marked declining gradient across the classes for these workers.

As would be expected occupational pensions vary considerably in amount. A survey in 1988–9 found that the weekly median pension of those aged between 55 and 69 and retired from non-manual jobs in rounded pounds was £81 for men and £26 for women, while for those from manual jobs the figures were much lower at £24 and £10 (*Retirement and Retirement Plans*, 1992, table 6.64). The same source (table 7.28a) showed that the average total usual weekly income of retired men declined across the classes (RG) from £183 for class I to £67 for class V.

Conditions at, and satisfaction with, work

The topics dealt with so far are aspects of the conditions of work. A more general though now dated view of this is provided by Townsend

Table 5.6 Employees' attitudes to work (percentages)

	Social class RG SEG					
	1	2	3	4	5 and 6	All
Would still work if no financial need	78	72	74	70	74	74
Job is more than just a living	85	80	59	46	50	64
Do the best I can even if it interferes with my life	72	66	39	43	43	52

N = 2945

Devised from table on p. 43, Hedges, 1994

(1979). As might be expected, the incidence of unusual hours of work, poor working conditions and amenities, lack of job security and welfare/fringe benefits increased across the social classes. In each case there was a marked difference between non-manual classes and manual, and within the latter between skilled, semi-skilled and unskilled workers. Such differences might well be expected to relate to how people feel or think about the work they do. A common question asked in surveys concerns people's satisfaction with their work. The GHS used to ask, 'Which of the statements on this card comes nearest on the whole to what you think about your present job: very satisfied, fairly satisfied, neither satisfied nor dissatisfied, rather dissatisfied, very dissatisfied?' Such questions can be seen as problematic because of the variation of meaning and expectations that we can assume surround such an idea. Perhaps surprisingly, very high levels of satisfaction were found: overall, some 79 per cent of men were 'very' or 'fairly' satisfied. Satisfaction was highest in classes (RG SEG) 1 and 2 and 4 at between 81 and 85 per cent and marginally lower in the other classes at 75 to 78. Dissatisfaction rose from around one in eight in class 1 to approaching one in five in class 6 (GHS 1977, table 4.8). In fact social class differences were far from dramatic, and other variables were significant. For example, women tend to be 'very satisfied' more than men (50 per cent as compared with 34 per cent), married persons more than single (43 as compared with 38 per cent), and part-time more than full-time workers (56 as compared with 39 per cent) (GHS, 1977).

Work is clearly an important aspect of life to those involved and one to which many have strong attachment. Table 5.6 shows relatively little class variation of pattern from the 74 per cent of employees who say they would work even if there was no financial need to do so. At the same time it is also clear that seeing one's job as more than just a living ranges from some four in five for classes 1 and 2 to half in 5 and 6 combined, with the first two standing out from all the others. This pattern is

Table 5.7 Percentage of employees reporting absence from work because of own sickness or injury*

	Social class RG					
	I	II	IIIN	IIIM	IV	V
Men	2.2	2.9	3.8	3.6	3.7	4.0
Women	3.8	4.7	4.9	4.4	5.3	4.6
All	2.4	3.7	4.6	4.2	4.5	4.4

* In previous week.
N = 148,426

Calculated from data supplied by Quantime Ltd from Labour Force Survey, Spring 1996

repeated for those who claim to do the best they can at work even if it interferes with their life.

Absence from work

Given the social class differences in health (see chapter 3), together with differing occupational health demands and hazards, the variation in absence from work because of own sickness or injury shown in table 5.7 can be seen as surprisingly small. Overall and for men classes I and II have the lowest rates. For women only class I has a much lower rate than overall and class IV is the highest, whereas for men the highest is V. It is also clear that women's absence is higher than men's in each class.

Of course, absence from work may be for other reasons. The last GHS (GHS 1983) to report on absence for work for any reason found that 5 per cent of classes (RG SEG) 1 to 3 compared with 8 per cent of classes 4 to 6 had been absent. Rates of absence did not appear to be related to the presence of dependent children for either sex, but not surprisingly the age of child did affect women's absence. Women with children under the age of 5 had an absence rate for personal and other reasons (including on account of children, but excluding own illness and injury) of 7 per cent, compared with 2 per cent of those with older children and 1 per cent with none.

Trade union membership

The percentages of employees who were members of trade unions, or staff associations, are to be found in table 5.8. Men are slightly more likely to belong than women, 31 compared with 28 per cent (which is in some contrast to membership of other types of organization: see

Table 5.8 Membership* of trade unions and staff associations (percentages)

	Social class RG						
	I	II	IIIN	IIIM	IV	V	All
Males	28	28	28	37	33	23	31
Females	31	44	20	25	13	17	28

* By employees in Great Britain.
N = 148,426

Devised from data supplied by Quantime Ltd from Labour Force Survey, Autumn 1996

chapter 9). There is no consistent class pattern to differences in membership. For men the highest level of membership is in classes IIIM and IV whereas for women it is classes I and II. For men the lowest membership is in class V, for women class IV. Data from an earlier, though not strictly comparable, survey (GHS 1983, table 7E) suggest that considerable change has taken place. Membership was much higher at 58 per cent of men and 50 per cent of women, with a similar class pattern to both, highest in classes (RG SEG) 4 and 5 and lowest in 1 and 2. Such change may well reflect changes in employment and the availability and popularity of trade unions. For example, the GHS found public sector employees more likely than those in the private sector to be members: 85 compared with 43 per cent of men, over three-quarters compared with a third of women. This difference reflected the fact that whereas 95 per cent of employees in the public sector said there was a trade union at work, this was true of only 58 per cent of those in the private sector. Within the private sector membership was much higher in larger establishments than in smaller ones.

Unemployment

The definition of unemployment is not straightforward. Not only are there different definitions, but these are changed: for example, there were nineteen changes in the official definition of unemployment between 1979 and the mid 1980s. Nearly all of these resulted in a reduction of the officially recorded unemployed – that is registered claimants (*Unemployment Unit Bulletin*, 1986). By 1997 the number of changes had risen to thirty-two and estimates were made that using the 1979 definition the jobless would be 3 million rather than 1.75 million (Milne, 1997). So the level of unemployment depends to an extent upon both how it is defined and how data are collected. However, whatever definition is used it is clear that between the 1970s and 1980s unemployment rose dramatically. The census records the unemployed as those stating they are 'seeking work': in 1971 some 4 per cent of the economically active were so recorded compared with 9 per cent in 1981, when the percentage of unemployed men rose tenfold across the classes from 2 per cent in class I (RG) to 21 in class V. The figures for women were lower overall and particularly in the manual classes. This difference may well reflect that some women 'do not regard themselves as seeking work if there is little chance of getting a job' *(Britain's Workforce,* 1985). A UK peak of 12 per cent was reached in 1985 and 1986 according to the official definition of people claiming benefits on the day of the monthly count, who on that day were unemployed and able and willing to do any suitable work (excluding students claiming during a vacation). The *Employment Gazette* up to September 1982 published figures for unemployment and notified job vacancies at unemployment offices broken down into non-manual and manual. These revealed a clear imbalance between the two: non-manual males represented 40 per cent of the workforce but only 20 per cent of the unemployed; in contrast the respective figures for manual classes were 60 and 80. Female unemployment was split more evenly – 58 per cent non-manual, 42 manual – reflecting more closely their proportions in the workforce at the time (63 and 37 per cent). Non-manual job vacancies at 46 per cent were more abundant in proportion to the unemployed (31 per cent) than were manual vacancies.

There are some reservations to be made to these figures. Not all unemployed persons registered as such; for example, a major motivation for registration was gaining social security benefits, but not all the unemployed qualified or were entitled to these. This applied particularly to women, who consequently were more likely than men to be excluded from such official figures. Further, it was estimated that notified vacancies at employment offices may have been only about a third of those existing in the economy. It should also be borne in mind that wide variations are to be found in unemployment and vacancies in different parts of the country. However, there are clear and general indications that unemployment among manual workers, particularly men, is both more common and less likely to be alleviated than that among non-manual workers.

A good view of the period and class distributions is gained from the GHS data in table 5.9. The definition used for the 1975 and 1985 figures was those out of work in the week prior to interview who were looking for work (or who would be but for temporary sickness) or who were waiting to take up a job already obtained; in 1994 the definition used (that of the International Labour Organization) was those waiting to take up a job or who had sought work in the past four weeks and would be able to start work in the next two weeks. The lowest part of the table shows the overall percentage of the unemployed rose across the classes:

Table 5.9 Percentage unemployed* by gender and social class, 1975, 1985 and 1994

	Social class RG SEG						
	1	2	3	4	5	6	All
Males							
1975	1	2	2	4	6	15	4
1985	1	3	6	11	19	30	10
1994	4	4	9	12	16	26	10
Females							
1975	4	2	3	3	4	1	3
1985	0	5	7	8	12	3	8
1994	3	3	6	4	10	9	6
All							
1975	1	2	3	3	5	7	4
1985	1	4	7	11	15	17	9
1994	4	4	7	11	12	17	8

* Of economically active persons aged 16 and over.
N = 10,692

Devised from table 7.5, General Household Survey 1994, 1996

sevenfold in 1975, seventeenfold in 1985 and just over fourfold in 1994. For the last two years the percentage of the middle classes unemployed was lower than the overall average, that for the working classes higher. This pattern is repeated for men, though both the gradients and the gap between the grouped classes are more dramatic. For example in 1994 the percentage of class 6 unemployed was six and a half times higher than class 1. The figures for women are much less marked, especially in 1975, though in 1994 the percentage in classes 5 and 6 was some three times higher than classes 1 and 2.

A further, recent view is provided by the LFS data based on the ILO definition of unemployment (see above) in table 5.10. As can be seen those claiming to be unemployed rose across the classes from 3 to 14 per cent overall, and for both men and women there was a sevenfold rise between classes I and V (3 to 21 and 1 to 7 per cent respectively). Women's rates were consistently lower then men's. Respondents were also asked how long they had been unemployed. The lower part of the table shows, perhaps surprisingly, that there is no overall class pattern to the duration of unemployment, though of course proportionally there are differences. For example, the middle classes have a lower percentage of unemployment for three or more years than the working classes, the percentage of the unemployed experiencing it ranging across the classes I to V as : 10, 13, 8, 18, 13, 17.

Table 5.10 Unemployment and length of unemployment* (percentages)

	Social class RG						
	I	II	IIIN	IIIM	IV	V	All**
Unemployment							
Men	3	4	7	9	13	21	10
Women	1	3	5	7	7	7	6
All	3	4	5	8	10	14	8
% unemployed for							
Less than 3 months	0.7	1.1	2.0	1.8	2.9	3.6	2.1
3 to 12 months	1.0	1.3	1.9	2.9	3.9	4.5	2.8
1 to 3 years	0.6	0.7	1.1	2.2	2.3	3.5	1.9
3 or more years	0.3	0.5	0.4	1.4	1.3	2.4	1.4

* Of economically active persons aged 16 or over in Great Britain, surveyed March to May 1996.
** Includes unclassified.
N = 148,426

Devised and calculated from data supplied by Quantime Ltd from Labour Force Survey, Spring 1996

Social Mobility

Mobility between social classes, both intra-generational (that is, upward or downward movement between social classes during a person's working life) and inter-generational (that is, the change in social class between two generations, typically father and children), has been surveyed since the Second World War, first in the classic British study of male inter-generational mobility by Glass (1954; for a review see Reid, 1977) and more recently by Goldthorpe et al. (1980; 1987). The latter authors argue that because of the nature of the social class scale they used (see appendix B for details) the seven classes do not form a consistent hierarchy. Consequently, they define upward and downward mobility only as movement into and out of classes I and II (the service class) regardless of origin or destination. Their basic data are contained in table 5.11, both parts of which use the social class of the respondents at time of interview and that of their fathers when the respondents were aged 14 years. The first part is an 'inflow' view, showing the social class origins of the respondents by their own class. Hence the left-hand column of figures shows that 25 per cent of those in class I originated in that class, 13 per cent were from class II, and so on down the column. The second part is an 'outflow' view, showing the social class achieved by respondents from different class origins. Hence the top row of

Table 5.11 Social class composition and distribution of respondents by father's class* when respondents were aged 14 (percentages)

Class composition

Father's social class (HG)	Respondent's social class (HG) I	II	III	IV	V	VI	VII		All
I	25	12	10	7	3	2	2		8
II	13	12	8	5	5	3	3		6
III	10	10	11	7	9	6	6		8
IV	10	12	10	27	9	7	8		10
V	13	14	13	12	17	12	10		13
VI	16	22	26	24	31	42	35		30
VII	12	17	23	18	27	28	37		25
			Each column = 100%						
All	14	12	10	8	12	22	22		100

Class distribution

Father's social class (HG)	Respondent's social class (HG) I	II	III	IV	V	VI	VII		All
I	46	19	12	7	5	5	7		7
II	29	23	12	6	10	11	9		6
III	19	16	13	7	13	16	16	Each	8
IV	14	14	9	21	10	15	16	row	10
V	14	14	10	8	16	21	17	= 100%	13
VI	8	9	8	6	12	31	26		30
VII	7	9	9	6	13	25	32		25
All	14	12	10	8	12	22	22		100

* Or other head of household.
N = 9434

Devised from tables 2.1 and 2.2, Goldthorpe et al., 1980

figures shows that of respondents with class I fathers, 46 per cent were themselves in that class, 19 per cent in class II, and so on across the row.

There are a number of ways in which these data can be viewed, and for a full discussion within the theory and literature of social mobility see chapter 2 of Goldthorpe et al. (1980). What is fairly obvious is that all classes are composed of men from the whole range of class origins, though the proportion whose class is the same or similar to that of their origins is much higher than would be expected if 'perfect' mobility existed, that is, if the social class system were completely open and social origin had no bearing on, or did not affect, one's achieved social class. If that were the case, it would be expected that the overall figures in the first part of table 5.11 would be the same, or approximately so, as those across the social classes. So, since 8 per cent of those surveyed had fathers from class I, they should themselves constitute that percentage of class I: in fact they are 25 per cent (three times higher) of that class. At the other extreme only 12 per cent of those in class I had fathers from class VII (the class that provided 25 per cent of those surveyed). The opposite pattern can be seen in respect of those in the working classes (VI and VII); for example, in the latter case, 37 per cent had origins in that class compared with 2 per cent from class I. The only class that gets very close to the idea of 'perfect' mobility is V (fifth row), where the percentages in classes I and II are 13 and 14, matching their overall figure of 13 per cent. Clearly, the general picture is far from one of 'perfect' mobility, there being a strong relationship between origin and destination.

This is further illustrated by the different view given in the second part of table 5.11. Here can be seen the social class distributions of sons from different class backgrounds – giving an indication of the chances of men from certain backgrounds achieving each class. For example, of those from class I, 65 per cent were in the service class (46 per cent in I and 19 in II), the percentages for class II being 52, 29 and 23 respectively. Of those from the working class 57 per cent stayed in that class. Social mobility, as defined by the authors (see above), was then of the order of 12 per cent of class I and 20 per cent of class II who entered the working class, and around 16 per cent of those from classes VI and VII who moved from working to service class. A conclusion drawn by the authors is that social mobility may be easier upwards than downwards. In other words, in the face of general upward mobility in society the service class appears to be fairly stable, its members remain in that class. This is interestingly related to intra-generational mobility, as illustrated by movement from class of origin to first job and then to current class/occupation of men aged 35 years and over. The first part of table 5.12 shows that while only 29 per cent of the sons of service-class fathers went directly into that class, by the time of interview some 63 per cent were there. In the third part, while 76 per cent of the sons of working-class fathers entered directly into that class only 48 per cent remained there, 8 per cent having moved to the service class and the rest to the intermediate class, while 6 per cent had moved from the latter class into the working class.

In reviewing the effects on social mobility of increasing educational opportunities and the growth in demand for educational qualifications, the writers suggest that, while the chances of mobility are increasingly influenced by educational attainment, there is little evidence of a decline in the importance of other avenues. This is especially evident since most of the increase in upward mobility they traced occurred before the expansion of higher education in the 1960s.

Table 5.12 Social class origins, first job* and job of men aged 35 and over (percentages)

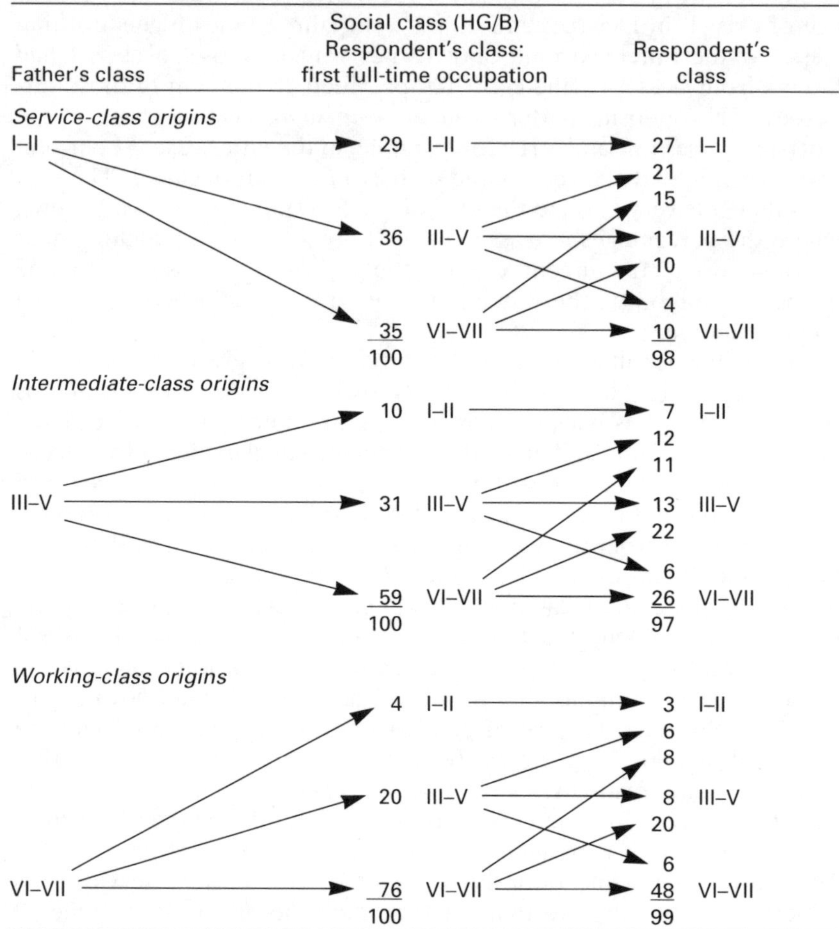

* First job following full-time education and not interrupted for more than two years except by National Service. Excludes holiday jobs or jobs held while waiting to take up apprenticeship. Trainees etc. classified as belonging to occupations which they were training for.
N = 5221

Devised from figure 2.1 and note p. 66, Goldthorpe et al., 1980

Obviously, social mobility is related to the job opportunities available to sons and the differences between those opportunities and those available to their fathers. Goldthorpe et al. observe that the decline in the proportion of manual occupations mainly affected women. The structure of male occupations has changed only since the inter-war period and, unlike women's, this change was not mainly towards the routine non-manual. As a consequence, male redistribution has been from manual to classes I and II. Similarly, they suggest that part of upward mobility may be due to differing social class birth rates, requiring working-class recruitment into the middle classes. Their conclusion is that a high level of social mobility is not incongruent with stability in the higher classes, both of which are trends demonstrated in their data. Indeed, Goldthorpe et al. show that upward mobility increased over time: younger men had better chances of gaining service-class jobs and a lower risk of downward mobility. However, this was not seen as indicating that Britain had become a more open society, since the increase is mainly accounted for by changes in the economic structure over the period considered. The *relative* chances of men from different classes displayed little change and the conclusion reached was:

> even in the presumably very favourable context of a period of sustained economic growth and of major change in the form of the occupational structure, the general underlying processes of inter-generational class mobility – or immobility – have apparently been little altered and indeed have, if anything, tended in certain respects to generate still greater inequalities in class chances.

Much the same conclusion is reached in a similar study of social mobility in the period 1972 to 1983 (Goldthorpe et al., 1987). Despite the change from one economic era to another, the relative chances of mobility remained much the same as they had been for most of the century. In the period there was a heightening both of opportunities created by structural changes and of risks from the return of large-scale, long-term unemployment (though as we have seen above, this was greatest in the manual classes). The combination of a deterioration of economic climate with a government since 1979 which explicitly rejected greater social equality is seen to have widened differences, especially, but not only, through the emergence of a highly disadvantaged underclass. Goldthorpe et al. suppose that in the long run tendencies towards greater inequality will widen the already marked inequalities of opportunity.

One of the few British studies to provide views of female social mobility based on their own employment is that of Abbott and Sapsford (1987). Since it differs in a number of important respects from Goldthorpe et al. – it was conducted later, covered the UK not just England and Wales, used a quota as opposed to random sampling, used MR rather than HG social class, and had fewer respondents – direct comparisons are limited. Table 5.13 gives the inflow and outflow views of female social mobility similar to those for males (table 5.11).

As can be seen from the first part of the table, there is considerable heterogeneity in classes A and B (though less than in the case of men),

Table 5.13 Social class composition and distribution of employed women, by father's class (percentages)

Father's class	Woman's social class MR A	B	C1	C2	D		All
Class composition							
A	50	17	13	5	2		11
B	24	35	23	12	4		20
C1	15	17	21	13	13		17
C2	9	23	33	56	54		38
D	3	7	10	14	27		14
	Each column = 100%						
All	2	23	37	13	25		100
Class distribution							
A	8	38	44	6	4		11
B	2	41	44	8	5	Each	20
C1	2	24	46	10	19	row	17
C2	(–)	14	32	19	35	=100%	38
D	(–)	12	27	13	48		14
All	2	23	37	13	25		100

(–) less than 1%.
$N = 1810$

Devised from tables 19 and 20, Abbott and Sapsford, 1987

while the working classes are more homogeneous. Of those with class D occupations, 27 per cent had origins in that class and 81 per cent came from working-class backgrounds, with only 6 per cent from A and B. For those in C2 the respective percentages were 56, 70 and 17. For those in class A, 50 per cent had the same class background, a further 24 per cent were from B and only 12 per cent had working-class origins. A greater variety of origins was found among women in class B. The lower part of the table shows that only 8 per cent of women who originated in class A stayed in that class, while 48 per cent of those from class D had remained in that class. Movement between the extremes was limited: less than 1 per cent from D to A and 12 per cent from D to B, and 10 per cent from A to C2 and D together. Some 39 per cent of women from class D had moved from manual to non-manual compared with 10 per cent from class A who had moved the other way. Overall 44 per cent were upwardly mobile from manual to non-manual (though 31 per cent went to Cl), and 56 per cent were downwardly mobile from classes A or B, 44 per cent to C2 and 12 to manual classes. The authors conclude: 'There is considerable female inter-generational mobility. Downward mobility occurs more frequently for women ... women of whatever origin are more likely than men to end up in routine non-manual jobs.' They also report that separate analyses of part- and full-time, married and single employees, all revealed similar patterns. They took this to indicate that sex rather than marital status or part-time employment is the key factor in labour market segregation.

Evidence suggests differences between the sexes in terms of intra-generational mobility. Chapman (1984), in a replication of the Goldthorpe et al. study which included women, found that men experienced more upward mobility than women and that women were less likely to be countermobile. Similar findings are reported by Greenhalgh and Stewart (1982), who found that single and full-time working females experienced less disadvantage than those married, divorced or working part-time. Martin and Roberts (1984), in a detailed and large-scale study of women's lifetime work histories, provide a valuable insight into the effects on women's employment of leaving to have children. They found that some 51 per cent of women returning to work changed social class, 37 per cent 'down' and 14 per cent 'up'. Part-time returners were more likely to be downwardly mobile (45 compared with 19 per cent) than were the full-timers. Subsequently, 60 per cent of returners stayed in the class they entered, 23 moved 'up' and 17 'down'. Mobility was affected by movement between part- and full-time work: moving to part-time work was more likely to lead to downward mobility, to full-time work upward mobility. Clearly, then, interruption in work history and part-time employment, related to women's domestic responsibilities, are important factors affecting female intra-generational mobility. However, a study of men's and women's inter-class and intra-class social mobility found that the level of social fluidity was similar (Marshall et al., 1988). This agrees with Goldthorpe and Payne's (1986) summation of research: that the forces making for class inequalities in mobility chances among women appear to operate to much the same degree and on the same pattern as men. The distinctive pattern of women's class destinations, into routine non-manual work and the lower levels of the service class, is the result of sex segregation in employment.

Abbott and Sapsford (1987) also addressed a further aspect of female social mobility, that of the relationship between class of father and that of husband, or marital mobility. Apart from being an aspect of women's intra-generational mobility it is also a measure of the openness of the class structure (see also chapter 6 'Class endogamy' and chapter 7 'Educational endogamy', which view social class and educational qualifications of partners. Table 5.14 reveals that while there is fluidity, most of it is short-range).

It is clear that marital mobility at the extremes is limited: a large majority of women from classes A and B and classes C2 and D married men of a class similar to that of their fathers. Some 78 per cent of

Table 5.14 Women's marital mobility (percentages)

Father's class	Husband's social class MR A	B	C1	C2	D		All
A	33	45	7	14	1		10
B	21	52	13	10	3	Each	19
C1	10	33	21	25	12	row	18
C2	5	24	12	47	12	=100%	37
D	4	14	10	44	28		15
All	12	32	13	32	11		100

N = 1495

Devised from table 11, Abbott and Sapsford, 1987

women of class A origin, and 73 per cent of class B, married men of either A or B; only 15 and 13 per cent respectively married men from the manual classes. Of class D daughters, 72 per cent had husbands from the manual classes and only 18 per cent from A and B, while the respective percentages for those from class C2 were 59 and 29. Not surprisingly, the most assortive mating occurred in class Cl. The study showed that overall 70 per cent of women married men from the same side of the manual/non-manual divide, 19 per cent with manual origins married men from non-manual classes, and 11 per cent with non-manual origins married men from the manual classes. In general the pattern of female marital mobility is similar to that of male intra-generational mobility, though there is more downward mobility for women through marriage than for men through occupation. Left unanswered by this and other studies is the exact nature and mechanism of this mobility. The data relate father's and husband's class, but fail to illuminate the role women's own class plays at the time of marriage, and the effects of intra-generational mobility of spouses.

Of course, in all forms of social mobility its incidence is dependent upon the number of social classes used to measure it. For example, Townsend (1979) demonstrated the difference between using the simple non-manual/manual dichotomy and an eightfold classification (HJ/A). With the first measure 19 per cent of the men in his survey had been upwardly and 14 per cent downwardly mobile in comparison with their fathers, and the respective figures for women were 20 and 13 per cent. In other words, around two-thirds of both sexes had not been mobile. Using the eight social classes and treating movement between them as equal gave the result of only 31 per cent of men being in the same class as their fathers, 41 per cent having been upwardly and 29 per cent downwardly mobile, with the figures for women being only marginally different from those for the men at 29, 42 and 29 per cent. A similar critical factor is the age and career stage at which father's and child's occupations are compared in order to identify social mobility. In tables 5.11 and 5.12 it was seen that sons and daughters had been involved in a considerable amount of intra-generational mobility, and fathers are likely to have been similarly involved. Ideally one would compare like with like – the occupation each held for the majority of their working lives or both at an age when further change is unlikely. Similarly, full work histories of both would greatly illuminate the changes in, and relationship between, intra- and inter-generational mobility. However, such data collection poses fairly severe problems for large-scale research.

A useful illustration of British people's views is provided by Harrop (1980), whose research was based partly on market research data. Perhaps surprisingly, the public had an accurate view of the amount of social mobility and of the proportion (two-thirds) of those who 'inherit' class from their parents, which accords closely with the data of Goldthorpe et al. When presented with ability, education and social background as factors for mobility, the public overwhelmingly chose ability as the most important (79 per cent of middle-class respondents and 62 per cent of working-class); education was a poor second at 15 and 25 per cent respectively. Even among those who chose education as the most important, almost 70 per cent saw the quality of education being dependent upon individual ability rather than social background. Hence the public have a very individualistic, or meritocratic, view of mobility in some contrast to that of most social scientists. The public's view, Harrop argues, allows it to have an optimistic view about the openness of society while recognizing the extent of parent–child class determination. The compatibility of these views is sustained because of the level of residential segregation of the classes and the way in which it obscures the class bias in the distribution of opportunity. Within-class interaction and comparison are much more common than across classes, with the result that differences in achievement are typically viewed as resulting from differences between individuals rather than as a product of the social structure.

6

Family, Children and Home

The Family

The family is almost certainly the oldest, the most basic and the most common of human institutions. Almost every society, throughout history and across the world, contains families. While dictionary definitions of the family are straightforward – 'a primary social group consisting of parents and their offspring, the principal function of which is provision for its members' (Hanks, 1979) – the actual form and nature of families in our society have a considerable range and have been and are subject to change (for a review of these and their implications see OPCS, 1987). Some of these aspects are explored in what follows, but initially we use what is the traditional and the majority concept and experience of the family, that based on marriage.

In our society the family through marriage has a legal status for all and a religious (or symbolic) significance for many. The latter is witnessed by the continued, relative popularity of church or religious weddings, in the face of a marked decline in church attendance (see chapter 8). Of those marriages which were the first for both partners in Great Britain during 1990, some seven out of ten had a religious ceremony, as did almost a third of those involving a previously married partner and one in five of those where both partners had been previously married (calculated from *Social Trends no. 23*, table 11.7). The legal and formal importance of the family and marriage is brought out by the fact that marital status, along with one's sex, age and occupation, is one of the pieces of information most commonly required for official and other purposes by a whole host of agencies. Family relationships lie at the basis of inheritance law and that surrounding responsibility for child care and education. Social and governmental agencies and research regard marital condition as a vital statistic and analyse and classify a whole series of other factors by it – sex, age, health, mortality, economic activity, the population and so on. Unfortunately for our purposes, not all such research cross-tabulates marital status and family data directly with social class. This is curious to the extent that the evidence is collected, particularly for example in the census, but is not published. At marriage the occupation of bride and groom and of their parents must be recorded, and at birth that of the father. Similarly, court proceedings, including divorce, usually contain reference to a party's occupation. This information is not, however, presented in the statistical returns. However, as Leete (1979) has pointed out, while the registration of births and deaths is subject to official returns, that of marriage is not, and therefore there is likely to be greater variation in accuracy.

Marriage

Other than the family and school, marriage is the commonest institution in our society, being experienced by all but a minority of people. For example, of those aged 45–9 years in 1990 only about 5 per cent of women and 9 per cent of men in our society had not been married (*Marriage and Divorce Statistics 1990*, table 1.1(b)). The estimated percentages of the population of England and Wales aged 20 and over in 1990 who were married, single, widowed and divorced were 63, 21, 10 and 7. While a similar percentage of each sex of those ages was divorced (men 6, women 7 per cent) men were more likely than women to be single (25 per cent compared with 18) and married (65 per cent compared with 60) and much less likely to be widowed (4 per cent compared with 15) (calculated from *Marriage and Divorce Statistics 1990*, table 1.1(a)). These sex differences are mainly accounted for by three facts: women tend to marry at an earlier age than men; men are somewhat less likely to marry at all (to some extent related to the fact that there are more men than women under the age of 50 and that people of that age currently account for around nine in ten of all marriages); and women, who live longer, are more likely to outlive their spouses.

Sex differences in age at marriage can be illustrated in a number of ways. For example, of those aged between 16 and 19 years in 1990 it is estimated that 29 in each 1000 women but only 5 in each 1000 men were married – a dramatic change from 1975 when the corresponding figures were 101 and 22 respectively. Both average and median age at marriage are markedly lower for women than for men. In 1979 Leete identified a growing surplus of single men at the younger marriageable ages, due to the unequal sex:birth ratio as well as to the fact that men tend to marry women from younger age groups than their own, which had been

Table 6.1 Cumulative percentages* ever marrying by age

	Social class RG						
	I	II	IIIN	IIIM	IV	V	All
Men							
20	0	3	5	4	10	8	6
25	65	47	44	46	44	52	46
40	84	73	71	74	68	67	72
50	93	89	84	86	81	74	85
Women							
20	0	17	19	21	25	23	20
25	35	65	66	69	65	79	66
40	62	87	81	86	71	98	82
50	(–)	93	87	94	86	(–)	91

* For example, right-hand column shows 6% married by age 20; 46% by age 25; etc. Social class of men and women in own right. Cumulative percentages based on national statistics.

(–) not available.

N = 1153

Devised from table 6, Haskey, 1983

affected by declining birth rates. In turn, this widens the gap between the marriage rates of the sexes and leads to more men marrying women older than themselves. In the long term, it seems likely that the proportion of men who never marry will be larger than the proportion of women, reversing the pattern established between the wars. The gap between the numbers of bachelors and spinsters grew quite dramatically – from 107 bachelors per 100 spinsters in 1961 to 123 per 100 in 1985. Calculation from *Marriage and Divorce Statistics 1990*, table 1.1(a), shows that the ratio of single men to women aged 20 and over in 1990 was 131:100.

Unfortunately for our purposes, marriage and marital status statistics are not regularly published or analysed by social class and hence there is little direct or extensive evidence about class variation in the incidence of marriage (or, for that matter, of divorce: see below).

An interesting analysis of a sample of marriages included the calculated percentages of men and women marrying by given ages as shown in table 6.1. These are based on the age-specific marriage rates and are therefore hypothetical to the same extent as life expectancy figures (see table 3.18). The proportion married by the age of 20 years rises across the classes more markedly for women than men (0 to 23 per cent compared with 0 to 8 per cent). For men aged 25 and over the married proportion is highest in class I; and with some variation, in general the non-manual classes are above, the manual below the overall figure. For women (whose class is based here on their own occupation) of the same ages, the pattern is almost the reverse of that of the men: in particular the percentage married in class I is lower than the overall figure and that for class V higher.

The figures also indicate class and sex differences in age at marriage. Members of the working classes and particularly women marrying at an earlier age have been illustrated by a number of earlier studies (for example Pierce, 1963; Gavron, 1966; Gorer, 1971). The *Household Composition Tables* (1975, table 47) provided the data for an extensive, different set of figures to be calculated, based on married couples' ages and the husband's social class. An analysis by Reid (1989a, table 7.1) showed that the percentage of married couples both of whom were under the age of 20 increased fourfold, from 0.3 in class I to 1.2 in class V. While there was a difference between the non-manual and manual classes, the largest difference was for class V, where the percentage (1.2) was some four times higher than for class I, half as high again as for class IV and nearly twice the overall figure of 0.7. A similar but even more marked pattern was found in the percentage of married men under the age of 20 which rose from 0.003 to 0.6 per cent across the social classes. Dunnell (1979) explored women's attitudes concerning the best age for marriage. While the most popular age for all classes was then 20–24, the percentage favouring the teens rose dramatically from 3 for class (RG) I to 12 for both classes IV and V. Conversely, those favouring marriage at 25 years or over declined from almost two-fifths of class I to less than a quarter for all the working classes.

Cohabitation

Living together as husband and wife without being legally married has considerably increased in the period since the GHS began to survey it regularly. For example, between 1979 and 1994 the percentage of single women aged 18 to 49 cohabiting trebled, from 8 to 24, and that for non-married (single, widowed, divorced, separated) women doubled, from 11 to 23 (GHS 1994, table 2.24). Of non-married men and women aged 16 to 59 one in five were cohabiting in 1994. Those most likely to cohabit among the non-married were women in their late 20s and men in their late 20s and 30s, about a third of these groups reporting it (GHS 1994, table 2.25). More than half of the surveyed couples marrying in 1986–7 reported having lived together beforehand. Analysis of cohabitation by social class revealed little systematic variation in rates among those aged 20 to 39, though women in classes RG SEG 1 and 2 had somewhat higher rates than those in the other classes, other than the numerically small group in class 7. Among men only class 4 had a percentage markedly different from the overall – 9 compared with 16 (Haskey and Coleman, 1986; Haskey and Kiernan, 1989).

Divorce

Divorce is the most obvious and dramatic indication of marriage breakdown, but by no means the only or necessarily the most common one. In 1990 the divorce rate (persons divorcing per 1000 married people) in England and Wales was 12.9, which was more than double the rate in 1971 (*Social Trends no. 23*). Of the divorces in 1990, 25 per cent were where one or both partners had been previously divorced.

National figures on divorce by occupation of the husband were published yearly in *Civil Judicial Statistics* until 1921, and research in the early part of this century suggested that only some 29 per cent of all divorces were working-class (as defined by husband's occupation at marriage: McGregor, 1957). Data on divorces in the 1960s, based on husband's occupation at time of divorce, displayed a quite different picture (*Statistical Review of England and Wales 1967*; Gibson, 1974). The calculated divorce rate was lowest in class I, followed by classes II and IV, higher in III (and markedly higher for IIIN than IIIM) and highest in class V – twice that for classes I, II and IV (RG).

Social and legislative change obviously affect both the incidence and the distribution of divorce, although the pattern in table 6.2 from a sample of divorces is similar to that prior to the Divorce Reform Act of 1969. As can be seen, with the exception of class IIIM, the standardized divorce ratios (for definition see note to table) and rates rise across the social classes, though the gradient is steepest between classes I and II and classes IV and V. The range from class I to V is more than four to one. A number of class-related factors affect divorce rates. For example, marriages at younger ages, particularly the teens, are at higher risk for divorce than later ones. As we saw above, teenage marriage is more prevalent in classes IV and V than in others, especially I and II. A similar situation is to be found in respect to married couples with premaritally conceived child(ren) (see below). However, such factors do not remove the clear influence of social class on divorce rates. As Haskey (1984) concludes, 'It is possible that social class is a good predictor of divorce differentials because it distinguishes different patterns of social norms, behaviour and expectations in the crucial period before marriage.'

Wives are more likely than husbands to be granted a divorce: of divorces in 1992, 72 per cent were granted to wives, 28 per cent to husbands and hardly any (0.2 per cent) to both (*Marriage and Divorce Statistics 1992*). There is a similar sexual bias in the petitions for divorce, though a majority were filed by husbands in the period 1901–5 and

Table 6.2 Divorce rates, standardized divorce ratios and class of decree*

	Social class RG						
	I	II	IIIN	IIIM	IV	V	All**
Divorce rate†	7	12	16	14	15	30	15
Standardized divorce ratio††	47	83	108	97	111	220	100
Decree to husband§							
Adultery	46	40	45	46	39	32	42
Behaviour	0	4	10	6	7	11	6
Separation	46	54	45	45	45	50	47
Decree to wife§							
Adultery	25	37	30	25	22	15	24
Behaviour	25	27	40	41	43	67	42
Separation	47	33	27	31	30	17	30
Decrees granted to wife	57	65	68	70	71	81	71

* Social class is of husband.
** Includes unclassified.
† Per 1000 husbands aged 16 to 59.
†† The number of actual divorces expressed as a percentage multiple of the expected number (calculated for ages 16 to 59 by multiplying the estimated number of married men in each class by national divorce rate).
§ Columns do not add to 100 because decrees of nullity and divorce for desertion are not shown.
N = 2164; 2168

Devised from tables 3 and 5, Haskey, 1984; table 3, Haskey, 1986

during and immediately following both world wars. Differences exist between the sexes over which of the five 'facts' for 'the irretrievable breakdown of marriage' (the sole grounds for divorce since the 1969 Act) were used in divorce proceedings. While 55 per cent of the divorces granted to women cited husband's unreasonable behaviour, 41 per cent of those granted to men cited wife's adultery.

Social class differences in the grounds for divorce are illustrated in the second part of table 6.2. The percentage of decrees for adultery granted to husbands is higher than to wives (42 compared with 24) and in both cases is somewhat more common in the middle than the working classes. Decrees for unreasonable behaviour are much rarer grounds for husbands than for wives (6 compared with 42 per cent) and rise across the classes. Wives with husbands in class V were two and a half times more likely to win their divorce on this ground than those with husbands in classes I or II. The class differences in adultery and unreasonable behaviour decrees might be seen to mirror commonly held views of class-based marital misbehaviour, but are just as likely to reflect differing class attitudes towards the acceptability of grounds for divorce. Decrees for separation are more commonly granted to husbands than to wives, and whereas in the case of husbands there is no class pattern, for wives there is a decline across the classes. Wives of husbands in classes I and II were more than twice as likely as those with husbands in class V to win their divorce on this ground. This difference may be related to the relative ease with which separate accommodation can be afforded or arranged in the 'higher' classes. The final row of the table shows that while the majority of decrees in all social classes is given to wives, this increases from 57 to 81 per cent from I to V.

Of course, as Haskey (1986) pointed out, the recorded ground for divorce cannot be taken as the root or actual cause of marital breakdown: 'whatever the client's reason for wanting divorce, the lawyer's function is to discover grounds' (Chester and Streather, 1972). The likelihood of success and/or the speed of divorce, together with the implications for children, finance and accommodation, are likely to affect choice of grounds and, indeed, which spouse pursues them.

Marriages are formally broken either by divorce or by the death of one partner, and, obviously, those divorced and widowed are eligible for remarriage. Consequently, marriage opportunities and rates are related not only to the basic demographics of the sexes and to differences in their length of life (see chapter 3), but also to the incidence of divorce and changing cultural factors surrounding marriage, divorce and second and subsequent marriages. In 1992 some 170 in every 1000 of persons aged 50 in England and Wales had been remarried (*Marriage and Divorce Statistics 1992*, table 3.12). In that year only 62 per cent of all marriages were the first for both parties; 21 per cent were the first for one party only (of the other parties 96 per cent were divorced and 4 per cent widowed); and 17 per cent were second marriages for both parties – of which 80 per cent were both divorced, 7 per cent were both widowed, and 13 per cent were mixed (calculated from *Marriage and Divorce Statistics 1992*, table 3.2).

A detailed view of remarriage in the two and a half years following divorce by a sample of couples is provided in table 6.3. While overall almost identical proportions of divorced husbands and wives remarried (34 and 33 per cent), there were marked social class differences. In the middle classes husbands were more likely than wives to have remarried (overall, 41 and 27 per cent), while in the working classes the situation was the opposite, with wives more likely to remarry at 35 compared with 31 per cent. Hence, remarriage of middle-class divorced husbands was almost a third higher than those from the working classes, and the reverse is true for their wives. The highest proportions of husbands and wives both remarrying were found in classes IIIN and IIIM. While there is no clear pattern to remarriage of both

Table 6.3 Percentage of divorced partners remarrying within two and a half years of divorce*

	Social class RG						
	I	II	IIIN	IIIM	IV	V	All**
Both	12	6	17	13	7	4	10
Husband only	32	32	29	20	22	25	24
Wife only	16	17	17	27	25	16	23
Neither	40	45	37	40	47	55	43
Husbands†	44	38	45	33	28	29	34
Wives†	28	23	34	40	31	20	33

* Class based on husband's occupation at time of divorce.
** Includes unclassified.
† Irrespective of partner.
N = 1084

Devised from table 2, Haskey, 1987

partners, generally the rate for husbands alone declines, and that for wives alone increases, across the classes. Interestingly enough, the social class pattern of remarriage was similar for partners with and without children.

In comparing these results with those of an earlier study by Leete and Anthony (1979), Haskey (1987) finds remarriage within two and a half years of divorce to have fallen appreciably. This suggests that there may have been either a trend away from remarriage or a change in its tempo. He concludes, 'It is virtually certain that cohabitation – whose prevalence increased substantially during the 1970s, particularly amongst divorced and separated women (Brown and Kiernan, 1981) – played an important role in such changes.'

The remarriage rate of divorced and widowed men is much higher than that for women. This is mainly due to differences in the sizes of the eligible populations. There are many more widows and divorced women, especially in the older sections of the population, than widowers and divorced men. Overall, the ratio of divorced men to women in 1985 was 78 to 100, and was due almost entirely to higher remarriage rates for male divorcees aged over 25 (Sparks, 1986). In 1991 this ratio was 74 to 100, while that for the widowed was 25 to 100 (calculated from *Sex Age and Marital Status, 1991 Census*, table 1). Leete and Anthony's (1979) study of divorced couples suggested that the fact that women generally have care of children after divorce does not explain why they have lower rates of remarriage than men.

One-parent families

While some are formed on purpose, many one-parent families are the result of broken marriages due to divorce, separation or death. Haskey (1991) estimated there were in excess of a million one-parent families in Great Britain in 1987–9, amounting to 14 per cent (over one in eight) of all families with dependent children in our society – an increase from 8 per cent in 1971–3. Between these two dates the percentage of all families with dependent children headed by a lone father remained fairly stable at around 1 per cent, while those headed by a lone mother rose from 7 to 13 per cent. In 1987–9 some 91 per cent of heads of one-parent families were women, two-thirds of whom were divorced or separated, 27 per cent single and 7 per cent widowed. Both the number and the proportion of single and divorced female lone parents rose fairly dramatically between 1971–3 and 1987–9, from 10 to 27 and 28 to 42 per cent respectively.

There appears to be little if any social class difference between lone and couple parents. A comparison of the class profiles of lone-parent and couple families carried out by the author revealed a very similar pattern (calculated from *Household and Family Composition, 1991 Census*, table 23). Haskey (1993) compared the social class profiles of lone and married parents and found that for both women and men they were fairly similar. He comments that this is perhaps surprising since while nearly all lone fathers and the majority of lone mothers had been married there is no reason to presuppose that they would be representative of the groups from which they came.

Class endogamy

Considering the evidence given elsewhere in this book concerning the relative segregation of people in different social classes in, for example, housing, employment, education, interests, leisure activities and so on, it is perhaps quite reasonable to anticipate that there would be some relationship between the social class origins, or class, of marriage partners (see also pp. 117–18). An intriguing early study was that of Berent (1954), which classified the social origins of the partners in some 5100 marriages into four classes. In 45 per cent of marriages the spouses shared the same class origin. Clearly such a relationship is very much higher than would be expected to happen by chance – if choice of partner was unrelated to class. Combining social origin with educational level revealed that 83 per cent of the marriages showed correspondence on one or other of the measures, 71 per cent on at least education, 45 on at least social origin; only 7 per cent had no correspondence on either.

Table 6.4 Ratio of observed to expected marriages in which bride and groom were in the same social class*

	Social class RG					
	I	II	IIIN	IIIM	IV	V
Bachelor/spinster	3.2	2.5	1.4	1.1	1.4	7.9
All	5.0	2.1	1.4	1.1	1.5	6.3

* On the assumption of independence of spouses' class, a ratio of over one indicates an association between them, the larger the stronger. Based on bride's and groom's own class.
N = 1153

Devised from table 2, Haskey, 1983

The higher accord on education than on origin is of interest given the relationship between the two (see chapter 7).

Similar findings are reported in the *Statistical Review of England and Wales 1967* and led the Registrar General to comment, 'It is of interest to note that despite trends to increased social mobility and more open social structure, there is a marked persistence of homogamy by couples in the sample.' Later studies have used partners' social class at time of marriage, rather than their origins (Leete, 1979; Haskey, 1983). Data from the latter study are at table 6.4, expressed as the ratio of the observed number of marriages with partners of the same class to the expected (calculated on the assumption that choice is independent). As can be seen, there is a distinct tendency for brides and grooms to be of similar social class at marriage. The ratios have a U shape, indicating that endogamy is most pronounced at the extremes and highest in class V.

A further view of this relationship can be gained from the census, by analysing the class of married/cohabiting couples in which both partners were economically active: see table 6.5. The first two parts of the table are read down the columns: hence the first part shows that 47 per cent of females in class I had partners in that class, while the second part shows the percentage of males by social class with partners in each class. The clear trend is for the occupations of partners to fall into the same class (the cells in bold type) or adjacent ones. The relative infrequency of one partner with a non-manual and the other with a manual job, or vice versa, is also shown. The differences between these two parts of the table are obviously related to the differing occupational structures of the sexes in our society (see tables 2.1 and 2.2). The third part of the table shows the same overall data expressed as the relationship between expected and observed frequency of couples being of the same class. The clear trend is for the occupations of partners in couple families to be in the same class (cells in bold type) or adjacent ones. The relative infrequency of their occupations being one in classes I or II and

Table 6.5 Relationship between partners' social class in couple families*

Female to male (percentages)

	Social class RG Wife/female cohabitant					
Husband/male cohabitant	I	II	IIIN	IIIM	IV	V
I	**47**	12	7	3	3	2
II	36	**50**	32	20	20	12
IIIN	6	9	**13**	8	8	6
IIIM	8	21	34	**47**	43	47
IV	3	7	12	17	**21**	24
V	(–)	2	3	5	5	**10**

Male to female (percentages)

	Husband/male cohabitant					
Wife/female cohabitant	I	II	IIIN	IIIM	IV	V
I	**11**	2	1	(–)	(–)	(–)
II	43	**45**	27	19	20	14
IIIN	34	37	**50**	40	41	32
IIIM	3	4	5	**9**	10	9
IV	7	10	12	21	**30**	25
V	2	3	5	11	16	**21**

*Observed to expected ratio***

	I	II	IIIN	IIIM	IV	V
I	**6.0**	1.5	0.9	0.4	*0.04*	*0.2*
II	1.1	**1.5**	0.6	0.6	*0.6*	*0.4*
IIIN	0.6	0.9	**1.3**	0.8	0.8	0.6
IIIM	0.2	0.6	1.0	**1.4**	1.3	1.4
IV	*0.2*	*0.6*	0.9	1.3	**1.6**	1.6
V	*0.1*	*0.5*	0.8	1.4	1.5	**2.7**

* Classified couples only.
** See note to table 6.4.
(–) less than 0.5%
N = 610,243

Calculated from table 18, 1991 Census, Household and Family Composition, Great Britain, 1994

the other in classes IV or V is shown in the cells in italic type at the top right and bottom left, which are all less than 1. The differences which occur between the social classes of partners have some obvious implications for social research, given the fairly consistent use of male social class to characterize families and children. For example, educational research typically relates children's progress to father's or male head of household's class. In some cases this measure could lead to unwarranted assumptions about home background. Two families in which the males were of the same class, but where the females' class differed widely, could be providing very different home environments, which might affect children's educational experience and achievements (see also chapter 7), and such families may have widely varying incomes and patterns of expenditure.

Children

Up to the Second World War social class was inversely related to family size: the smallest families were those of the 'highest' classes, and family size increased across the classes, the 'lowest' having the largest families (*Demographic Review 1977*). The popularization of efficient birth-control methods, particularly the 'pill' in the early 1960s, affected the traditional pattern of family size (see also next subsection). By 1961 social class RG II had replaced I as that with the smallest families; by 1971 it was class IIIN and the absolute differences in mean family size were small, though relative differentials remained. Unfortunately for our purposes the 1971 census was the last to have questions on fertility. At that time the mean family size of women who had been married twenty-five to thirty years (assumed to have completed their childbearing) followed a U-shaped pattern across the social classes, with the lowest number of children in class IIIN (1.86) and the averages rising in both directions to class I (2.04) and to class V (considerably higher at 2.47). The non-manual classes were below and the manual above the overall mean of 2.14 (*Demographic Review 1984*, table 4.33).

A rather similar social class pattern was found for general fertility. Werner (1984), by combining births within and outside marriage, calculated the average number of children born to women by the age of 25 in the social classes (RG, based on the chief economic supporter of the household) to be: I 0.24; II 0.4; IV 0.79; V 0.96. The percentage of women who became mothers by the age of 25 rose across the classes from 19 in class I to 55 in class V.

Despite a dramatic rise in the average age of mothers at the birth of their first baby in the past two decades, class differences remain. As can be seen in table 6.6, while 37 per cent of married mothers in 1994 in classes IV and V combined gave birth before the age of 25, this is true of only 13 per cent of those in classes I and II combined. At the same time only one in five of the former compared with 45 per cent of the latter were aged 30 or over at the birth of their first child. This pattern of earlier motherhood for the working than the middle classes is much less pronounced than it was in the 1970s and 1980s. The percentage of

Table 6.6 Distribution of mother's age at birth of first child* (percentages)

	Social class RG			
	I and II	IIIN	IIIM	IV and V
Under 20	1	2	3	5
20–24	12	19	25	32
25–29	42	47	45	42
30 and over	45	32	27	21

* Of married mothers; social class is that of husband. Of births in calendar year 1994, England and Wales.

Calculated from table 11.1, Birth Statistics 1994, 1996

Table 6.7 Mean age of women at first live birth within marriage and median interval between marriage and first live birth*

	Social class RG				
	I and II	IIIN	IIIM	IV and V	All
Mean age at birth of first live child (years)					
1984	27.8	26.4	25.1	23.8	25.8
1994	29.6	28.3	27.6	26.8	28.3
*Median interval between marriage and first live birth*** (months)					
1984	38	34	27	20	29
1994	33	30	27	24	28

* Social class of husband, for England and Wales, 1984 and 1994.

** Of women married once only: interval for remarried women shows little variation over time or class from 18 months. Median is the number of months in the middle of the range, so that half the intervals are above and half below that number.

Devised from tables 11.3 and 11.4, Birth Statistics 1994, 1996

first-time mothers aged under 25 in 1971, 1984 and 1994 fell from 44 to 25 to 13 for classes I and II combined and from 79 to 67 to 37 for classes IV and V combined (*Demographic Review 1984; Birth Statistics 1994*).

Mother's mean age at birth of first child declined across the classes by some three years in 1994, a gap of a year less than a decade before (first part of table 6.7). As the data are for married women, it is obvious that age of marriage, which is class-related, affects the situation. So does the interval between marriage and first birth, the median time of which in 1994 declined from 33 to 24 months from classes I and II combined to IV and VI combined. This difference between these two classes increased from 16 to 23 months between 1972 and 1978 (Werner, 1988), and then fell to 18 in 1984 and to 9 months in 1994.

Table 6.8 Social class profiles of births within marriage and jointly registered births outside marriage and the percentage of first births conceived before marriage* (percentages)

	Social class RG				
	I and II	IIIN	IIIM	IV and V	All
Births in marriage**	39	12	32	18	100
Jointly registered births	19	8	42	31	100
% of first births conceived before marriage†	9	10	12	15	11††

* Of total live births with details of father, England and Wales, 1994.
** Marriage to birth interval 8 or more months.
† Marriage to birth interval 0 to 7 months.
†† Includes 'others'.

Calculated from data in tables 11.1, 11.2 and 11.5, Birth Statistics 1994, 1996

Not all babies are conceived in marriage or born into families. Table 6.8 shows that the percentage of babies conceived prior to, but born in marriage increases across the classes from 9 in classes I and II combined to 15 in IV and V combined. Class analysis of births outside marriage is only possible when such births are jointly registered by both parents (which happened in 61 per cent of such registrations in 1984: *Birth Statistics 1984*). It is clear from the table that the distributions of births inside and outside marriage are different, with proportionally more jointly registered births in classes IIIM and in IV and V combined than in I and II combined and in IIIN. There was a threefold increase in such registrations in the middle and a doubling in the working classes between 1984 and 1994 (*Birth Statistics 1994*). Werner (1985) reported that a survey of a sample of records showed that the majority of parents jointly registering births were resident at the same address.

Family planning

One factor commonly assumed to be related to family size and spacing is the use of contraception. This is not an entirely straightforward factor, since some families were limited before effective contraception was available, and not all methods of contraception are reliable means of avoiding pregnancy. At a simple level it can be said that the use of contraceptives lessens the likelihood of unwanted pregnancies and is more likely to result in families of planned size (assuming, of course, that 'planned' means limited and/or spaced births).

Contraceptive use changed rapidly between 1970 and 1983; overall use by ever-married women increased, the 'pill' replaced condoms as the most popular non-surgical method, the use of unreliable methods of 'withdrawal' and 'safe period' declined together with abstinence and 'cap', while the use of IUDs (the coil) doubled and sterilization increased sixfold (GHS 1983; Cartwright, 1987). The same trends were observable in respect to social class use. In 1970, of married women not planning to become pregnant, over 90 per cent of those in the middle classes were using mechanical or chemical contraceptives, compared with just over two-thirds of those in classes (RG) IV and V (Bone, 1973). Some clear differences existed in the type of contraceptive used: the middle classes made more use of the pill and cap and less of withdrawal than the working classes, though there was little variation in the use of condoms and IUDs. By 1975, Bone (1978) recorded greater similarity between the classes – especially in respect to the pill which was then used by 42 per cent overall. The growth in the use of the pill and IUDs was matched by a decline in the least effective methods, withdrawal and safe period, though the former remained more prevalent in the working classes. These changes may be seen as due to the considerable increase in the use of family planning services, related to a growth in their provision at this time. This growth in use was greatest in the working classes, so that while use still declined across the classes in 1975, it was less marked than in 1970.

Among recent mothers the percentage using the pill more than doubled between 1967–8 and 1984. In the first year mothers in social class I were the most likely to be using it, and use declined across the classes to V (32 to 13 per cent). This pattern was reversed in 1984, when class V mothers used it most – three in five. While all classes' use had increased, the increase in class I was marginal, that in V dramatic and that in the rest substantial. In 1975 there were no class variations in the use of IUDs by recent mothers (Cartwright, 1978); their use had increased only in classes I and II by 1984, to 13 per cent, compared with all other classes at 8 per cent (Cartwright, 1987). Condoms were used by a higher percentage of the middle than the working classes in 1984, 29 compared with 22 per cent. Sterilization had by the mid 1980s become a very popular method of contraception, second only to the 'pill': the percentage among married or cohabiting women or their partners was 27, with a member of working-class couples somewhat more likely to have been sterilized than middle-class at 28 compared with 25 per cent. Overall male sterilization was more common than female (14 per cent compared with 12) and was accounted for by the differences among middle-class couples – where 15 per cent of men and 10 per cent of women were sterilized – as there were no differences between the sexes in the working classes (GHS 1984).

By the 1990s such differences had further narrowed according to self-

Table 6.9 Contraceptive use with a partner in past year* (percentages)

	Social class RG						
	I	II	IIIN	IIIM	IV	V	All
Men							
Pill	29	28	32	30	31	36	30
Condom	40	35	34	34	36	56	37
Sterilization**	22	28	24	20	17	6	22
IUD/diaphragm	10	9	7	6	5	3	7
Withdrawal	8	6	6	8	7	9	7
Safe period	5	3	3	2	2	4	3
Other†	2	2	0.6	0.6	1	2	1
Abstinence	3	2	2	1	2	2	2
None	14	14	16	22	23	18	18
Women							
Pill	22	24	36	24	33	37	29
Condom	29	27	27	20	23	32	26
Sterilization**	23	28	21	28	19	13	24
IUD/diaphragm	13	10	9	8	8	8	9
Withdrawal	4	3	4	4	5	6	4
Safe period	4	2	2	2	2	1	2
Other†	2	2	1	1	1	2	1
Abstinence	1	1	0.6	0.7	1	2	1
None	19	19	19	25	24	23	21

* Year prior to interview; respondents who had had sexual intercourse with opposite sex. Percentages over 1 rounded; columns do not add to 100% because more than one method used.

** Female and/or male.

† Includes pessaries, sponge, douche and other unspecified.

N = 15,042

Calculated from table 8.3, Wellings et al., 1994

reported use, there being few clear class patterns in use of types of contraception (see table 6.9). However, among both men and women the working classes are more likely than the middle classes and the overall average to not use any form of contraceptive. Reliance on the pill varied over the classes, with class I use lower (markedly lower for women) than that in class V. Among men condom use was higher in classes I and V (40 and 56 per cent) than other classes which were close to the overall 37 per cent; this pattern is repeated in respect to women but with lower proportions and with class IIIM being lowest. The middle classes were more likely to use intercourse-related methods particularly female barrier ones (IUD/diaphragm), and the 'safe period'. The study also found variation within the overall figures for sterilization: more women reported reliance on male than female sterilization in all but classes IV and V, in which classes the reverse was true. This pattern reflects the findings of Hunt and Annandale (1990) that sterilized women were of a lower class than those with a sterilized partner, which might be partly explained by the fact that manual women had a larger number of children.

A further aspect of family planning which has grown in importance since the Act of 1967 is abortion. The *Report of the Committee on the Working of the Abortion Act* (1974) contained a social class analysis of abortions, though since there are no available figures for pregnancy by class it is not possible to estimate any differences in termination rates. The estimated abortion rate as a percentage of live births (for married women only) was highest for (RG) class II at 6.9, followed by I at 5.2, with III, IV and V almost the same at 4.5–4.6. The estimated abortion rate per 1000 women aged 15 to 44 years was somewhat different: II at 8.3, III and V at 6.2 and 6.1, I at 5.5 and IV at 4.7. As might be expected the percentage of NHS as opposed to private abortions increased across the classes from 61 in class I to 86 in class V, though class II had the lowest at 59.

Sexual activity and behaviour

Obviously, most of the topics covered so far in this chapter centre on sexual activity and the ways in which this is affected by, or interacts with, social institutions. While there is considerable interest in, and a number of very detailed studies of, sexual behaviour, few fit the purposes of this book. One that does is the *Health in England 1995* survey, which among the range of topics it covered included sexual behaviour.

As is clear from the data in the top part of table 6.10 the age of first sexual intercourse is typically younger among the working than the middle classes. Since the legal age for intercourse is 16 and the activity was self-reported it is perhaps surprising that 12 per cent of men and 14 per cent of women claimed to have experienced it below that age. The percentage of men reporting this experience almost doubles between classes I and II combined and classes IIIM, IV and V combined, while for women there is a clear divide between the middle classes at 12 and the working at 16 per cent. At the other extreme those who report never having had a sexual partner are highest for men and women in classes IV and V combined at 23 and 20 per cent. In the case of women this proportion is markedly higher than all other classes, with I and II combined having the lowest (7 per cent), while for men class IIIN, at 19 per cent, is also higher than the other classes. All but a very small minority of both sexes who had had intercourse experienced it before the age of 25, a large majority before they were 20.

Wellings et al. (1994) argue that class differences in the age of first

Table 6.10 Age at first sexual intercourse and number of sexual partners in last twelve months* (percentages)

	Social class RG				
	I and II	IIIN	IIIM	IV and V	All**
Age at first sexual intercourse					
Men:					
Under 16	14	17	27	25	12
16–17	28	29	31	31	29
18–19	25	17	18	11	19
20–24	18	12	11	9	13
25 or over	5	6	3	1	3
Never had sexual partner	11	19	10	23	15
Women:					
Under 16	12	12	16	16	14
16–17	29	34	33	31	31
18–19	28	22	29	21	24
20–24	22	19	12	12	17
25 or over	3	2	–	1	2
Never had sexual partner	7	12	10	20	13
Number of sexual partners					
Men:					
None	15	25	17	31	21
One	72	64	65	49	63
Two or more	13	12	19	20	16
Women:					
None	15	17	15	26	19
One	77	76	71	63	72
Two or more	8	7	13	11	9

* Of persons aged 16–54 years, who reported having a sexual partner, England, 1995.
** Includes unclassified.
N = 2667; 2467

Devised from tables 8.3 and 8.12, Health in England 1995, 1996

intercourse have persisted in the UK longer than in America and Europe and found that there was no lessening of the class effect through the successive age cohorts they surveyed. In their study the percentage of those who had experienced sexual intercourse before the age at which they would recommend it for young people today increased across the classes (RG) I to V, from 11 to 21 for men and 8 to 19 for women. They also report that while there are no obvious reasons to expect class differences in the frequency of heterosexual intercourse they found a weak trend for those in classes IV and V to report a lower frequency of sex in the four weeks prior to interview. While recognizing that this may have been caused by differences in marital status and age they also suggest it may be influenced by the nature of work – manual workers being more likely to do physically demanding work, with more overtime and unsocial hours. Their study contained questions on homosexual contacts and both men and women in classes I and II were more likely to report same-gender genital and other sexual contact than the other classes. In this case they raise an issue which in fact relates to all research in this area, that levels of tolerance and acceptance of sexual practices may affect reporting. In this case Wellings and Wadsworth (1990) had found tolerance and acceptance of homosexual practice rose with social status.

The lower part of table 6.10 displays some interesting differences, but few clear patterns, in the number of sexual partners in the twelve months prior to interview. In the case of men and women with two or more partners the proportion in the working classes is higher than in the middle, the overall average dividing them, though the percentage of men is higher than women – 16 compared with 9. For both sexes the percentage with one partner declines across the classes, more markedly for men than women – 72 to 49 and 77 to 63 per cent. This reflects the higher proportion of the working classes, particularly IV and V, with no or two or more partners.

Adoption and fostering

On the other hand there are families who are unable to produce children of their own, some of whom seek to adopt or foster children. (Of course, it is also true that some parents with children of their own adopt or foster other children, and not all fostering and adoption is done by families.) Somewhat dated research suggests that adopters and fosterers have different social class profiles, as do the backgrounds of the children involved. Grey (1971) in a study of 3400 adoption application files found classes I and II provided a third of prospective adopters from 20 per cent of the population but less than 10 per cent of the natural mothers offering children for adoption. In contrast, the comparable percentages for classes IV and V were, respectively, 14, just over 20, and almost 30. Some caution is necessary in respect to the figures relating to natural mothers since for 30 per cent the class data were not available. However, the over-representation of the upper non-manual classes among adopting parents was confirmed by data from the National Child Development Study (see next section), in which very definite social class differences were found between adoptive homes, those of the whole cohort and the population as a whole. The proportion of adopted children in (RG) class I homes was twice as large as that for the other two groups; and they were more likely to be in non-manual homes and less likely to be in manual homes than the other groups (Seglow et al., 1972). The NCDS also found that the proportion of adopted children living in non-manual homes at ages 7 and 11 was some five times higher than for illegitimate children and much higher than for legitimate children (Lambert and Streather, 1980).

In contrast to adoption, both foster parents and natural parents of fostered children have been found to come predominantly from the manual classes, particularly classes IV and V. Holman's (1975) study of foster children found 60 per cent of natural, and 38 per cent of foster, parents were semi-skilled or unskilled (see also George, 1970). Hence, the evidence clearly suggests that at the time of these researches there was a marked social class divide between adoption and fostering.

Bringing up children

Social differences in the rearing and care of babies and young children have received detailed attention in social research since the Second World War. Three large national cohorts of children – all those born in Great Britain in a single week of 1946 (National Survey of Health and Development, NSHD), 1958 (National Child Development Study, NCDS) and 1970 (Child Health and Education Study, CHES) – have been and are being followed through life. A further source is the smaller-scale but more detailed study conducted by a husband-and-wife team on overlapping samples of mothers and children in Nottingham (Newson and Newson, 1963; 1968; 1976; 1977).

Obviously the evidence on child rearing from these studies is now rather dated and its relationship to what goes on now is limited because of the dynamic nature of the activity. It is also true that most of the evidence from these studies is based on mothers' answers to questions in interviews. Doubts may be raised about the accuracy of such reports (see for example Yarrow et al., 1964; Davie et al., 1972). Respondents from different social classes may vary in their awareness of what is a socially acceptable answer, in their familiarity with current professional opinion and literature about child rearing and in their anxiety about giving what they consider to be socially acceptable responses. Given the purpose of this book, and the nature and extent of the material to hand, the data used in this section have been chosen to emphasize differences. It should be remembered that in many areas of child care and rearing social differences are very small or non-existent.

Infant feeding

Breastfeeding of babies displays considerable change over time and distinct social class differences. In the 1930s the majority of babies were breastfed. Interest in infant feeding methods arose when it was

Table 6.11 Incidence and duration of mothers breastfeeding babies* (percentages)

	Social class RG						
	I	II	IIIN	IIIM	IV	V	All**
At birth	86	79	73	59	53	41	63
1 week	81	70	62	48	42	32	53
2 weeks	77	67	59	45	39	29	50
6 weeks	68	56	47	33	27	20	39
4 months	48	39	28	20	16	10	25
6 months	40	34	22	16	15	9	21
9 months	22	18	13	10	8	4	11

* Based on current or last occupation of husband/partner.
** Includes those without husbands/partners and those unclassified.
N = 5413

Devised from tables 2.50 and 2.51, Infant Feeding 1990, 1992

discovered, in 1946, following the introduction and popularization of modified cow's milk, that only 45 per cent of babies were breastfed at the age of 2 months (Douglas, 1948). The social class variations recorded then were also found for children born in 1958 (Davie et al., 1972). At that time, while over two-thirds of babies were initially breastfed, only 43 per cent were so fed at the end of their first month. Initial breastfeeding declined from 78 per cent in class I to 64 in class V, but more marked was the difference in the length of breastfeeding: of mothers in class I who did it initially, 25 per cent stopped within a month compared with 44 per cent of mothers in class V. A study in England and Wales in 1975 (Martin, 1978) showed that breastfeeding had dropped from 68 to 51 per cent overall and that the social class differences had increased. While over three-quarters of class I babies were breastfed and of these nearly a quarter were still so fed at 6 months, less than two-fifths of those in classes IV and V were initially breastfed and only 10 per cent of those were so fed at 6 months. The popularity of breastfeeding rose again by 1980 to an overall percentage of 65 and in all classes. There was a clear divide between the non-manual and manual classes. Length of breastfeeding had also risen: the percentage of mothers who initially breastfed their babies and who were still doing so at 6 weeks rose from 46 to 63 and at 4 months from 26 to 40 (*Infant Feeding 1980*).

The figures in table 6.11 for 1990 suggest little change from 1980. There are clear social class differences: the 'higher' the class, the more likely the baby is to be breastfed and the longer the time of such feeding. Social class I babies are twice as likely to be initially breastfed than class V. This difference grows with length of breastfeeding, to almost three and a half times at 6 weeks, more than four times at 4

Table 6.12 Age at which mothers introduced solid food to babies (percentages)

	Social class RG						
	I	II	IIIN	IIIM	IV	V	All**
6 weeks	2	5	8	10	10	15	9
8 weeks	9	13	17	20	22	24	19
3 months	57	61	70	69	73	72	68

* Based on current or last occupation of husband/partner.
** Includes those without husbands/partners and those unclassified.
$N = 5413$

Devised from table 6.5, Infant Feeding 1990, 1992

months (the age recommended by the DHSS working party of 1974) and five and a half times at 9 months. At each stage the overall average divides the middle from the working classes.

As in breastfeeding the age at which babies are given solid food has been found to be related to social class, though as can be seen in table 6.12, the overall pattern is reversed. At 6 weeks the percentage of babies introduced to solid food rises across the classes from 2 to 15, at 8 weeks from 9 to 24, and there are still differences at 3 months. Again the overall average at each age divides the middle from the working classes. It might be expected that these differences reflect the higher prevalence of bottle feeding in the working classes: however class differences remained when the classes of breast- and bottle-feeding mothers were separately analysed (*Infant Feeding 1990*).

Use of medical and day care services

Local authorities provide under statute a number of clinics and services for mothers, babies and children. The use of these is class related, as the examples in table 6.13 display. While two-thirds of all mothers-to-be attended antenatal clinics there is a clear and consistent decline across the classes in the percentage having attended from 92 in class I to 53 in class V. Virtually all children from class I had had some immunization by the age of 5 compared with 93 per cent of class V. This pattern is seen in the two examples of immunization given in the table, being more marked in the case of measles than whooping cough.

A survey carried out in 1990 found that overall more than half the children surveyed in classes (RG) I to IIIM had working mothers, 43 per cent in class IV and 36 in V; while the proportion in part-time work, overall 33 per cent, showed little variation. Not surprisingly working mothers with pre-school age children were more likely to make use of

Table 6.13 Percentage of mothers* of first babies who attended antenatal classes and of children immunized by age of 5

	Social class RG						
	I	II	IIIN	IIIM	IV	V	All**
Attended antenatal classes	92	86	80	69	60	53	67
Immunized†							
Whooping cough	97	96	95	93	92	87	
Measles	70	66	64	57	55	47	
Never immunized	0.2	1.0	1.2	2.6	3.6	7.0	

* By social class of husband/partner.
** Includes those without husband/partner.
† Of those from classified households who answered.
$N = 5413$; 13,135

Devised from table 3.9, Infant Feeding 1990, 1992; calculated from tables A20.20, A20.25 and A20.40, British Lending Library Supplementary Publication no. 90,119, being an unpublished appendix to Butler and Golding, 1986 (CHES)

day care services than non-working: 92 per cent compared with 66. Table 6.14 shows that among non-manual working mothers just under 30 per cent of children were regularly looked after by their fathers compared with around a half of the manual working mothers. Care by other relatives also increased across the classes, grandparents being used by 18 and 25 per cent in classes I and II and 44 per cent in classes IIIN, IIIM and V. The use of paid care may reflect different class attitudes as well as income. The percentage of class I using childminders is twice that of class V and the use of other paid carers, like nannies and mother's helps, was exclusively by classes I and II. These patterns, albeit with lower incidence, were found among non-working mothers of pre-school age children.

Talking and social adjustment

There is very little systematic evidence on any scale about social class differences in the way in which children are taught, or learn, to talk. The medical examination of children in the NCDS included a speech test and an intelligibility of speech report, which gave an indication of how successfully children learnt to talk. The test required children to repeat a series of short sentences designed to cover English letter sounds and most of the combinations of sounds used in normal speech. Davie et al. (1972) argue that some of the observed differences may in part have been due to doctors' preference for 'middle-class speech'

Table 6.14 Percentage of pre-school age children with working mothers* using day care services**

	Social class RG						
	I	II	IIIN	IIIM	IV	V	All
None	7	11	8	7	4	3	8
Father	29	27	29	45	50	47	36
Grandparent	18	25	44	44	35	44	34
Brother/sister	1	1	1	3	3	–	2
Other relatives	1	6	10	8	9	9	7
Friend/neighbour	14	8	5	11	9	18	10
Registered childminder	18	16	14	8	6	9	12
Nanny/mother's help/au pair	14	9	–	–	–	–	4
Playgroup	21	21	25	27	24	15	23
Nursery class/ school	21	18	16	14	20	18	17
Day nursery	9	9	11	9	6	12	9
Parent and toddler group	29	23	21	17	15	18	21

* By social class of head of household.
** Columns do not add to 100% because more than one service could be used regularly.
N = 5525

Devised from table 4.6(a), Day Care Services for Children, 1994

(though this would not account for the overall better performance of girls than boys). Overall the percentage of children who made no mistake in the speech test was 47, with a range from 65 for class (RG) I to 36 for class V. The increasing percentage of children making errors across the classes was particularly stark for those making ten or more errors: 1 to 6 per cent (1972, tables A147 and A149).

One assumed objective of the socialization of the children in the family is to prepare them for life in other groups. In our society the first other group universally entered into is the school class. The NCDS provided Bristol Social Adjustment Guide (BSAG) scores (Stott, 1963) for the children in the study. In this test teachers chose from a series of behaviour descriptions those which best fitted the child in question. Scoring produced three groups: 'stable', 'unsettled' and 'maladjusted'. It should be noted that these are not clinical terms, but merely an indication of behaviour, and that while many of the behaviour deviations noted in the BSAG are abnormal by any standard, a proportion of them reflect school and teacher norms which are likely to be middle class. In general the percentage of 'unsettled' and 'maladjusted' children rose across the classes (RG) I to V, from 17 to 27 and 6 to 22 per cent respectively (Davie et al., 1972, table A232). However, the marked differences occurred only between classes IIIN and IIIM and between IV and V for both types. Boys, as might be expected, were more often seen by their teachers as being 'unsettled' (25 compared with 19 per cent) or 'maladjusted' (17 compared with 10) than were girls.

An analysis from CHES defined three groups of children:

Difficult Destroys belongings, fights other children, is irritable, steals, is disobedient, tells lies, bullies.
Troubled Often worried, often solitary, miserable or tearful, fearful or afraid, fussy or overparticular.
Hyperactive Very restless, squirmy or fidgety, cannot settle.

Boys were more likely than girls to exhibit the characteristics of the difficult and the hyperactive child, but there was little sex difference in those associated with the troubled child (Butler and Golding, 1986). There were strong social class associations with the behavioural content of the descriptions, that is an increasing prevalence across the classes from I to V. For example, the percentage of children whose mothers reported that they had temper tantrums at least once a week increased markedly across the classes from 6 for class I to 23 for class V. This pattern is clearly demonstrated in the range of behaviour attributes listed in table 6.15. While the magnitude of class differences varies, only one – sucks finger/thumb – decreases across the classes.

Discipline and obedience

As is shown in table 6.15 according to mothers' reports, children from different social classes vary in their degree of obedience and disobedience. Perhaps surprisingly, the NCDS found that overall some 40 per cent of 7 year old children were seen as never being disobedient, girls more than boys, with a range from 45 per cent in social class (RG) I to 36 per cent in class V. Class V children were more likely to be seen as frequently disobedient (5 per cent as compared with 2 per cent in class I) (Davie et al., 1972, table A227). Given that these figures were based on mothers' reports, and that the study lacked a definition of 'disobedience' (whose meaning can vary widely), too much weight should perhaps not be put on them. The same report does, however, contain references to specific kinds of behaviour – 'fighting' and 'destroying belongings' – which show similar social class differences (1972, tables A225 and A217).

Similar findings were reported by Bone (1977) of children aged 1 to 4 years. Mothers were questioned on a range of areas of behaviour, eating, toilet training success, ease of control and relationships with other children, and their replies assessed on degree of difficulty as perceived by the mother. Overall, 'difficult' children were identified as 10

Table 6.15 Prevalence of 5 year old children's behaviour attributes as reported by mothers (percentages)

	Social class RG					
	I	II	IIIN	IIIM	IV	V
Destroys belongings	1.2	2.5	3.0	4.2	5.5	8.2
Fights with other children	1.5	2.1	1.9	4.7	5.4	8.9
Irritable	5.3	7.5	8.0	12.5	12.8	22.0
Takes things	0.5	0.9	1.4	2.0	2.3	4.2
Disobedient	5.6	5.9	7.4	10.2	10.9	14.3
Tells lies	0.8	0.7	1.6	2.3	3.3	4.5
Bullies others	0.5	0.5	1.1	1.5	1.6	4.2
Often worried	3.8	4.4	5.3	6.2	5.3	6.2
Miserable or tearful	1.1	1.2	1.6	2.5	3.5	3.9
Fearful or afraid	5.4	5.9	6.0	6.6	7.6	7.9
Fussy or over-particular	6.6	7.4	8.0	9.8	10.1	13.5
Restless	18.5	21.5	24.9	30.3	33.7	41.9
Squirmy or fidgety	7.5	9.1	11.7	11.6	12.3	18.7
Unable to settle	2.6	3.8	5.0	7.8	8.2	12.5
Not much liked	0.2	0.5	0.4	1.8	1.6	3.4
Bites nails	8.9	8.2	10.7	12.1	12.9	12.8
Sucks finger/thumb	26.8	21.1	19.8	14.9	14.0	12.7

N = 13,135

Devised from table A7.16, British Lending Library Supplementary Publication no. 90,119, being an unpublished appendix to Butler and Golding, 1986 (CHES)

per cent of the sample, with a rise across the classes (RG) from 7 for class I to 12 for classes IV and V. Interestingly enough, the clearest relationship was between 'difficult' children and the mother's age at the child's birth. Younger mothers were more likely both to have 'difficult' children and to be wives of manual workers.

Mothers' attitudes towards methods of discipline and punishment have been shown to vary by social class in studies by Newson and Newson (1968; 1976). They found that smacking was a common practice among mothers of 4 year olds, and that a sizeable proportion of those who disapproved of it actually used it. The main social class difference was that mothers in classes I and II were over-represented in the 'smack less than once a week' category – 33 per cent as compared with the overall average of 22 per cent – and class V under-represented at 11 per cent. The latter were over-represented in the more frequent smacking category – 79 per cent compared with the overall average of 68 per cent. According to the Newsons, classes I and II were more likely to use punishments other than smacking, usually verbal methods, both in general and for specific reasons, with a steady increase in their use across the classes from 10 per cent in classes I and II to 46 per cent in V.

Table 6.16 Mothers' scores on corporal punishment index* (percentages)

	Social class RG					
	I and II	IIIN	IIIM	IV	V	All
High (5 or more)	21	27	34	31	40	31
Medium (3 and 4)	30	33	29	32	33	31
Low (0 to 2)	49	40	37	37	27	38

* Based on mothers' replies to questions concerning: physical punishment used when child is very slow, refuses to do something, is rude, has picked up bad language (1 point each); frequency of smacking (1+ per day = 3, 1+ per week = 2, 1+ per month = 1); 2 points if implement used, 1 for threat of implement or for trousers taken down or skirt up. Maximum total = 10.

N = 700

Devised from tables 42 and 43, Newson and Newson, 1976

By the time children reached the age of 7 years, physical punishment appeared to be less generally used, though social class differences remained. Table 6.16 displays mothers' scores on an index of corporal punishment (for details see note to table). The scores have been divided into three nearly equal levels. High scores rise over the classes, the proportion in class V being nearly twice that in classes I and II combined. Mothers used physical punishment considerably more for boys than for girls. The Newsons report that its use was particularly marked in class V, where girls were much more likely to receive such punishment than in other classes. A further interesting and related aspect of mother–child interaction is what mothers do when their child asks a question to which they do not know the answer. Willingness to 'bamboozle' the child by concealing ignorance, bluffing or duping varied considerably by social class. More than two-thirds of mothers in classes I and II combined, but only a fifth of those in V, reported avoiding it completely. High scores varied from 11 per cent in classes I and II combined to 39 per cent in IV and V. Unlike the use of physical punishment, this behaviour did not display differences based on the sex of the child.

The Newsons further analysed mothers' answers to ten of their questions as an index of child-centredness which they claimed gave 'a meaningful indication of mothers' underlying attitudes'. Overall, the index was used to divide the mothers into three similar-sized groups scoring high, medium and low. The social class differences were stark. About half of the non-manual-class but only a quarter of the manual-class mothers scored 'high'. At the extremes, while 60 per cent of classes I and II had 'high' and 10 per cent 'low' scores, the equivalent figures for class V were 16 and 57 (Newson and Newson, 1976, tables 34 and 35). Mothers of boys and those with large families were found to be less child-centred than others. Again this appears to be partly a further function of class, since both large families and low scores on the index were clearly related only in the working class.

A further difference between the social classes was found in respect to father's role in child rearing, which, as might be expected, varied with the age of the child. Overall the data showed a larger percentage of participating fathers at ages 1 and 4 years in the middle as opposed to the working classes, together with a decline across the classes I and II to V: 57 to 36 per cent and 64 to 49 per cent respectively being identified by mothers as having 'high' participation. At age 7 the measure of father's participation was less demanding in terms of practical services, centring instead on common interests and involvement with the child. A more modest, though consistent, class trend remained – class I at 47 and class V at 34 per cent – due almost entirely to fathers and sons, since there was no significant class trend with respect to daughters. Middle-class fathers of sons were the most participant, probably reflecting, according to the authors, the development of increasingly sex-based interests and activities. Mothers were also asked how their husbands compared with themselves in strictness with the child. Middle-class mothers were less likely to think their husbands stricter than themselves, and this was because they agreed on strictness (in classes I and II disagreement was 45 per cent; in V, 80 per cent). Finally it was found that the level of participation by the father was related to the wife's agreement about strictness. Where the father was 'high' on participation, 43 per cent of all mothers said that they agreed with their husbands on strictness, compared with 31 per cent where fathers participated at a moderate or low level.

Variation in the help mothers received from fathers is also illustrated in CHES (Osborn et al., 1984). In this particular study a composite 'social index' measure was used to define five groups from most advantaged to most disadvantaged; these had a strong relationship with RG's social classes (over 80 per cent of the two extreme groupings were class I or class V). Comparing the most advantaged with the most disadvantaged families it was found that fathers in the first group were more likely to help with housework and shopping, taking the child to school and putting the child to bed, than those in the second, but there was little or no social variation in respect to day or evening baby-sitting.

The Home

While the majority of our society live in homes that house families composed of married or cohabiting couples with or without children, it is fairly obvious that many people do not. Some people live alone, by choice or circumstance, live with others who do not constitute a family, or live temporarily or permanently in institutions. For this reason and

Table 6.17 Type of home accommodation, by social class of head of household* (percentages)

	Social class RG SEG						
	1	2	3	4	5	6	All**
Detached house	39	39	17	15	7	5	19
Semi-detached house	34	29	31	37	33	30	32
Terraced house	18	20	32	34	40	37	29
Purpose-built flat/ maisonette	5	6	14	10	15	23	14
Converted flat, maisonette, rooms	4	4	6	3	4	4	4
With business premises, other	0	2	(–)	1	1	1	1

* Of households with economically active heads.
** Includes economically inactive heads.
(–) less than 0.5%.
N = 9788

Devised from table 3.44, General Household Survey 1991, 1993

the demands of large-scale research, the main unit of study for homes and home circumstances is the household (for definition see appendix C).

The GHS 1994 surveyed almost 10,000 households, which had a mean size of 2.44 persons and were composed of: married or cohabiting couple with dependent children, 25 per cent; married or cohabiting couple without dependent children, 36 per cent; lone-parent family, 9 per cent; one person, 25 per cent; other (including two or more unrelated adults or families), 4 per cent. All save one-person households may also have contained other non-family members. These types of household contained the following percentages of the people surveyed: 42, 34, 9, 10 and 5. The mean household size has decreased from 2.91 persons in 1971, to 2.67 in 1979, to 2.51 in 1989, to 2.44 in 1994, mainly owing to an increase in one-person households (17 to 25 per cent) and a decrease in those with five or more members (14 to 8 per cent).

Type and tenure of dwelling

The GHS regularly surveys households' accommodation. In 1994 four out of five households in Britain lived in houses, the other fifth in flats, maisonettes, rooms and shared premises. Some 67 per cent of dwellings were owned or being purchased by their occupants (25 and 42 per cent

Table 6.18 Type of home tenure by social class of head of household*

	Social class RG SEG						
	1	2	3	4	5	6	All**
Owner-occupied	89	87	77	74	54	43	67
Owned outright	11	13	12	14	12	11	25
With mortgage	78	74	65	60	42	32	42
Rented	11	13	24	27	47	57	32
Council	1	3	10	17	29	42	20
Housing association	1	1	4	3	4	7	4
With job/business	3	3	2	1	4	0	1
Unfurnished private	2	3	4	4	5	5	4
Furnished private	4	3	4	2	4	3	3

* Of households with economically active heads, Great Britain, 1994.
** Includes economically inactive heads.
N = 9507

Devised from table 11.11(b), General Household Survey 1994, 1996

respectively), 20 per cent were rented from a local authority and 12 per cent were privately rented. Tables 6.17 and 6.18 show that while households of all social classes live in all types of dwellings and use all types of tenure, there are distinct class patterns to both. Just over nine out of ten households in class 1 occupy houses compared with 72 per cent of those in class 6, and while similar proportions of all classes inhabit semi-detached houses, the percentage in detached houses declines across the classes 1 to 6 from 39 to 5, and that for terraced houses increases from 18 to 40 for class 5 and 37 for class 6. The proportion of households with accommodation other than houses is three times higher in class 6 than in class 1. Of course, given the differences in income of the classes (see chapter 4) and the range in costs of accommodation, there will be big variations in the size, condition and location of dwellings within these types. Private rents and mortgage repayments have been shown to decline markedly across the classes (GHS 1977).

While owner-occupancy drops across the classes from almost nine in every ten class 1 households to 43 per cent of those in class 6, council renting rises much more steeply from 1 to 42 per cent. Renting from a housing association is also rare for households in classes 1 and 2 at 1 per cent, and only higher than average for class 6 at 7 per cent. Other renting displays little social class variation and no pattern. This tenure pattern is not simply the result of differences in income, since owner-occupancy is higher in the middle than working classes even when incomes are matched.

The pattern of household tenure changed quite considerably between

Table 6.19 Social class profiles of homeless persons using a range of facilities* (percentages)

	Social class RG						Never
	I	II	IIIN	IIIM	IV	V	worked
Hostel residents	2	12	12	22	24	14	13
Private sector leased accommodation	–	11	19	16	20	10	24
Night shelter residents	–	3	7	23	30	26	11**
Homeless adults sleeping rough, using day centres	1	7	6	30	23	21	13

* Based on current or last job.
** Includes 2% armed forces.
$N = 530$

Devised from tables 4.2, 4.8, 4.12 and 4.17, Psychiatric Morbidity amongst Homeless People, 1996

1977 and 1985. The proportion of owner-occupied homes grew by 10 per cent, while local authority and other renting declined by 6 and 3 per cent. These changes are at least partly due to the sales of council housing (especially to tenants exercising their 'right to buy' under the 1980 Housing Act) and the continuing decline in the stock of private rented accommodation (in 1971, 20 per cent of households so rented their homes: GHS *Introductory Report*, 1973). While all the social classes followed these general trends, the largest percentage increase in owner-occupancy in the manual classes was in class 4 and the lowest in 6.

It should be remembered that the social classes vary in size (see chapter 2) and that no conclusions concerning the proportions of each type of dwelling in Britain can be made. The GHS makes no breakdown of house accommodation other than for the types shown. A now dated study found that caravan households were predominantly skilled and other manual – the non-manual, especially the professional, being under-represented in relation to the general population (Consumer Council, 1967).

The homeless

For obvious reasons there are few data on the social class of those without homes. However, table 6.19 contains the social class profiles of the homeless using a range of facilities who took part in a medical survey. Any comparison of these profiles with that for the population (see table 2.1) shows a clear over-representation of the working and under-representation of the middle classes. The proportion of those who had never worked is also very high.

Accommodation and amenities

A number of criteria and measures might be used to assess the adequacy of a household's accommodation. A long-standing one is the bedroom standard in which the number and type of people in a household were related to available bedrooms, according to rules which allocated a bedroom for: each married couple; each other person over 21 years; each pair of same-sex persons aged 10 to 20; each other person aged 10 to 20 with children under 10 of same sex (otherwise given bedroom on own); each pair of children under 10 (remainder given bedroom on own) (Gray and Russell, 1962).

There is clear evidence that the general level of housing accommodation has significantly risen in the past three decades. In 1960 in England and Wales, 6 per cent of owner-occupiers, 14 per cent of council tenants and 15 per cent of other renters had accommodation below the bedroom standard (GHS 1972). Between 1971 and 1977 the overall percentage of households below the bedroom standard fell from 7 to 4 per cent, and this occurred in all social classes (RG SEG) other than 1 (in the order of 2 per cent for classes 2 and 3, 3 per cent for classes 4 and 5, and 4 per cent for class 6) (GHS *Introductory Report*, 1973; GHS 1977). In 1982, 4 per cent of households still had homes below the bedroom standard and the proportion rose fourfold from classes 1 and 2 to 6. Since the standard may be regarded as minimal (especially in respect to sharing by persons aged 10 to 20) the proportion above it may be regarded as a better indicator. In this case the percentage declined from class 1 at 83 per cent overall (38 per cent one bedroom above, and 45 per cent two or more above) to class 6 at 53 per cent (40 per cent one above, and 13 two or more above). These are, of course, overall figures covering all types of household. Predictably, small adult households were most likely to have accommodation above the bedroom standard (48 per cent two or more), large family households most likely to fall below it (18 per cent) (unpublished data from GHS 1992, supplied by OPCS; see Reid 1989a, table 7.26).

A more detailed, further view of housing deprivation is provided by a study based on three measures from an analysis of census returns: overcrowding (less than one room per person), lack of or sharing bath and/or WC, and shared accommodation. Table 6.20 displays the considerable improvement in a decade in the proportion of households with accommodation without deprivation and some closing of the range of class differences – from 89 and 62 per cent in 1971 to 91 and 82 in 1981.

Table 6.20 Housing deprivation in 1971 and 1981 (percentages)

		Social class RG					
		I	II	IIIN	IIIM	IV	V
No deprivation*	1971	89	84	82	74	70	62
	1981	91	90	90	88	85	82
Overcrowded** only	1971	1.9	3.0	4.6	8.4	9.0	11.4
	1981	1.4	2.3	3.6	6.6	8.0	9.6
No/shared bath/WC only	1971	2.4	4.7	7.1	11.1	12.5	16.0
	1981	0.4	0.9	1.3	2.1	2.5	3.5
Multiple deprivation	1971	3.1	2.8	3.9	4.7	5.8	7.9
	1981	1.3	1.1	1.3	1.3	1.8	2.1

* Percentages rounded.
** Less than one room per person.
N = 1 per cent census sample

Devised from tables 4.14 and 4.15, Housing Deprivation and Social Change, 1994

Similarly, multiple deprivation declined. While the overall rates of households with only overcrowding, or only no or shared bath and/or WC, declined over the period, the class gradients remained. In the first case the incidence stayed at around six times higher in class V than I, while for the second the incidence increased from six to almost nine times.

Alongside the very clear overall improvements in housing conditions between 1971 and 1981, which have continued, there remain marked class differences in overcrowding. The top part of table 6.21 shows that in 1991 overcrowding in class V households was four times that in class I and that its incidence rose over the classes. The second part of the table provides a somewhat different view of household accommodation based on an index derived from allocating households points (indicated in brackets) on the following housing features: owner-occupancy, of detached house (2), of non-detached house (1); more than two rooms per person (2), between one and two rooms (1); central heating to all rooms (2), to some (1); exclusive use of bath/shower (1), of inside WC (1); dwelling self-contained (1). The maximum score was thus 9 and was achieved by less than 8 per cent of households in the 1991 census, though 60 per cent scored 7 or more and just over 7 per cent scored 4 or less. The table shows that the mean score for all households declines across the classes – 7.6 to 6.1– with only classes I and II being above the overall mean score of 6.9. A similar pattern can be seen but with somewhat lower mean scores for couple and lone-parent families.

Table 6.21 Household overcrowding and mean score on housing condition index,* 1991

	Social class RG						
	I	II	IIIN	IIIM	IV	V	All**
Overcrowding†	1	1.6	2.3	3.5	3.6	4.0	
Housing condition index††							
All households	7.6	7.4	6.9	6.7	6.3	6.1	6.9
Couple with children	7.4	7.3	6.8	6.5	6.1	5.8	
Lone-parent family	7.5	6.8	6.2	6.0	5.6	5.7	

* Both measures rounded to first place of decimal.
** Includes unclassified.
† Less than one room per person. Expressed as odds ratio based on difference from class I.
†† For definition see text.

Devised from table 9.8b, Housing Deprivation and Social Change, 1994; and from data supplied by Angela Dale, The Cathie Marsh Centre for Census and Survey Research, University of Manchester, from the same source

Domestic amenities and consumer durables

There is evidence, mainly from market research sources, to show social class differences in the ownership of domestic amenities and consumer durables. A selection of these is in table 6.22 and, as might be expected, the general pattern reveals that the 'higher' the class, the higher the frequency of ownership. There are some exceptions. Nearly all households in each class have at least one TV set, though there is some variation in proportions with more than three sets. The percentage with video recorders is also very similar, save for class E. Satellite and cable TV is highest among C2 and D households and lowest among A, B and E. Ownership of nearly all of the other items listed declines across classes and is particularly marked in respect to dishwashers (52 to 5 per cent), CD players (42 to 20 per cent) and home computers (49 to 18 per cent). As might be anticipated from social class differences in types of household accommodation, the percentage with gardens declines from class A to E. With the exception of class E, the class similarity in the proportion of households with allotments suggests that there are reasons for 'ownership' other than lacking a garden.

Overall, these tendencies are such as to suggest that ownership is merely the result of being able to afford to purchase or rent the amenity or durable. This is supported to the extent that lower income groups have lower levels of ownership of most domestic amenities, though other factors are also involved, such as perceived needs and values, together with exposure to advertising, availability, and so on.

Table 6.22 Percentage of households owning certain consumer/household goods and having a garden and/or allotment*

	Social class MR						
	A	B	C1	C2	D	E	All
Television							
1 set	22	24	27	25	30	46	29
2 sets	32	39	39	40	38	33	38
3 or more sets	44	36	33	34	31	16	32
None	1.8	1.3	1.6	1.0	1.4	3.9	1.7
Video recorder	87	86	85	88	83	63	83
Satellite/cable TV	14	14	18	23	22	13	18
Automatic washing machine	76	72	70	71	65	55	68
Combined washer/dryer	15	14	12	10	7	5	10
Dishwasher	52	35	20	14	8	5	18
Microwave oven	68	70	67	69	61	45	65
Have garden	91	91	86	85	82	76	85
Have allotment	2.7	2.4	2.0	2.6	2.2	1.6	2.2

	Social class RG SEG						
	1	2	3	4	5	6	All
Telephone	99	97	92	88	80	71	90
Central heating	95	94	85	82	76	72	85
CD player	42	47	35	35	27	20	37
Home computer	49	37	29	27	19	18	30

* Percentages over 3 rounded.
N = 25,296; 6033

Devised from data supplied by BMRB from Target Group Index, 1994; and table 3.52, General Household Survey 1991, 1993

Moving home

Evidence that we live in a mobile society is provided in table 6.23. Overall just less than a third of households surveyed in 1982 (the last GHS to include this topic) had moved within the previous five years. The percentage declined across the classes 1 to 6 from 44 to 25. It is evident that class 1 is the most mobile since the percentages who had moved twice or three or more times (9 and 11 per cent) were much greater than the other classes whose percentages were close to the overall of 6 and 5 per cent. Of course, it has to be remembered that

Table 6.23 Household moves in past five years (percentages)

	Social class RG SEG						
	1	2	3	4	5	6	All
Had not moved	56	66	64	69	72	75	68
Once	24	24	22	22	20	17	21
Twice	9	5	6	5	5	5	6
Three or more times	11	5	8	4	4	3	5

N = 11,970

Calculated from unpublished data supplied by OPCS from General Household Survey 1982, 1984

Table 6.24 Percentage of male movers who moved given distances in the year prior to census*

	Social class RG SEG						
	1	2	3	4	5	6	All**
Moved up to 19 km	61	69	72	87	81	85	76
Moved between 20 and 79 km	15	14	12	6	8	6	10
Moved 80 km or more	25	17	16	7	11	9	14

* Economically active and classified only with a different address one year before the census.

** Includes unclassified.

N = 152,494

Calculated from table 6, 1991 Census, Migration, Great Britain (10 per cent) part 2, 1994

these figures relate to all types of household, varying in size, composition and age, factors related both to moving and reasons for moving. The most popular general reasons for considering moving were: insufficient accommodation, dissatisfaction with present environment, reasons connected with employment or education. The main reasons for not moving, having considered it, were: cost of, or inability to find, suitable housing; job-related problems; and personal reasons such as those to do with health, marital factors or bereavement.

Other studies have shown that moving home within, as opposed to beyond, the local area is class-related, and that it is likely to be due to different reasons. For example Davie et al. (1972) found that of families with children who had moved, the percentage which moved out of the local area declined from 63 per cent in class I (RG) to 27 per cent in class V. It can be conjectured, on the basis of social class differences in home tenure and accommodation, family size and formation, and employment and income, that the middle classes move more frequently for work-related reasons and the working classes because homes are or become unsuitable. Table 6.24 illustrates clear class differences in the distance of moves: over four-fifths of male movers in the working classes moved within 19 km compared with but three-fifths in class 1, of whom a quarter moved 80 km or more. Moves within these two distances are also higher in the middle than the working classes.

7

Education

In the past education has been fairly extensively analysed in terms of social class. The origins of interest in the relationship between social class and education are clearly both historical and political. The development of the British education system, from the point where education was wholly the preserve of the rich, through forms of voluntary education for the poor, to compulsory education for all, has been characterized by concern about social class and about equality. The introduction of universal education following the Forster Act of 1870 had produced, by the late nineteenth century, 'two distinct educational systems – elementary for the working class and secondary for middle-class children' (Silver, 1973). Vestiges of this situation remain today, notably in the continuance of independent and 'public' schools alongside those provided by local education authorities (LEAs). The Education Reform Act of 1988 included provision for schools to 'opt out' of LEA control to become grant maintained, together with the development of City Technology Colleges (CTCs). There has been some growth in the independent sector. It seems likely that these changes led to some growth of segregation in education. It remains to be seen what the effect of the present government's proposals will be on the situation.

Empirical research into the relationship of social class with education was initially systematized in the inter-war period, mainly through the interest of psychologists, notably Burt (1937; 1943), in relating intelligence and educational performance to social background and class. After the Second World War the field blossomed, and between the mid 1950s and the 1960s became a veritable industry, with a wealth of government and academic social science research into a host of topics, and using a variety of approaches.

Two factors coincided to promote this flourishing interest in social class and education. The first was a continuing concern about social equality in education among some educationalists, the public and politicians. In the 1950s and 1960s this focused particularly on how the 1944 Education Act (which in abolishing the payment of fees in secondary schools was seen as removing an obvious source of social inequality) actually worked out in practice. The ensuing empirical research revealed, briefly, that many working-class children were still being kept out of grammar schools, but by 'academic' rather than financial criteria, and that those who did get in progressed less well than expected. This led to suspicions that academic selection involved social selection, and that equal educational opportunity did not necessarily result in equality of achievement. The debate caused by this research culminated in calls for the abolition of selection, the introduction of comprehensive schools, and more subtle educational reforms of the curriculum and of teaching methods.

The second important influence was the emergence and development of sociology and in particular of the sociology of education. Whether the discipline merely heightened existing interest or actually created the new research developments is open to debate. It seems probable, however, that sociology did more than just provide a body of empirically minded researchers who thought social class an important concept for explaining how society worked. It also needed to be recognized that the theoretical emphasis in the application of sociology to education was, at least to the end of the 1960s, very clearly that of structural functionalism. (Simply, structural functionalism is a particular sociological perspective according to which society is viewed as a set of interrelated social systems or parts.) As Banks (1968/1971) wrote: 'One of the major strengths of the structural functionalist approach to education is the placing of educational institutions firmly in their relationship with the wider social structure ... Consequently ... the sociology of education has developed as a largely macrocosmic study.' Certainly during the late 1950s and the 1960s researchers tried to explain classroom performance, and the functioning of schools and of the educational system, in terms of their relationships with other parts of society. Most important among these were family and social background, of which a commonly considered aspect was social class. This interest resulted in a fairly substantial body of data which described reasonably well the relationship between parental social class and children's educational achievement. Explaining the results was harder, however, particularly when it came to demonstrating how social class affected children's educational performance – and this situation remains true today (for a review see Reid, 1986; 1992).

Since then changes have occurred that have resulted in a dearth of large-scale studies of social class and education. The sociology of education has incorporated an interpretative perspective, attempting to view social reality more through the eyes of the participants, and this has given rise to in-depth, small-scale research (though social class has remained a prominent factor). LEA secondary schooling has been transformed, albeit incompletely and in varied form, into a comprehensive system. Although the debates that have raged over comprehensive schools clearly demanded a basis of fact from research, few substantial data on social class have emerged, perhaps because both sides have had too much at risk to undertake it. Governmental interest, which had been expressed in a number of commissions and reports, together with questions on education in the census, subsided. The single, notable exception is in Scotland where the Centre for Educational Sociology monitored school leavers from 1977 (see below; and see McPherson and Willms, 1987; 1988). The net result is that for some aspects of our interest here, only dated material is available.

While interest in social class and education has declined, research into other aspects of stratification has grown in the last three decades. On the one hand the educational attainments of ethnic groups, originally of young immigrants from New Commonwealth countries, and later their children and grandchildren, were identified as a cause of concern. This led, in the late 1970s, to the setting up of a governmental Committee of Inquiry into the Education of Children from Ethnic Minority Groups, which produced two reports: *West Indian Children in Our Schools* (1981) and *Education for All* (1985). On the other hand, there was a growth of interest in the educational performance of the sexes, or perhaps more accurately in what was seen as the under-performance of females. Such interest coincided with the development of feminism, legislation on sexual equality and the establishment of the EOC. Hence the change in emphasis can be seen as the product of significant social change in Britain, bringing to the forefront other aspects of inequality. It was certainly not caused by a solution of social class inequality. As we shall see, the changes led to the neglect not only of class in itself, but also of class within ethnicity and sex. Ignoring problems does not make them disappear and in this case may seriously detract from a proper understanding of related areas. One implication for our review here is that in large measure the forms of stratification have to be viewed separately. Having looked at some aspects of the social context within which the research took place, we can now turn to the findings, first in respect to adults and then to children.

Adults and Education

Educational qualifications

Everybody accepts that some occupations are open only to those with particular educational qualifications – especially, for example, the professions – having learned in school that qualifications are importantly related to occupation. Hence they would anticipate a relationship between adult education and social class. The most useful source of data here would be the census. Questions on schooling and education were included up to 1971, but the last published by social class were those from the 1961 census (*Education Tables (10% Sample), 1961 Census*). The questions, with the exception of one concerning post-18 and above A level or SCE qualifications or equivalent (see appendix C), were dropped from the 1981 census, perhaps because of the more comprehensive, though sample-based, data from the GHS, which are used here. However, the 1997 census test on 100,000 households contained a question concerning qualifications at fifteen levels, though its inclusion does not mean that it will appear in the census of 2001 (*Census News*, 1996).

There are two alternative ways to view the relationship between adult social class and education: one can look either at the educational qualification composition of the classes, or at the social class of those holding differing levels of qualifications. The first is to be found in table 7.1. The first part gives the overall picture: the 'higher' the social class, the smaller the percentage without formal qualification and the larger that with higher qualifications. The extremes are fairly dramatically marked: 78 per cent of class 1 have gained higher educational qualification, while 74 per cent of class 6 have gained no qualification. The percentage with degrees or equivalents ranges across the classes from 60 to 0. There is a fairly clear divide between the middle classes (1–3), in which the majority (between 92 and 68 per cent) had at least GCSE grades A–C or equivalent, and the working classes, in which large proportions (40 to 74 per cent) had no qualification. While there are very clear differences in the qualifications of members of the social classes, it should also be noted that each level of qualification is represented in each class. Perhaps surprisingly, some 3 per cent of class 1 were without qualification, and 1 per cent of classes 4 and 5 had degrees or equivalents.

The lower parts of table 7.1 reveal that within the same pattern there are clear differences between the sexes in terms of both social class (see lowest part) and qualifications. Women are under-represented in classes 1, 2 and 4, and over-represented in the others, particularly 3 (see also chapter 2). Women were less likely than men to be graduates (8 compared with 13 per cent) and marginally more likely to have no qualification (32 compared with 30 per cent).

The second view is in table 7.2, in which the same data are recast to show the social class distribution of holders of various levels of educational qualifications. Here it can be seen that higher education is extremely strongly associated with non-manual occupation, lack of qualification with manual. Overall 97 per cent of those with degrees and four in five of those with other higher education qualifications were in

Table 7.1 Highest educational* qualifications gained** (percentages)

	Social class RG SEG						
	1	2	3	4	5	6	All
Degree†	60	17	12	1	1	0	11
Higher education below degree	18	18	18	8	4	1	13
GCE A level†	8	15	11	12	5	2	10
GCSE grades A–C†	6	21	27	22	19	11	21
GCSE grades D–G††	1	8	11	14	12	9	11
Foreign or other	3	4	3	3	4	3	3
No qualifications	3	17	19	40	56	74	31
Men							
Degree†	58	19	19	1	1	1	13
Higher education below degree	20	17	19	9	3	1	13
GCE A level†	9	17	17	13	6	2	13
GCSE grades A–C	7	19	20	21	18	11	19
GCSE grades D–G	1	7	6	15	12	8	10
Foreign or other	3	4	5	2	4	3	3
No qualifications	3	17	15	38	56	75	30
Women							
Degree†	70	13	9	2	1	0	8
Higher education below degree	11	19	17	5	4	1	12
GCE A level†	7	12	9	8	4	2	8
GCSE grades A–C†	5	26	29	25	20	12	25
GCSE grades D–G††	1	9	13	12	12	10	12
Foreign or other	4	3	3	3	3	3	3
No qualifications	2	17	20	45	56	73	32
Social class of sample							
All	6	17	33	23	14	6	
Men	9	22	17	36	12	4	
Women	2	12	52	8	16	9	

* For definitions see appendix C.

** By persons aged 25 to 69 and economically active (either in work or unemployed in week prior to interview), excluding those in full-time education and the armed forces, Great Britain; data for 1991 and 1992 combined.

† Or equivalent.

†† Or equivalent, and commercial qualifications, apprenticeship.

N = 18,398

Devised from table 8.3a, General Household Survey 1992, 1994

Table 7.2 Social class distribution of persons* with given educational qualifications** (percentages)

	Social class RG SEG						
	1	2	3	4	5	6	All
Degree†	33	28	36	3	1	0	
Higher education below degree	9	25	46	16	4	0	
GCE A level†	5	26	35	27	7	1	
GCSE grades A–C†	2	17	41	24	13	3	
GCSE grades D–G††	1	13	35	31	15	5	
Foreign or other	6	20	32	19	16	6	
No qualifications	1	9	19	30	25	15	Each row =100%
Men							
Degree†	40	32	24	3	1	0	
Higher education below degree	14	30	25	26	3	0	
GCE A level†	6	29	22	36	6	1	
GCSE grades A–C†	3	23	19	42	12	2	
GCSE grades D–G††	1	17	10	55	15	3	
Foreign or other	8	26	23	27	14	3	
No qualifications	1	12	8	47	23	9	
Women							
Degree†	20	19	58	2	1	0	
Higher education below degree	2	19	71	3	5	0	
GCE A level†	2	19	58	9	10	2	
GCSE grades A–C†	0	12	62	8	13	4	
GCSE grades D–G††	0	9	58	9	16	8	
Foreign or other	3	13	45	9	21	10	
No qualifications	0	6	33	12	28	21	

* Persons aged 25 to 69 and economically active (either in work or unemployed in week prior to interview), excluding those in full-time education and the armed forces, Great Britain; data for 1991 and 1992 combined.
** For definitions see appendix C.
† Or equivalent.
†† Or equivalent, and commercial qualifications, apprenticeship.
N = 18,398

Devised from table 8.3b, General Household Survey 1992, 1994

the non-manual classes; 70 per cent of those without qualification were in the manual classes.

There are some marked gender differences to the general pattern, mainly due to the sexes' distinctive occupational structures (as seen in table 7.1), but also reflecting sex differences in the age and career pattern of the economically active in the sample. For example, a much higher percentage of women with degrees and other higher education are to be found in class 3 (58 and 71 per cent respectively, compared with 36 and 46 per cent for men). This follows from the inclusion in that class of such predominantly female occupations as primary school teaching, social work and paramedical jobs, which require such educational qualifications.

It should be noted that the data in tables 7.1 and 7.2 cover persons aged 25 to 69 years and therefore reflect a considerable period of educational history. In particular, over the period the educational differences between the sexes have closed – see table 7.7 and section 'Children's Schooling and Education' in this chapter. This is also illustrated by age group differences in GHS samples. For example, the percentages of those without qualifications in 1992 were the same, at 14, for men and women aged 20 to 29, whereas for those aged 50 to 59 they were 41 for men and 54 for women and for the ages 60 to 69, 55 and 68. Between 1975 and 1992 the percentage of women with degrees increased from 2 to 6 and that of men from 6 to 11 (GHS 1992, tables 8.2 and 8.7).

As suggested above, the relationship between adult's social class and educational qualifications and experience, and that between education and class, can be explained fairly straightforwardly. As we have seen, however, these relationships are not exact: not all people with higher education are to be found in the middle classes, nor are these classes made up exclusively of people with higher education. It may be assumed that this is due not only to changes in the occupational structure of society, together with changing educational entry demands over time, but also to changes in educational opportunities and achievements of successive generations, as well as the importance of factors other than education in both getting a job and furthering a career.

Education, earnings and unemployment

A further aspect of the relationship between education and social class is the connection between education and income. Table 7.3 shows the median earnings (for definition see p. 82) in 1992 of holders of various educational qualifications by sex. It reveals that the higher the educational qualifications, the higher the earnings. For both men and women earnings declined across the qualification levels, somewhat more markedly for women than men. Male degree holders earned almost twice as much, 97 per cent more, than males without qualifications, while the figures for females were one and a third times, 37 per cent more. These ranges have considerably changed since 1985 when the comparable percentages were males 70 more, females 91 more (GHS 1985, table 7.13). Overall, there is a strong relationship between

Table 7.3 Usual weekly gross earnings by highest educational qualification*

	Highest qualification attained**						
	1	2	3	4	5	6	All[†]
Median weekly earnings (£)							
Men	433	310	277	242	226	220	259
Women	346	278	201	183	173	146	192
Women's earnings as % of men's	80	90	73	76	77	66	74

* Persons aged 20–69 in full-time employment (31 hours or more, 26 for teachers/lecturers, including overtime), excluding full-time students who worked in reference week, Great Britain, 1992.

** Codes: 1, degree or equivalent; 2, higher education below degree level; 3, GCE A level or equivalent; 4, GCSE grades A–C or equivalent; 5, GCSE grades D–G or equivalent; 6, no qualifications. For definitions see appendix C.

† Includes those with foreign and other qualifications.

Devised from table 8.6, General Household Survey 1992, 1994

qualifications and earnings, though not a complete one: not all holders of educational qualifications earned more than those without, nor were all high income earners holders of qualifications. The table also reveals distinct differences between the sexes. At each educational level women earned less than men. Overall, women's median earnings were 74 per cent of men's (up from 68 per cent in 1985), although women with degrees and other higher educational qualifications had earnings somewhat closer, at 80 and 90 per cent. The largest difference was among those without qualifications where the figure was 66. Only part of the overall sex earnings difference is explained by the fact that women in the workforce are overall marginally younger and work slightly fewer hours. More of the difference is accounted for by the varying occupations (with different levels of income) followed by the sexes, what amounts to sex segregation in employment (see chapter 2; and see Webb, 1989).

The differing age structure and deployment of men and women in the same occupation produces earnings differences despite equal pay. In school teaching, for example, the average earnings of male teachers in maintained schools in 1992–3 was £22,500 and of females £19,900 (*Education Statistics for the United Kingdom 1995*). This difference reflects both incremental differences and the male predominance in secondary as opposed to primary schools (the former having more and better-paid posts of responsibility) and among head and deputy head teachers.

Education can be shown to be related not only to occupational class and income but also to unemployment. Of those below retirement age only 5 per cent of men and 4 of women with higher education (here, qualifications above A level GCE standard) were unemployed, compared with 14 and 6 per cent of those without qualifications. Among those aged 20 to 29 the percentage differences were even more marked at 7 and 6 and at 33 and 9 respectively (GHS 1992, table 8.5). While graduate and professional unemployment has received a good deal of media attention, their rates compared favourably with the less well qualified. The *Labour Force Survey 1990 and 1991* revealed that proportionally more of the unemployed were without educational qualifications: 43 per cent compared with 25 per cent of the employed. Almost 11 per cent of economically active persons of working age without qualification(s) were unemployed, compared with less than 3 per cent of those with degrees or other post A level or equivalent qualifications and just less than 6 per cent of those with GCE or equivalent qualifications (overall unemployment among those with qualifications was 6.7 per cent). The pattern of lower unemployment rates being related to higher levels of qualifications was broadly true for each age group and the sexes. It was particularly marked among those aged 16 to 24 years where one in five of those without qualifications were unemployed compared with around 7 per cent of those with O and A levels or equivalents (*Employment Gazette*, 1991, table 13). It appears, then, that educational qualifications provide something of a buffer against unemployment.

Educational endogamy

As in the case of occupation (see tables 6.4 and 6.5) so with education: people tend to have marriage/cohabitation partners of similar backgrounds to themselves. The first part of table 7.4 shows men's qualifications by those of their partner (and is read column by column), the second women's by their partner's (and is read row by row). As can be seen the patterns are far from assortive: the qualifications of partners, particularly towards the extremes, are related. Since, as we have seen above and is further illustrated in the table, men in general are better qualified than women, the relationship between their own and their partners' qualifications is less strong than that of women's partners. For example, of men with degrees 32 per cent are married to or living with women with degrees, a further 23 per cent have partners with other higher education and 8 without qualifications. The percentages in respect to women are higher at 66, 11 and 1. Of those without educational qualifications 63 per cent of men and 56 per cent of women have partners without, and very few with degrees or other higher education.

Table 7.4 Men's and women's highest educational qualification by their partner's* (percentages)

Men's qualifications by women's

Women's highest qualification**	Men's highest qualification** 1	2	3	4	5	6	7
1	32	5	6	3	1	2	0
2	23	19	11	10	5	8	5
3	8	9	11	9	5	6	4
4	20	30	36	34	20	18	16
5	6	14	13	14	19	13	11
6	4	2	2	2	2	22	2
7	8	20	20	28	47	30	63
All men	12	13	12	16	10	3	33

Women's qualifications by men's

Women's highest qualification**	Men's highest qualification** 1	2	3	4	5	6	7	All women
1	66	11	12	7	2	1	1	6
2	27	22	13	16	5	3	15	11
3	15	18	19	19	8	3	19	7
4	11	16	18	23	8	2	22	23
5	6	15	14	18	15	4	28	12
6	15	8	11	12	8	27	19	3
7	3	7	7	12	13	3	56	38

* Wife/husband or cohabiting partner; persons aged 25–69 not in full-time education.

** Codes: 1, degree or equivalent; 2, higher education below degree level; 3, GCE A level or equivalent; 4, GCSE grades A–C or equivalent; 5, GCSE grades D–G or equivalent; 6, foreign or other qualifications; 7, no qualifications. For definitions see appendix C.

N = 4645, 4485

Devised from table 8.4, General Household Survey 1992, 1994

Children's Schooling and Education

Schooling and qualifications

Unfortunately for our purposes, available research findings preclude a comprehensive review of social class and education based on up-to-date data. The main weight of research has been with parental social class and children's terminal educational qualifications (16+ and 18+ examinations and further and higher education). It is possible, however, to trace social differences in participation and performance throughout the educational system even if in places this requires the use of research from the past three decades or so. Some of the earlier data from this period are dated in that together with general educational change, LEA secondary education has been reorganized and higher education considerably expanded. The extent to which these and other changes have affected the relationships outlined below is, without specific empirical evidence, open to some debate.

While the statutory age for entry into the educational system in Britain is 5, provision is made for younger children. LEAs provide places in nursery schools and day nurseries – the latter open for longer hours and terms than do the former, which are similar to infant schools – together with nursery classes in infant schools. The most dramatic growth in such provision has been in private voluntary playgroups, which are self-supporting and often initiated by parents, together with private nurseries. The GHSs showed that in 1972 the middle classes were better catered for by, or took greater advantage of, pre-school education than the working classes. The percentage attending nursery school declined from 14 of class 1 (RG SEG) to 7 of classes 4 and 6. For day nurseries and playgroups the differences were more marked, though not as regular, although the divide between working (7 to 12 per cent) and middle (9 to 14 per cent) class was greater than for nursery schools. This may have indicated middle-class 'self-help' – that is, voluntary playgroups. In both forms of pre-school education the middle classes were above, and the working classes below, the average. A government White Paper, *Education: A Framework for Expansion* (1972), called for expansion and though the proposed level of provision was not reached, even by the end of the 1980s, change did take place. Between 1972 and 1976–7 the overall percentage of children in either form of provision increased from 22 to 34 per cent. In particular, the percentage of working-class children in nursery schools or classes just about doubled, from around 7 to 14 per cent, and day nursery and playgroup provision changed similarly. Playgroup provision continued to decline across the classes, from 25 per cent for classes 1 and 2 to 14 per cent for classes 5 and 6. On the other hand, nursery schooling showed little social class variation. Even so it may be argued that in terms of need, assumed by the White Paper to be greater among the 'disadvantaged', the resulting change amounted to little more than a numerical equality of provision. Most of the increase was in part-time provision (*Statistics of Education 1979*), and the change took place during a period of sharp decline in the number of children in this age group. Data on this aspect of education are no longer collected by the GHS.

Whether, and how, such experience affects subsequent performance at school is not clearly indicated by research. What has been shown, however, is that by the age of 7, the differences in performance of the social classes in infant or first schools in the essentials of reading and arithmetic are marked. The test scores of some 15,000 7 year olds from the NCDS revealed social class V (RG) children were six times as likely to be 'poor' readers as those from class I (48 per cent compared with 8). The study also pointed out that the lower the level at which a 'poor reader' was defined, the more marked was the imbalance in terms of social class. Hence a social class V child was some fifteen times more likely to be a non-reader at the age of 7 than a child from class I (Davie et al., 1972).

There was a clear division between the middle and the working classes. The average of poor readers was some 13 per cent for the former and 34 per cent for the latter. Class I was distinguished from the other middle classes by having a lower percentage of poor readers and a higher percentage of the best readers. Conversely, class V stood out from the other working classes by having markedly poorer scores. These early class differences increased with further schooling.

> For a given 7-year score the children whose fathers were in non-manual occupations are, at the age of 11, about 1.0 years ahead of social classes III manual and IV, who in turn are about 0.4 years ahead of social class V. This, of course, is additional to the existing differences at the age of 7, which were respectively 0.9 years and 0.7 years. Thus the overall differences at 11 have increased to 1.9 years and 1.11 years respectively. (Fogelman and Goldstein, 1976)

This divergence of attainment test scores between the social classes observed at ages 7 and 11 was found to continue through secondary school. Fogelman et al. (1978) commented that their figures implied that at 16 years only about 15 per cent of children in social class V could be expected to score above the mean of non-manual children. These findings are perhaps surprising. It could be held that schools ought to operate so that initial differences are at least not heightened, while it might be argued that their purpose should be to equalize differences by improving the performance of disadvantaged pupils.

The most crucial stage of schooling is clearly the leaving examinations. Table 7.5 provides a dramatic view of the relationship between social class and secondary school examination achievement among Scottish school leavers. At each level of achievement the percentage passing declines across the social classes from I to V, and this can be compared with the overall percentage (the dashed line) which neatly divides the non-manual from the manual classes. As can be seen, at the extremes 95 per cent of children from social class I left school with at least some qualification and 58 per cent had three or more higher SCE passes, compared with only 45 and 4 per cent respectively of those children from class V.

Table 7.5 School examination performance* of all Scottish leavers** (cumulative percentages)

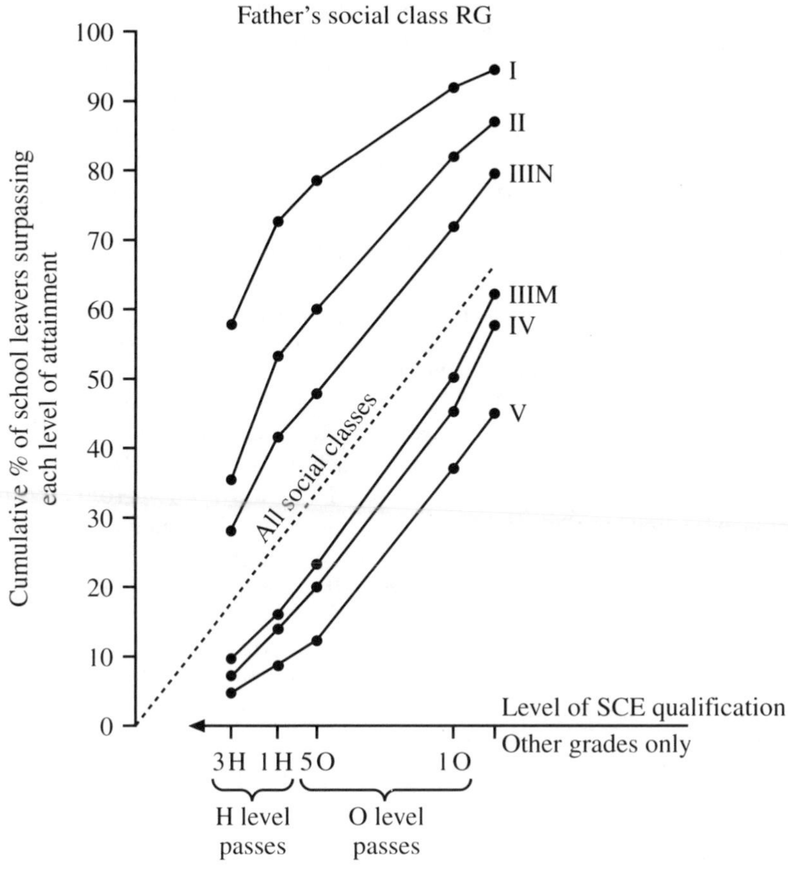

*For definition see Appendix C.
**Data for 1975–6.

Devised from figure 1, Burnhill, 1981

Such differences have been noted in a variety of surveys over a considerable period (for a review see Reid, 1981; 1989a). Few of these surveys have held constant other factors which can be seen to affect educational achievement. Consequently, although the data from *Higher Education*, 1963 (table 5, appendix 1, part 2) are dated they remain interesting because they hold constant both the type of school attended (grammar) and the measured IQ ranges of the children studied. Other than for children of the highest IQ range (130 or more) at the GCE O level stage, differences in achievement existed between middle- and working-class children in distinct favour of the former. In the middle IQ range (115–29) a quarter more middle-class children gained five or more GCE O levels than did the working class, two-thirds more gained two A levels, and more than twice the number entered degree-level courses. Note, however, that these are not measures of pure achievement. They also involved staying on at school and using educational qualifications to enter higher education rather than employment. Hence part of the difference in A level success between the classes was due to differences in entry to sixth forms. Even at the highest IQ range the percentage of those who gained two A levels and subsequently went on to degree courses was 86 per cent for the middle class and 60 per cent for the working class. Very similar results were reported in a further study (*Statistics of Education 1961*, Supplement) which held constant the type of school and the grade of the 11+ secondary school selection examination. Here, although the overall achievements at O level were higher, the social class differences remained. They were again revealed in the NSHD cohort study, in which ability measured at the age of 15 was held constant but not the type of school attended (Douglas et al., 1968). It showed that the percentage of the top ability group (16 per cent) who had gained five or more O level GCEs (including at least three from English language, mathematics, science and a foreign language) varied from 77 per cent for the upper-middle-class children across the classes to 37 per cent for lower-working-class children. These findings were again broadly supported by Rutter et al. (1979) who, having controlled for verbal reasoning, found parental occupation to be related to the examination performance of children in their sample of London schools. The relationship was particularly strong among children in the middle band of ability and slightly less so for those in the higher ability band.

The data in table 7.6 show the highest educational qualification gained by a large sample of adults related to the social class of their fathers. The 'expected' pattern – the 'higher' the class, the larger the proportion with qualifications – is clear. For example the overall percentage with degrees falls across the classes from 32 for those with fathers from class 1 to 3 for those with fathers from class 6, a difference of almost elevenfold. This is mirrored by a rise in the percentage without qualification from 7 to 60. These two gradients, particularly that for degrees, are more marked in the case of women (24 to 1, and 7 to 66) than men (41 to 5, and 7 to 54). There are clear differences at each level of qualification between the middle and working classes, with the first being above the average, the second below.

As is fairly obvious, such data based on adults hide educational attainment changes over time. Younger people are more likely to have gained qualifications. Table 7.7 illustrates these differences both overall

Table 7.6 Highest educational qualification* attained,** by father's social class (percentages)

	Social class RG SEG						
	1	2	3	4	5	6	All
Degree†	32	17	16	6	4	3	10
Higher education below degree	19	15	17	10	7	5	11
GCE A level†	15	13	12	8	6	4	9
GCSE grades A–C†	19	24	25	21	19	15	21
GCSE grades D–G††	4	9	7	12	12	10	10
Foreign or other	4	4	4	3	2	2	3
No qualifications	7	19	18	40	50	60	35
Men							
Degree†	41	21	22	7	5	5	13
Higher education below degree	15	15	19	12	9	5	13
GCE A level†	17	16	14	12	10	7	13
GCSE grades A–C†	15	20	20	18	18	15	18
GCSE grades D–G††	2	7	5	11	11	11	9
Foreign or other	3	4	4	3	2	2	3
No qualifications	7	17	16	36	44	54	31
Women							
Degree†	24	12	12	4	2	1	7
Higher education below degree	23	15	16	7	6	5	10
GCE A level†	14	10	9	5	3	1	6
GCSE grades A–C†	22	29	28	23	20	16	24
GCSE grades D–G††	6	11	10	13	12	8	11
Foreign or other	5	4	4	3	3	2	3
No qualifications	7	20	20	45	54	66	38

* For definitions see appendix C.

** By persons aged 25 to 59, excluding those in full-time education, Great Britain; data for 1990 and 1991 combined.

† Or equivalent.

†† Or equivalent, and commercial qualifications, apprenticeship.

N = 19,669

Devised and calculated from table 10.6a, General Household Survey 1991, 1993

and for classes 1 and 6 in respect to the percentages aged 30–39 and 50–59 holding higher education and no educational qualification. For both sexes the overall percentage with higher education in the younger age group is higher than in the older and that for those without qualifications markedly lower, the women's differences being greater proportionally than the men's.

In fact, sex differences in educational achievement have dramatically

Table 7.7 Percentage of men and women aged 30–39 and 50–59 with higher and no educational qualification, by father's social class*

	Social class RG SEG					
	Men			Women		
	1	6	All	1	6	All
Aged 30–39						
Higher education	54	7	27	53	7	20
No qualifications	4	51	24	6	54	28
Aged 50–59						
Higher education	51	9	20	42	5	13
No qualifications	22	65	45	13	81	57

* Columns do not add to 100 because other qualifications are not shown.
N = 10,630

Devised from table 10.7, General Household Survey 1991, 1993

changed in a relatively short period of time. This change has been particularly marked in terms of the percentage of 17 year olds at school gaining three or more A level GCEs. In England, Wales and Northern Ireland in 1975–6 more males than females achieved this level (9.7 compared with 6.9 per cent); by 1985–6 the gap had narrowed to 10.2 and 9, and by 1991–2 females out-performed males (16 compared with 14.7 per cent) (*Education Statistics for the United Kingdom 1993*, table 34(I)). Similarly more female than male pupils left school in Great Britain with GCSE/SCE grades A–C in any subject (72 compared with 62 per cent), though this achievement showed variation by subject. Again there has been change: in the past boys have out-performed girls in mathematics, but now the performance of the sexes is almost identical at 16+. A higher percentage of boys gain good grades in physics (20 compared with 10) and chemistry, while girls gain higher grades in English (59/45), French (29/18) and biology (18/12) (*Education Statistics for the United Kingdom 1993*, table 32). These differences have been seen to disadvantage women in the labour market (see for example Skeggs, 1989), though in educational terms boys can be seen as missing out as well.

An interesting view of the relationship between parental class and education and their children's performance is provided from a random sample of English and Welsh 17–20 year olds attending full-time the final year of an A or S level GCE or equivalent course (*Young People's Intentions to Enter Higher Education*, 1987). Table 7.8 illustrates a very clear relationship between the number of A level passes and the social class of the head of the student's household. The percentage of those gaining three or more passes declines from 70 for males and 68 for females in class I to 42 and 33 respectively in classes IV and V com-

Table 7.8 Number of A level GCE passes by gender and head of household's social class (percentages)*

	Social class RG					
	I	II	IIIN	IIIM	IV and V	All
Boys						
3 or more passes	70	58	49	39	42	54
2 passes	16	20	22	23	21	20
1 pass	14	22	29	38	37	26
Girls						
3 or more passes	68	47	45	36	33	47
2 passes	15	24	23	27	26	23
1 pass	17	29	32	37	41	30

* Percentage of those who took A levels and passed at least one.
N = 4473

Devised from table 10.8, Young People's Intentions to Enter Higher Education, 1987

bined. A similar gradient can be seen in respect to two or more passes which is the normal minimum requirement for entry into degree courses. The study also found that the 'higher' the social class the higher the average A level points score and that the percentage with no passes increased across the classes from 5 to 16 per cent for males and from 3 to 15 per cent for females (1987, table 10.9).

As we have seen there is a strong relationship between social class and qualifications, and this is clearly illustrated again in the case of A level GCE students' parents in table 7.9. The percentage of students

Table 7.9 Students'* parents' educational qualification by head of household's social class (percentages)

	Social class RG					
	I	II	IIIN	IIIM	IV and V	All
Both had degrees or higher	36	17	4	2	0	13
One had degree or higher	49	35	21	10	8	28
One or both had post-18 qualification (not degree)	5	12	16	17	11	12
Neither had post-18 qualification	10	36	59	71	80	47

* Those taking A level GCE only.
N = 4473

Devised from table 10.3, Young People's Intentions to Enter Higher Education, 1987

with parents who had degrees declines sharply from 85 for one or both and 36 for both in class I, to 8 and 0 respectively in classes IV and V combined. Conversely, the proportion of parents without post-18 qualification declines from one in ten in class I to eight in ten in class IV/V. The study reports, as might be expected, that analysis by parental class and qualifications displayed similar trends. For example, participation in higher education declined across the classes for both measures, the percentages ranging from 58 to 40 for class, and 62 to 37 for qualifications. Participation was higher in families where only the mother had a degree than where only the father had one (58 compared with 49 per cent) (1987, tables 10.4 and 10.5).

So far our review has taken social class as an individual characteristic. However it can also be used to characterize areas. Schooling is presently administered by LEAs, which display a wide range in the percentage of pupils living in households whose heads have non-manual occupations, from 50 per cent in Surrey to 11 per cent in Knowsley, as compared with the average for all English LEAs which is 28 per cent. The DES *Statistical Bulletin 13/84* related these differences to the proportion of age groups gaining 18+ and 16+ qualifications and found a very strong relationship. For example, the percentage of pupils gaining one or more A level GCEs in Surrey was 22, in Knowsley 8 and overall 15. The comparable percentages for five or more O level GCE higher grades or equivalent were 33, 12 and 23 respectively. The survey included a number of other socio-economic factors – measures of population density, household amenities and overcrowding, non-white children, unemployment, supplementary benefit payments, infant mortality and family size – which all to varying degrees displayed a relationship with educational achievement, though none matched the statistical significance of the social class measure in respect to attainment. Several educational and resource variables, together with overall expenditure, were also associated with attainment but were 'of small degree' and much lower than the socio-economic variables. As the *Statistical Bulletin 13/84* clearly indicates, any comparison of the educational attainment of LEAs 'would be seriously misleading if the socio-economic background of pupils were not taken into account'. Of course, it has to be recognized that the LEAs are large and diverse, displaying considerable intra-area variation. However, this type of research reinforces that on individuals, in identifying class as an important and fundamental variable in educational achievement.

More recent studies, using a similar approach but limited to the 32 London LEAs, have revealed differences both in Key Stage 2 SATs results at 11 and the gaining of five GCSEs (McCallum, 1996; reported in Dean; Russell; and Robinson and White 1997). In the first the LEAs were divided into four groups of 8 on the basis of the proportion of economically active heads of household in social classes (RG) IV and V. The average SATs scores for English, mathematics and science were combined. Analysis showed that 7 of the 8 LEAs with the lowest proportion of classes IV and V had average test scores in the top scoring group of 8 LEAs, while among those with the highest proportions of classes IV and V, 7 were in the lowest scoring 8. For GCSEs the 8 LEAs with the highest proportions of children from classes I and II contained 5 of the LEAs with the best GCSE results, and the 8 with the lowest contained 5 with the worst. McCallum (1996) claims: 'This surely provides compelling evidence that GCSE results are not independent of social factors.' Batey and Brown (1997) looked at the HE participation rates in a range of neighbourhood types and found that those from the most privileged (indicative of classes I and II) were up to seven times more likely to enter HE than those from the most deprived (indicative of classes IV and V).

There is a certain crudeness in the normal use of father's occupation as the single criterion of a child's social class. Not only has mother's social class been shown to be related to educational performance (see p. 182), but we can suspect that fathers and mothers are important in combination. Moreover, it is obvious that aspects of social class beyond occupation have important effects, or are related to such performance. Particularly important here, and as has been demonstrated in research, is the educational level of parents. Certainly, as was seen above, adult social class and occupation are related to education level. Studies with more information about their subjects reveal interesting insights. One of my own (Reid, 1969), for example, identified some sixteen 'family characteristics' related both to educational success and to 'middle-classness'. Detailed analysis revealed a small number of 'working-class' children (defined by father's occupation) who had *more* of these characteristics than many of the 'middle-class' children. They had, for example, middle-class, educated mothers and grandparents and came from educationally responsive and supportive, materially well-off, small families. These children were among the most successful in the whole sample and were the most successful working-class part of it. The reverse was also true: some 'middle-class' children had few of the 'family characteristics' and were not successful. The use of the simple occupational definition of class could be seen to misplace some success and failure. What is being argued, therefore, is that the class chances in education, as outlined above, may in fact be more blatant than they appear. More sophisticated criteria of social class than father's occupation might well reveal greater differences in educational performance between the classes.

Type of secondary school

The empirical research interest in the secondary schooling of the social classes in Britain really stems from the 1944 Education Act. After this

Act secondary schools were either selective, offering chances of public examination and entry into HE, or non-selective, normally leading to termination of schooling at the minimum school-leaving age. A document published at the height of this period of concern, *15–18* (1960) – often referred to as the Crowther Report – revealed sharp social class differences in secondary schooling. For example, in social class I (RG) only about a quarter of boys attended non-selective schools, while nearly half went to selective schools and 22 per cent to independent schools; in classes IV and V over 80 per cent went to non-selective, less than 20 per cent to selective, and virtually none to independent schools.

Two main changes took place in secondary schools after this time. First, before the raising of the statutory minimum school-leaving age to 16 years in 1973, many of the non-selective schools introduced opportunities for education beyond the minimum leaving age, and for sitting public examinations. Second, most but not all areas introduced comprehensive secondary education. There was, and is, however, wide variety in the comprehensive schemes existing in different areas of Britain. For example, the DES identified fourteen types of comprehensive school (including sixth-form but not tertiary colleges) just on the criterion of age of the children attending them (*Comprehensive Education,* 1978). Data from the mid 1970s (GHS 1976, table 7.1) showed that the middle classes had a higher percentage in the remaining selective schools – that is, grammar and independent – and a lower percentage in secondary modern schools, the opposite being true of the working classes. Classes other than class 1 all had remarkably similar percentages in comprehensive schools, around the average of 64. Some general observations can be made about the effects of secondary school reorganization. The proportion of working-class children in non-selective schools rose slightly from around, or over, 80 per cent to more than 90 per cent, and that of class 1 (RG SEG) children rose sharply from 24 to 52 per cent between the late 1950s and the mid 1970s. This does not necessarily mean that any particular school was better balanced in terms of the social class backgrounds of its pupils than before. Many comprehensive schools are neighbourhood schools, catering for children from a limited area surrounding the school, and many such areas are occupied predominantly by one social class or another. Hence some comprehensives could be described as working class, and others as middle class. Given local variations in the development and organization of comprehensive schools, together with the lack of recent research, it is not possible either to substantiate or to refute the suggestion that comprehensivization brought closer together the educational experience of the social classes.

Apart from differences in the social class composition of types of secondary school, they also show variation in terms of their pupils' performance in public examinations (see also table 7.17). In 1995 the remaining few selective schools had the largest percentage (95) of

Table 7.10 Educational outcomes of comprehensive schools and colleges by the social class composition of intakes (percentages)

	Mostly working class	Mixed, more working class	Equal working/ middle class	Mixed, more middle class	Mostly middle class	All
5 or more GCSE grades A–C	26	28	47	51	55	39
% staying on*	50	55	58	60	65	56
A level GCE points score**	9.6	12.2	13.8	14.3	14.3	12.7
Attendance below 90%†	50	15	10	5	1	21
% of schools	27	34	13	20	6	100

* All-through schools only.
** England only. Passes scored: grade A, 10; B, 8; C, 6; D, 4; E, 2. (See also note to table 7.17.)
† Schools only.
N = 1542 schools

Devised from table 4.6, Benn and Chitty, 1996

pupils gaining five GCSE grades A–C, followed by the independents (86) and comprehensives (41), while for average GCE A level scores (for definition see note to table 7.10) the order was independent 22, selective 20 and comprehensive 15 (Robinson and White, 1997, chart 6, figures rounded). It is far from straightforward to discern the extent to which such differences are due to differences in the social class and/or ability intakes, or the education they provide, for example, the better staff–pupil ratios of independent schools (see below) or for that matter the balance between these factors and the extent to which types of schools may vary in their ability to 'add value' to their pupils' performance. An Audit Commission (1993) study *Unfinished Business* concluded that 'no single type of institution appeared markedly more effective at A levels than the others'.

An unusual view of the effects of the social class composition of schools on educational outcomes is provided by a survey in 1994 of 1424 comprehensive schools and colleges (Benn and Chitty, 1996). School respondents were asked to identify their pupil intake according to the five broad social class categories in table 7.10. As can be seen a clear relationship between social class of intake and outcome is displayed. For example, the percentage gaining GCSE grades A–C rises across the categories from 26 for 'mostly working class' to 55 for 'mostly middle class'. However, the figures for 'mixed' intakes are generally closer to the next 'higher' than 'lower' group. Benn and Chitty suggest that social class mixing 'might produce its own positive effect' and note that this effect was found in several other parts of their survey. A similar gradient can be seen in respect to the percentage staying on at 'all-through' schools, and a less marked one for A level GCE scores in England. The most marked differences are for schools with less than 90 per cent pupil attendance, which ranges across the school types from 50 to 1 per cent.

It is clear that the existence of independent, fee-paying schools as an alternative to those provided by LEAs has and continues to segregate education along class lines. The term 'independent' refers to independence from the LEA system and not, as many suppose, to financial independence. While parents pay fees, it has been estimated that various forms of state subsidy for such schools in 1979 amounted to between £350 and £500 million, comparable to the sums received by either of two of the then major nationalized industries (Rogers, 1980). And this was prior to the Conservative government's introduction of the assisted places scheme.

In the UK in 1992–3 some 6.5 per cent of children of all ages attending schools (other than special schools) were in independent schools, the percentage rising with age: 5 for 8 year olds, 8 for 14 year olds and 18 for those aged 17 and over. Slightly more male than female children attended them, 6.7 compared with 6.2 per cent (calculated from *Education Statistics for the United Kingdom 1994*, table 13). The number of pupils at such schools increased between 1975–6 and 1991–2 from 573,000 to 619,000 (8 per cent) (*Social Trends no. 24*, table 3.7), and in the decade up to 1992–3 their number of pupils increased by 2 per cent, while maintained schools decreased overall by 7 and secondaries by 20 per cent (*Education Statistics for the United Kingdom 1994*, table A). Independent schools enjoy considerably better teacher–pupil ratios than maintained schools, in 1991–2 1:10.6 compared with 1:18.4 for all maintained and 1:15.2 for secondary (*Social Trends no. 24*, table 3.26).

A number of studies have shown independent schools to be middle-class institutions. The first part of table 7.11 shows the percentage of each social class (based on father's occupation when respondent was aged 14 years) of privately educated men aged 20 to 60. As can be seen, a third of social class I attended private primary school and the percentage declined dramatically across the classes to only 0.3 per cent of class VIII, a pattern repeated with slightly higher percentages for private secondary schools (36 to 1 per cent respectively). Notice that the only exception to the pattern of decline across the classes is class IV (small proprietors/self-employed artisans/own-account workers other than professionals) which had higher percentages than class III (routine non-manual).

The second part of the table is the last GHS survey of children in this area. These data are based on parents' answers and may underestimate independent schools to the extent that not all parents may have appre-

Table 7.11 Attendance at private primary and secondary schools (percentages)

*Males only**

	Social class HG/A								
	I	II	III	IV	V	VI	VII	VIII	All
Private primary	33	14	7	10	2	1	0.9	0.3	5.8
Private secondary	36	16	7	11	3	2	0.9	1	6.5

*Males and females***

	Social class RG SEG						
	1	2	3	4	5	6	All
Independent primary	15	11	5	2	(–)	(–)	5
Independent secondary	26	12	6	1	1	1	5

* Aged 20 to 60 years in 1972; percentages over 1 rounded; private secondary schools are HMC, direct grant and independent non-HMC; class of fathers when respondents were aged 14.

** Children in GHS samples 1976 and 1977; class is of head of household where father was not member of household.

(–) less than 1%.

N = 8029; 4384

Devised from table 4.3, Halsey et al., 1980; table 5.1, General Household Survey 1977, 1979

ciated that 'direct grant' schools (other than Catholic ones) had become independent by the time of the inquiry. Here again there are strong class differences: the proportion of class 1 attending independent primary schools is more than fifteen times greater than that of classes 5 and 6, and that for independent secondary schools twenty-six times greater. Notice also the very marked differences between the middle and working classes, and within the middle between each of the classes.

This relationship was again found in the survey of A level GCE students (see also above) and their place of study. Table 7.12 shows that in the case of both sexes the proportion at independent schools declines from over a third of class I to less than one in ten of classes IV and V combined, while the proportion in maintained schools and FE colleges rises.

Much research in the field has been on public schools, defined by the Public Schools Commission (1968) as those independent schools in membership of HMC, GBA and GBGSA. While difficult to define or characterize accurately, they are the longer-established, most prestigious independent schools and were mainly boys' and boarding schools. In 1984, 4.4 per cent of males aged 14 attended HMC schools compared with only 0.5 per cent of females (based on information supplied by

Table 7.12 Type of educational institution attended by A level students* (percentages)

	Social class RG					
	I	II	IIIN	IIIM	IV and V	All
Boys						
Independent	35	25	13	8	8	21
Maintained	56	62	69	78	74	66
FE college	9	13	18	14	18	14
Girls						
Independent	35	18	14	6	7	17
Maintained	56	66	66	72	70	66
FE college	10	16	20	22	22	18

* By students aged 17–19 taking A level GCE only; social class is of head of household.
$N = 4473$

Calculated from table 10.6, Young People's Intentions to Enter Higher Education, 1987

ISIS). Hence such schools are almost exclusively male and middle class; the Commission reported that only 1 per cent of pupils were from the working classes while 85 per cent were from classes I and II, which comprised but 18 per cent of the male population at the time. It would be difficult, then, to disagree with the Commission's finding that public schools are 'socially divisive', in that they recruit and segregate a very particular group of children from the majority. Similarly, Halsey et al. (1980) concluded from their survey of male education: 'The private schools represent a bastion of class privilege compared with the relatively egalitarian state sector.' The significance of 'public' schools lies not only with their almost exclusively middle-class intakes but also with the destinations of their output. Public school products are remarkably successful in securing elite jobs in our society, which is clearly demonstrated in table 7.13. Of particular note is the very high proportion of MPs who served the DES whose own education was at HMC schools. Of the twenty-one ministers in John Major's Cabinet in 1990, nineteen went to independent school and seventeen to Oxford or Cambridge University (*The Guardian*, 29 November 1990).

The table also indicates the strong relationship between attendance at Oxford and Cambridge Universities and elite positions in our society, and suggests a powerful relationship between attendance of independent school and Oxbridge. This is spelt out in table 7.14, which shows that the independent school minority constituted almost half those admitted to Oxbridge.

Table 7.13 Percentage of public school and Oxbridge educated holders of various elite positions*

	Public school	Oxbridge
Politics		
Conservative MPs	62**	45
Labour MPs	14	16
Liberal Democrat MPs	50	30
Parliamentarians serving DES 1964–84:†		
Conservative	79	63
Labour	31	34
The establishment		
Civil Service (under-secretary and above)	50	61
High Court and Appeal judges	83	83
Law Lords	89	89
Church of England Bishops	59	71
Ambassadors	69	82
Commerce		
Directors of major life insurance companies	92	50
Directors of clearing banks	70	47
Chairmen of clearing banks	83	67
Directors of Bank of England	78	89
Chairmen of merchant banks	88	59

* Of total of group whose education was known; 'public school' means membership of HMC, GBA or GBGSA, generally excluding other independents. Dates: for politics, 1992; for establishment, 1984; for commerce, 1981.

** Of whom 21% attended Eton, Harrow or Winchester.

† A further 3% Labour and 4% Conservative attended other independent schools.

Compiled and devised from: Who's Who, 1984; Whitaker's Almanac 1984; Sampson, 1982; Butler and Kavanagh, 1984; 1992; The Times House of Commons (1964–84)

Higher education

The most comprehensive, though now dated, research in this area is *Higher Education* (1963, often referred to as the Robbins Report). This showed how very sharply separate the social classes, based on father's occupation at the time the sample left school, were in terms of entry to higher and further education. At each level of education the percentage entering declined across the social classes. Some 33 per cent of those from class I (RG) backgrounds undertook degree courses compared with only 1 per cent from classes IV and V. Put another way, the chances of a child from social class I entering degree-level education were thirty-three times greater than those of a child from classes IV and

Table 7.14 Percentage of 8, 14 and 17 year olds,* university** and Oxbridge entrants† educated at maintained and independent schools

	Maintained schools	Independent schools
8 year olds	95	5
14 year olds	92	8
17 year olds	82	18
University entrants	72	28
Oxbridge entrants	51	49

* Percentages for the UK, 1992–3.
** Pre-1992 universities' home accepted applicants from schools in England and Wales, 1993.
† Oxbridge percentage is of home accepted applicants from schools, 1995, excluding 9 per cent in both universities categorized as 'other'.

Devised or calculated from: table 13, Education Statistics for the United Kingdom 1994; table 9B, UCCA, 1994; table 1, Cambridge University Reporter, 1996; table 1, Oxford University Gazette, 1996

V. At the other extreme, while almost two-thirds (65 per cent) of classes IV and V neither gained qualifications nor entered post-school education, this was true of only 7 per cent of class I and 20 per cent of class II (*Higher Education*, 1963, appendix 1, table 2; and see Reid, 1989a, tables 8.16–8.18).

An interesting aspect of this research was that it also related children's educational achievement to mothers' occupation before marriage. Comparison, in terms of the simple non-manual/manual dichotomy, of both parents' social class with their children's level of education presented a very similar picture. The sample's educational attainment related nearly as closely to mothers' social class, defined by occupation before marriage, as it did to that of fathers at their children's school-leaving age. *Higher Education* suggested that a mother's occupation is an indirect measure of her education, and comments, 'But his [the father's] occupation ... presumably affects his family's income and children's education directly, whereas in the case of the mother the effect of her education, rather than that of her occupation before marriage, is presumably the more direct.'

The situation did not change with the expansion of universities and other forms of higher education following the recommendations of *Higher Education.* As can be seen in table 7.15, despite a growth in the number of entrants to universities between 1970 and 1977 (from 63,000 to 78,000), the percentage of students from class 1 rose from 30 to 36 per cent while that of the working classes (class 4 in this classification, see appendix B) fell from 28 to 24 per cent. On the more sophisticated age participation rate (see table note for definition), class 1 rose from 29

Table 7.15 Social class* profile of age group, university entrants and age participation rates, 1970 and 1977

	Social class UC				
	1	2	3	4	All
1970					
Profile of age group	9	7	21	63	100
Profile of university entrants	30	14	28	28	100
Age participation rate**	29	17	11	4	8
1977					
Profile of age group	10	9	21	61	100
Profile of university entrants	36	16	24	24	100
Age participation rate**	33	18	11	4	9

* Class 4 includes all manual.

** The percentage that entrants in each class constitute of the age group in each class.

Devised from table 6, Edwards and Roberts, 1980

to 33 per cent, while classes 3 and 4 stayed constant at 11 and 4 per cent respectively. In fact the extremes differed even more. Edwards and Roberts (1980) calculated that males in class I (RG) had in 1976 a 58 per cent chance of entering university and an 85 per cent chance of some form of higher education, while for females the respective percentages were 38 and 56. At the other extreme, males from class V had only a 1.4 per cent chance of university and a 2.1 per cent chance of any form of higher education; females of that class had the lowest chances of all at 0.8 and 1.2 per cent respectively.

Much the same picture over a longer time period emerges from Halsey et al.'s (1980, table 10.8) comparison of different male age cohorts' university attendance. Of those born between 1913 and 1922, 7.2 per cent of classes I and II (HG/A) and 0.9 per cent of the working classes went to university, while of those born between 1943 and 1952, 26.4 per cent of classes I and II and 3.1 per cent of the working classes went to university. The increase over this considerable period of time for both groups of classes is of the order of three and a half times, which almost matches the overall participation rate increase from 1.8 to 8.5 per cent. As a consequence, the difference between the two sets of classes remained constant, some eight times higher for classes I and II than for the working classes. The greatest absolute increments of opportunity throughout that period of expansion went to classes I and II.

The social class imbalance in the intakes of universities has persisted through their expansion following the Robbins Report, the growth of polytechnics and their incorporation into the university system in 1992.

Table 7.16 Social class profile* and age participation index of undergraduates

	Social class RG						
	I	II	IIIN	IIIM	IV	V	All
Social class profile	17	44	13	17	8	2	100
Age participation index**	79	45	31	18	17	12	32
Working population	5	29	24	21	16	6	100

* Classified home students accepted onto degree courses, 1995.
** The same as age participation rate, defined in note to table 7.15.
N = 218,809

Calculated from table H2.1, UCAS, 1996; and devised from table 1.2, Robertson and Hillman, 1997

Between 1960 and 1995 the overall age participation rate in higher education increased from 5.4 to 32 per cent (Robertson and Hillman, 1997, table 1.1). During the same period the percentage of undergraduates from classes (RG) I and II rose from 55 to 60, while that for those from the working classes fell marginally from 28 to 27. While the proportion of non-manual economically active heads of household increased over the period, from a third to a half, their advantage was sustained (Robinson and White, 1997). Table 7.16 shows the social class profile of accepted, classified home students to degree courses in 1995 and displays a clear over-representation of classes I and II and the under-representation of the working classes. The second row indicates that very nearly four in five of the age group in class I became undergraduates, compared with only one in eight in class V, and that the middle classes were at or above the overall participation rate of 32, the working classes well below it.

Table 7.17 provides a further view of the social class composition of applicants for, and admissions to, universities founded before 1992. The now familiar pattern is clear: class I, which makes up 5 per cent of the working population, presents 18 per cent of applicants and gains 22 per cent of acceptances; for class II the respective figures are 29, 45 and 47. The opposite is true for the working classes: for example, class IIIM, which is 21 per cent of the population, provides only 16 per cent of candidates and secures 13 per cent of acceptances, and this disproportion increases through class IV to class V where 6 per cent of the population make only just over 1 per cent of both candidates and those accepted. There are also differences in the social class composition of candidates and those accepted (compare the first and second rows): classes I and II are a slightly larger proportion of acceptances than of applicants, while the working classes are a lower proportion of acceptances than of applicants.

Table 7.17 Social class profiles and A level GCE scores* of university applicants** and accepted applicants

	Social class RG						
	I	II	IIIN	IIIM	IV	V	All
Applicants†	18	45	12	16	7	1.5	100
Accepted applicants†	22	47	12	13	6	1.2	100
Accepted as % of applicants	65.2	58.6	55.4	50.6	51.2	48.0	57.6
A level GCE score††							
Applicants	19.6	18.0	17.3	16.1	16.2	15.5	17.8
Accepted applicants	22.4	21.2	20.6	19.6	19.6	18.8	21.1

* Based on best two or more passes, grades scored A = 10, B = 8, C = 6, D = 4, E = 2 (assumes same numerical values for each/same grade in different subjects are equal and that grades from different examination boards are equal).
** Classified, home applicants, with A levels.
† Percentages over 2 rounded.
†† Calculation includes only those with two or more A level passes or equivalent.
N = 33,041 applicants; 30,000 accepted applicants

Devised and calculated from tables 8a, 8b and 8c, UCCA, 1994

These differences can be defended from the implication that they reflect a social bias in selection by the universities, in as much as the classes also vary in terms of pre-entry examination performance. The average GCE A level scores of both applicants and those accepted decline somewhat across the social classes (a range of 4.1 for applicants and 3.6 for those accepted: see table note for scoring). Overall, 58 per cent of applicants were accepted, the percentage declining from 65 to 48 between classes I and V.

As might be expected there are social differences in applications to and attendance at different types of HE institutions and courses. For example, post-1992 universities (formerly polytechnics) attracted some 60 per cent more applicants from the working classes than the pre-1992 ones in 1991–2. However, the profiles of admissions to degree courses in the two types are almost the same. The percentage of working-class students admitted to post-1992 universities for HND courses is somewhat higher than for degrees, 33 compared with 28 (Robertson and Hillman, 1997, tables 1.4 and 1.5). Again these figures suggest little change over time. Social class analysis of students at polytechnics in the early 1970s found a clear middle-class bias in their backgrounds, especially for those on degree courses (64 per cent; working class 26; unclassified 11), though non-degree courses were only slightly lower (57 per cent;

working class 30; unclassified 14). However, the representation of classes I and II (46 per cent) was lower than at universities (Whitburn et al., 1976). The proportion of working-class students on non-degree courses was higher than for degree courses, 30 compared with 26 per cent, and was particularly high at just over 40 per cent on non-degree courses in engineering, technology and science. There was also considerable variation in the social class compositions of individual polytechnics: the middle-class percentage varied from 41 to 70.

Similarly some older studies of individual universities have displayed considerable differences in the social origins of their students. This could indicate social class differences in choice of, or opportunity to enter, particular universities. In 1960–1 the average proportion of undergraduates from the manual classes for all universities was 25 per cent (*Higher Education*, 1963). At one extreme 13 per cent of male and 6 per cent of female undergraduates were from the manual classes in Oxford and Cambridge (Kelsall et al., 1972, table 22). This matches the figures of 10 and 12 per cent for both sexes in two Cambridge colleges (anonymous) reported elsewhere (Hatch and Reich, 1970). At the other extreme, Musgrove et al. (1967) showed that 41 per cent of the entrants to Bradford University, then a newly emerging technological university, came from manual backgrounds.

There are also differences in the class composition of successful applicants for first degree and HND courses both regionally and by country. The percentage of such students from the working classes (RG IIIM to V) is 27 for the UK and England (ranging from 19 for East Anglia to 30 for the North West), 25 for Scotland, 30 for Wales and 35 for Northern Ireland (figures, based on classified applicants only, calculated from *Regional Trends 1996*, table 4.13).

It is interesting, though not surprising perhaps given the vastly differing social class chances of university entry, that performance once at university is not affected by social class (Hogarth et al., 1997; Metcalf, 1997). This lack of relationship between social class and class of degree was established in the 1960s and has been sustained (Brockington and Stein, 1963; Kelsall, 1963; Newfield, 1963; Dale, 1963). Class chances in respect to HE are, of course, related not simply to the point of entry, but also, as we have seen, to class chances throughout schooling. Indeed, it is argued by many that in order to increase working-class participation in HE, reform of the schooling system, and particularly the primary stage, is necessary (see for example Robinson and White, 1997).

In some contrast to the relative lack of change in the class composition of undergraduates, that for gender has altered considerably. In 1971 females were 32 per cent of those admitted to university degree courses; this rose to 43 in 1988 and reached equity in 1993 (UCCA, 1994). Half the home students admitted to degree courses in all HE institutions were female in 1995 (UCAS, 1996, table A2). Women continue to be over-represented in arts, language and education degrees and under-represented in sciences and particularly engineering, and constitute a minority of the academic staff of universities and an extremely small one of professors.

This chapter has demonstrated that, contrary to much popular belief that educational achievement is solely or mainly dependent on individual ability, there are extremely important social aspects. Educational experience and achievement are clearly related to social class. One of three views can be adopted: either our present systems of schooling and education are better equipped to cater for certain classes; or the classes are variously equipped to take advantage of what the systems offer; or there is an interplay between systems and class. All the views have strong implications for the educational system.

8

Religion, Crime and the Law, Politics and Opinion

This chapter deals with topics which at first glance seem rather diverse and perhaps unrelated. Politics and religion are areas of life which are typically seen as more personal and intimate than many of the others reviewed in this book. This is because they involve belief and feeling, and are surrounded by social values. For example, there exists a profound social acceptance of an individual's right to his or her own views, and also the right to secrecy, in voting and in relationship with God. It is not surprising, therefore, that these areas are often emotionally charged: they arouse passion and enthusiasm, particularly when like-minded people gather, or attempt to bring new recruits into the fold.

Probably most of us who are involved in a social organization centring on politics, religion or leisure (see chapter 9) are aware to some degree of social class exclusiveness or emphasis. Certainly many of the organizations themselves exhibit such an awareness. Sometimes this is explicit and assertive as in the case of some golf clubs, working men's clubs, trade unions, chambers of commerce, professional associations, and so on. More typically the awareness is expressed defensively, and exclusive social class labels or associations are deliberately avoided. Political parties and churches are in general careful to avoid, or to reject, such labels (for example, the working-class label of the Labour Party, or the middle-class/aristocratic/establishment image of the Conservative Party and the Church of England). An alternative tack is to emphasize the existence of minority social groups within the organization – be they based on class, ethnicity or sex – and sometimes then to claim that this proves their openness.

Such factors as individuals' desire for privacy of beliefs and feelings, and the concern of institutions with their public image, may partly explain why empirical research in these fields tends to be limited, in both scope and depth, in contrast to some other areas. A further explanation for the comparative paucity of empirical research in this area is that there are recognized methodological problems associated with the investigation of opinion and attitudes. This is particularly true of large-scale research, the concern of this book, since private and deep-seated factors can only really be explored by using long in-depth interviews, which are not a feature of social surveys. Finally, the institutions involved are often not particularly research-minded. This reflects in some cases the nature of their organization and in others a resistance to inquiry combined with the power to sustain it. A prime example of the latter is the Freemasons.

A good case in point are the churches, whose information about the numbers of their members and attenders is often based only on rather dubious estimates. Gaine (1975), in reviewing the literature on religious practice and belief, concluded: 'It must be strongly emphasized that the above conclusions are highly tentative and cannot be made more definite due to the absence of agreed statistics and scientific study of the factors involved. In particular, the effects of social class, education, and locality need to be studied.'

Religion

As Matthijsen (1959) pointed out, 'It is one of the idiosyncrasies of the English people to regard inquiries into a person's religion as something unheard of.' This idiosyncrasy may go some way towards explaining the relative lack and limited scope of empirical research in this field in Britain. For example, it was only in the 1851 census that attendance at religious worship was investigated, and then only on a voluntary basis. The 1997 census test on 100,000 households did contain a question on religion asking 'Do you consider you belong to a religious group?', and listing: no, Christian, Buddhist, Hindu, Islam/Muslim, Jewish, Sikh, any other. Its inclusion does not mean that it will appear in the census of 2001 (*Census News*, 1997). In contrast the Northern Ireland census has always produced a volume of *Religion Tables* (*Northern Ireland Census 1991*), based on Christian denomination affiliation, analysed and published by social class until the 1971 census. Extensive and systematic data do not exist at present for Britain, even for a particular denomination, and consequently reliance has to be placed on smaller-scale researches.

Religious groups in Britain use a variety of methods to arrive at their membership numbers, ranging from the careful annual recording of those holding membership cards by the Methodists, to counts of those attending services by others. These and various estimates are regularly brought together in the *UK Christian Handbook* (Brierley and Wraight, 1995) to provide an overview. This suggested that in 1994 some 6.5 million, about 14 per cent of UK adults, were church members, of whom 31 per cent were Roman Catholic, 27 Anglican, 20 Free Church and 22 other (calculated from Brierley and Wraight, 1995, table 9a). Church membership declined overall by 19 per cent between 1975 and 1994, and in all the major denominations, with only New, Pentecostal and Orthodox Churches displaying an increase. The majority of Christian church members are either young or old people, and women outnumber men (Thompson, 1988). The percentage of the population having a looser affiliation than membership is very much higher. It has been argued that the religious communities encompass about 42 million, or 72 per cent, of the UK population. A percentage breakdown of this is: Anglicans 62; Roman Catholic 14; Presbyterian 6; Baptist/Methodist 5; other Trinitarian 4; non-Trinitarian 3; Hindus 1; Jews 0.7; Muslims 3; Sikhs 1; other 0.7 (calculated from, Brierley and Wraight, 1995, table 312, percentages over 1 rounded). All Trinitarian denominations and Jewish religious communities declined between 1975 and 1994, whereas non-Trinitarian and non-Christian ones increased. Hindus, Muslims and Sikhs together now outnumber Baptists and Methodists.

A number of social surveys have shown that the general public are quite willing to associate themselves with religious, mainly Christian, denominations. Table 8.1 contains the results of a recent poll in which 87 per cent said they had an affiliation with a Christian religious denomination and 60 per cent saw themselves as being Church of England/Scotland. There are but marginal differences for the classes from the overall 60 per cent claiming Church of England/Scotland, and the 13 per cent Roman Catholic, allegiance. However, the percentage of class AB claiming Free/Nonconformist allegiance is twice that of the overall and four times higher than class C2. ABs are also more likely than other classes to associate themselves with 'other' denominations. The percentage claiming no allegiance rises from 10 to 16 across the classes.

There are clearer class differences in going to church. Attendance once or more a week is a minority habit at around 12 per cent – the same percentage as recorded in a similar study in 1979, but lower than that in 1972 when 15 per cent claimed attendance at least once a week (NOP, 1972). Regular attendance is highest in class AB, at 19 per cent, lowest in C2, at 8, with classes C1 and DE close to the overall. There is less variation in the proportions attending at least once a month, while those never attending a place of worship rises over the classes from 36 in AB to 52 in DE.

Some 44 per cent of those interviewed thought religion was very or fairly important in their lives, the percentages being highest at 25 for 'very' and 30 for 'fairly' in AB and lowest for 'very' in C2 and DE.

Table 8.1 Religious denomination, attendance at place of worship, importance of religion in own life and opinion on the influence of religion on British life (percentages)

	Social class MR				
	AB	C1	C2	DE	All
Denomination					
Church of England/Scotland	56	60	62	59	60
Free/Nonconformist	8	4	2	3	4
Roman Catholic	13	15	13	12	13
Other	13	9	9	9	10
None	10	12	15	16	13
*Attend place of worship**					
Once a week or more often	19	12	8	11	12
At least once a month	10	11	9	8	10
Less often than once a month	34	31	34	30	32
Never	36	46	48	52	46
Importance of religion					
Very important	25	17	13	14	17
Fairly important	30	25	25	27	27
Think religion is losing its influence on British life	79	75	74	70	74

* Apart from marriages, funerals, etc.
N = 1091

Devised from table 1 of data supplied by The Gallup Organization Inc., from survey conducted 11–18 July 1996

Almost three-quarters of respondents thought religion was losing its influence on British life. It is interesting that slightly fewer in class DE thought this, given that they were less likely to attend worship, claim denominational allegiance, or see religion as 'very important' than other classes.

The unpublished data from the 1991 census for Northern Ireland in table 8.2 provide a further, more detailed view of self-declared religious affiliation by the economically active population. Those who did not answer the question are not included: interestingly enough they amounted to some 7 per cent, both overall and in each class. The first part of the table shows the social classes by religious denomination, which can be compared with that for the population (right-hand column). If there was no relationship between class and affiliation then the figures in each column would be the same. The second part of the table shows the percentage of each religious denomination by class. While a range of minor differences can be seen, the pattern is of the

Table 8.2 Social class by religious denomination and religious denomination by social class in Northern Ireland (percentages)*

	Social class RG						
	I	II	IIIN	IIIM	IV	V	All
Roman Catholic	31	37	31	40	38	39	36
Presbyterian	26	27	28	23	24	22	25
Church of Ireland	17	18	21	20	22	23	20
Methodist	4	4	6	4	4	4	4
Other	12	9	10	8	8	8	9
None	10	6	5	5	4	3	5
	Each column = 100%						
Roman Catholic	3	25	19	26	18	8	
Presbyterian	4	27	24	22	16	7	Each
Church of Ireland	3	22	23	24	19	9	row
Methodist	4	25	28	21	16	7	=100%
Other	5	27	24	21	16	7	
None	7	31	23	21	14	5	
All	4	26	22	24	17	8	

* Percentages of economically active persons who stated a denomination or none.
N = 687,265

Calculated from unpublished data supplied by Northern Ireland Statistics and Research Agency, from the Northern Ireland Census 1991

similarity between the Roman Catholics and the Church of Ireland which have working-class majorities of 52 per cent, and the Presbyterian, Methodist and other denominations with middle-class majorities of between 55 and 57 per cent. The percentage declaring they had no affiliation declines over the classes I to V from 10 to 3 (which is in contrast to the parallel figures in table 8.1).

Gender and age differences in religious behaviour and beliefs have long been recognized. A NOP survey conducted in 1985 (reviewed in Reid, 1989a, table 9.3) found that seven in ten of those interviewed stated that they believed in God or a supreme being: 77 per cent of females, 65 per cent of males, with the percentage rising across the age groups, from 59 of those aged 18 to 34 years to 86 of those aged 55 and over. Of the believers, half said they never attended religious services nowadays (females 57, males 44 per cent) and only about one in five that they attended weekly or more often (females 22, males 15 per cent).

In Northern Ireland not only do most people (87 per cent) think of themselves as church members but attendance is higher there than in the rest of the UK (Cairns, 1992). Table 8.3 shows Catholic and Protestant attendance by class and age group. While weekly attendance increases by age group for both Churches, it is clear that the class differ-

Table 8.3 Church attendance by Catholics and Protestants by age groups in Northern Ireland (percentages)*

		Social class RG					
		I and II		III		IV and V	
		Catholic	Protestant	Catholic	Protestant	Catholic	Protestant
18–34	Weekly	81	40	76	21	78	20
	Never	4	14	6	22	2	28
35–54	Weekly	93	45	87	46	84	38
	Never	0	11	3	6	2	15
55+	Weekly	100	58	91	44	86	52
	Never	0	9	6	20	1	15

* Columns do not add to 100% within each age group because only weekly and never attendance is shown.
$N = 1272$

Devised from tables 10.2 and 10.3, Cairns, 1992

ences are much more marked for Protestants than Catholics, particularly in the youngest age group where weekly attendance in classes I and II combined is twice that for classes III, IV and V combined. Never attending church is very much higher among Protestants than Catholics in each age group and there are class differences. The pattern for Catholics for all three age groups is the same with class III having the highest proportion never attending. In the youngest age group of Protestants the percentage rises across the classes from 14 to 28, while among those aged 35 to 54 years class III has the lowest proportion, whereas among those above that age the same class has the highest.

A more detailed view of religious beliefs is provided in table 8.4 (the questions asked are in the notes to the table). Some 16 per cent of respondents, one in five men and one in eight women, rejected belief in a personal God or spirit/life force and a further 11 per cent did not know what to think. Of the seven out of ten who had a belief, three subscribed to a personal God and four to a spirit/life force. Belief in a personal God is higher among women than among men (39 compared with 23 per cent), is higher among those aged over 65, and declines from class AB to C2 but is highest for DE (probably partly reflecting both its age and its sex composition). Belief in a spirit/life force declines across the classes: it is higher for men than women but shows very little relationship with age. Perhaps surprisingly, almost half of those interviewed believed Christ to be the Son of God, the proportion rising across the classes. It is also interesting that, while 52 per cent believed in heaven, only half as many accepted reincarnation and even fewer believed in hell or the devil. The Bible was seen as essential to the survival of the Church by the majority, though 45 per cent viewed the Old and 39 per

Table 8.4 Religious beliefs* (percentages)**

	Social class MR				
	AB	C1	C2	DE	All
1 God					
There is a personal God	33	30	25	38	31
There is some sort of spirit/life force	48	46	41	35	41
I do not really think there is any God/spirit/life force	14	14	19	16	16
I do not know what to think	5	10	14	11	11
2 Christ					
Son of God	47	48	42	56	48
Just a man	35	33	34	29	32
Just a story	6	8	11	7	8
3 Believe in					
God	71	70	59	73	68
Devil	22	25	17	23	21
Heaven	49	55	44	59	52
Hell	20	25	17	24	21
Reincarnation	23	27	24	25	25
4 Believe that					
Bible is essential	63	65	63	62	63
Church will survive	31	26	30	30	29
5 Old Testament					
Divine authority	6	7	7	17	10
Needs interpretation	40	44	37	34	38
Stories/fables	51	39	50	40	45
6 New Testament					
Divine authority	9	13	9	20	13
Needs interpretation	46	45	36	34	39
Stories/fables	42	33	45	35	39

* Answers to questions:

1 Which of these statements comes closest to your belief?
2 Do you believe Jesus Christ was the Son of God or just a man or just a story?
3 Which of the following do you believe in?
4 Do you think that the Bible is essential to the Christian Church, or would the Church survive even if the idea that the Bible is of divine authority were to be rejected?
5 Which of these comes nearest to expressing your views about the Old Testament: it is of divine authority and its commands should be followed without question; it is mostly of divine authority but some of it needs interpretation; it is mostly a collection of stories and fables?
6 As for 5 for New Testament.

** Columns do not add to 100% because don't knows and no answer are not shown.
$N = 1000$

Devised from data supplied by The Gallup Organization Inc., from a survey conducted 10–14 July 1986

Table 8.5 Religious beliefs of 13 to 15 year olds* (percentages)

	Social class RG					
	I	II	IIIN	IIIM	IV	V
I believe in God	51	45	42	38	38	33
I believe Jesus really rose from the dead	39	34	31	28	27	27
I believe in life after death	47	42	45	43	45	42

* Based on questionnaire answers (agree strongly/agree) by a cumulative sample of 23,856 school children age 13 to 15 between 1989 and 1996.
N = 23,856

Devised from unpublished data supplied by Leslie J. Francis, Trinity College Carmarthen

cent the New Testament as stories or fables. Only small minorities saw the Testaments as having divine authority, 10 and 13 per cent respectively. There are no clear class differences in these beliefs. Comparison of data from a parallel survey in 1979 (Gallup Polls, 1979) suggests that there may have been a lessening of traditional Christian beliefs. Between the two surveys the overall percentage believing in a personal God is lower by 4, that in Christ as the Son of God by 7 and in heaven by 5, while those believing the Old and New Testament to be stories/fables has grown by 12 and 9 per cent. However, it still seems reasonable, in view of the data, to conclude that the population in general, while rejecting institutionalized religion, to a considerable degree maintains acceptance of some of its beliefs.

Similar findings are gained from more intensive surveys such as that reported by Gerard (1985). Three-quarters of those surveyed reported a belief in God, three-fifths saw themselves as 'religious persons' and half regularly felt the need for prayer, meditation or contemplation. Only 4 per cent identified themselves as convinced atheists, but since about half of these also claimed denominational attachment or expressed some form of Christian belief in answering other questions, the true figure was probably nearer 2 per cent. The study used a scale of religious commitment based on a series of questions on two dimensions, religious disposition and institutional attachment. Overall 19 per cent of respondents had high scores, males 15 per cent and females working 20, non-working 26 per cent. Age groups had more marked differences than social classes; the relevant percentages of high scorers were 18 to 24 years, 9; 25 to 44, 14; 45 to 64, 27; 65 and over, 28; class (MR) AB, 20; Cl, 21; C2, 17; DE, 21. A range of other social factors was analysed, but when age was held constant other differences tended to disappear.

Table 8.5 contains data from a large-scale and ongoing survey of the religious beliefs of 13 to 15 year olds. Belief in God declines from a bare majority of class I to a third of class V; that in the resurrection of Jesus, while lower overall, displays a similar pattern. Belief in life after death appears higher overall than in God, this difference being most marked in the working classes. Studies using a more in-depth attitude scale towards Christianity with 10–11 and 14–15 year olds have revealed that such attitudes are related to social class in two different ways. Children from higher social class backgrounds were more likely to have parents who attended church and to do so themselves and positive attitudes were associated with attendance. On the other hand children from lower class backgrounds were found to have more conservative social attitudes which tended to be associated with positive attitudes towards Christianity (Francis et al., 1990; Gibson et al., 1990).

Obviously there is a difference between claiming an allegiance to a denomination and being involved in religious affairs. Less direct questioning in the context of inquiries into other areas, notably leisure, has produced what might well be more valuable evidence of religious involvement. Sillitoe's (1969) study of leisure, for example, asked questions about club membership, including religious organizations. Sex differences were quite marked, females being more likely than males to be members of religious organizations (11 compared with 7 per cent). Membership for both sexes declined across the classes and was highest in the middle classes.

Greater detail of the relationship between religious affiliation and practice is provided in an analysis of the Roman Catholic pastoral research census data (Moulin, 1968). A door-to-door census was conducted in six parishes, four in Southwark and one in Westminster (both in London), and one in Northampton. This identified 15,851 Roman Catholics of whom 42 per cent were observed at Mass at their parish churches on the subsequent Sunday. Catholics were over-represented in social classes (RG) I and V and under-represented in II and IIIN in comparison with the population of the areas of the parishes. Observed attendance at Mass ranged from 61 per cent in social class I down to 36 per cent in classes IV and V; the middle classes had percentages of 49 and upwards, the working classes 36. A slightly higher percentage of the working classes had not been confirmed, and they were less likely to be members of Catholic organizations. The percentage having received Catholic school education increased across the social classes I to V from 49 to 71. While this may well reflect the provision of, and opportunity to attend, such schools, the survey also indicates that the majority of Catholics who were converts came from the middle classes, and obviously would not have attended Catholic schools. The study found all the factors outlined above to be related to attendance at Mass, supporting Moulin's view that, since religious behaviour is a social act, only people integrated – through such factors as education, marriage and organizations – into the religious community will display such behaviour (in this case, attending Mass).

A study in Scotland found differences in the class of people belonging to the Church of Scotland and the Catholic Church. In the former 11 per cent were from class I (RG), 29 from II and 8 from IV and V; in the latter the percentages were 0, 20 and 20 (Sissons, 1973). Even more local studies have been undertaken. For example, Burton (1975) compared the social class profiles of two midlands Methodist churches with that of their locality. He found that members and leaders were predominantly middle class, in contrast to the local population (see also Harris and Jarvis, 1979). In a suburban church 93 per cent of members and all leaders, compared with 46 per cent of the neighbourhood, were middle class, while for an estate church the figures were: members 56 per cent, leaders 83 and locality 16 per cent. At the same time adherents, those who were involved in the churches' activities but who had not taken out membership, were 12 per cent working class in the suburban church and 69 per cent in the estate church. Hence, while the general picture of churches as middle-class institutions may be sustained, local, and probably denominational, variations exist. A similar situation existed with respect to Sunday school pupils, the majority of whom had church-attending parents, and of their teachers, who were predominantly middle class (Reid, 1979; 1980a).

Anglo-Jewry has had its social class structure investigated in a particularly novel way (Prais and Schmool, 1975). The study involved collecting information about Jewish burials and then securing social class information from death certificates. None of the Jewish sample was in social class (RG) V, whereas 13 per cent of the population in the area were. Jews were also under-represented in class IV (14 compared with 22 per cent), equally represented in class III, and over-represented in classes I and II (4 compared with 2 per cent and 34 compared with 14). The study also revealed differences between the two-thirds sample who were synagogue members and those who were not. The latter were more similar to the area's population, in particular to have been in social class IV (22 compared with 14 per cent). The authors suggest that this may be due to differences in meeting the expenses of membership.

The topics of religious membership, practice and belief continue to reflect Gaine's (1975) review conclusion quoted at the end of the introduction to this chapter.

Crime and the Law

Data in this field are far from comprehensive and have a number of limitations. In particular crime presents some problems for research. The incidence of law-breaking is much greater than is revealed by official statistics, for much crime goes unnoticed or undetected, is not reported, or is not followed by prosecution. For example, data from the British

Crime Survey and the GHS suggest that the amount of crime actually committed is perhaps four times that recorded (*Criminal Statistics England and Wales 1994*). While most commentators recognize a relationship between crime and social class, the situation is far from clear because of variations in the detection and prosecution of different types of crime in our society. In particular, we can suspect that much 'white-collar' crime, associated with the middle classes, remains invisible to the official eye. In any case criminal statistics are neither recorded nor analysed by social class.

A number and variety of studies over time have shown criminals and delinquents to be predominantly male and working class (Douglas et al., 1966; Mays, 1970; Wadsworth, 1975; Home Office Research Unit, 1978; Rutter et al., 1979). A clear sexual and age bias in law-breaking is evident among those convicted of crimes, of whom, in 1993, 89 per cent were male (about eight times more males than females) and 54 per cent were under the age of 25 (calculated from *Criminal Statistics England and Wales 1994*, tables 9.1 and 9.2). Other than in sexually specific crimes such as rape, prostitution and homosexual this gender bias, with some variation, is evident in all types of crime (for an earlier review see Stratta, 1989). Some 12 per cent of those convicted were aged under 18 and a further 20 per cent aged 18 and under 21. Similar patterns exist among those cautioned over as opposed to convicted for crime.

The relationship between social stratification and crime is reflected in the composition of the prison population, though not necessarily accurately because of variations in detection, prosecution and sentencing. Surveys of the prison population have shown it to have marked differences from the population at large. In comparison prisoners are mainly male (96 per cent), younger on average (40 per cent compared with 16 under the age of 25 and 1 compared with 26 aged 60 or over), less likely to say that they were 'white' (82 per cent compared with 95) and less likely to have stayed at school beyond the statutory age (*The National Prison Survey 1991*). As can be seen in table 8.6 there were large social class differences, the proportions being equal only in respect to IIIM, with prisoners over-represented in classes IV and V combined (37 per cent compared with 18) and under-represented in the middle classes (16 compared with 45), and these figures neglect the fact that 9 per cent of prisoners had never worked or were unclassified.

A random survey of 1000 sentenced male prisoners revealed much the same picture with some further detail (*Survey of the Physical Health of Prisoners 1994*). Some 35 per cent were from class (RG) IIIM, 1 per cent from class I and 14 from classes I and II compared with 36 per cent in the general male population of the same age. Older prisoners were more likely than younger ones to be from the middle classes, 38 per cent of those aged 45 to 54 compared with 11 per cent of those under 25. Younger prisoners were more likely than older to be from classes IV

Table 8.6 Social class profile of prisoners and their reasons for first getting into trouble with police* (percentages)

	Social class RG			
	I, II, IIIN	IIIM	IV and V	Other**
Prisoners	16	37	37	9
Male labour force of working age	45	37	18	–
% who played truant	14	28	35	
Reasons for first getting into trouble with police†				
Mixing with the wrong crowd	51	56	60	
Family problems	30	34	40	
Having no job	46	60	65	
Having no money	46	60	65	
Drink or drugs	27	40	46	
Boredom	6	7	9	
Emotional problems	3	4	4	

* Answers from convicted, non-civil, non-segregated prisoners other than first-time offenders, England and Wales, 1991.

** Includes those who had never worked and those with undefined and unofficial jobs.

† Respondents were shown a list as above. Percentages add to more than 100 as more than one answer could be given.

N = 3844

Devised from tables 2.6, 2.36 and 10.9, The National Prison Survey 1991, 1992

and V – 41 per cent of those under the age of 25 compared with 19 per cent of those aged 45 to 54 – and to have never worked.

Table 8.6 further shows differences in the percentage of prisoners who played truant from school which rises steeply over the classes and at 30 overall was ten times higher than in the general population. The reasons that prisoners felt had led them to be involved in crime also vary by class. Middle-class prisoners gave fewer reasons than the others. With the exceptions of boredom and emotional problems which were identified by small numbers, the proportion for each reason rises across the classes, with the gradient being particularly sharp for drink and drugs and for the class-related factors of having no money or job.

Some investigations have been made into self-reported crime. A recent, topical survey was into young adults' drug misuse. Respondents were shown a list containing the real and street names of sixteen substances which were either illegal drugs or prescription drugs not prescribed by a doctor. Perhaps surprisingly more than two in every five respondents claimed to have used drugs, 14 per cent in the month before interview. These figures are interesting in that only 8 per cent of the public think that taking hard drugs should not be a criminal offence (see table 8.14). As can be seen in table 8.7 the percentage reporting ever having taken drugs is higher in the middle than the working

Table 8.7 Self-reported drug misuse*

	Social class RG						
	I	II	IIIN	IIIM	IV	V	All**
Ever used drugs	48	45	46	41	41	42	43
Used drugs in last month	14	15	19	11	13	18	14
Respondents' households	6	22	12	30	17	5	

* By persons aged 16–29, social class of head of household. Illegal drugs or prescription drugs not prescribed by doctor.

** Includes unclassified.

N = 9646

Devised from table B.5, Drug Misuse Declared, 1996

classes, the highest rate being in class I. Use in the last month, typically reflecting regularity and implying more damaging usage, while overall somewhat higher in the middle classes, had the highest rates in classes IIIN and V – where the authors argue household incomes are not necessarily very different. They found that both types of drug use were highest in poorest households, followed by the richest and then middle-income households.

There are very few studies relevant to our concerns of either those committing, or being the victim of, particular types of crime. One interesting example relates to burglary. The GHS found on the basis of self-report that in 1991 the overall rate of burglary in Great Britain was 40 per 1000 households. Households in which the head was aged under 30 and was not 'white', and in which the accommodation was rented and a flat or maisonette, were more likely to have been burgled than were their opposites. As can be seen in table 8.8, households with middle-class heads had higher rates reporting burglaries than those with working-class ones, 43 compared with 36 – and, not surprisingly perhaps, a much higher rate for burglaries in which more than £200 of goods was stolen (23 and 15). Such households were also more likely to report all burglaries to the police, though this difference is only marked in respect to those where the value of stolen goods was £200 or less.

Not only are men more likely to commit crime but they are also more likely to be the victims of crime: they are twice as likely as women to be robbed, five times as likely to be seriously wounded and three times as likely to be a victim of minor assault. Such figures hide subcategory differences, for example domestic violence, the victims of which are very predominantly female. For both sexes 16 to 24 year olds were the most likely and those 60 and over the least likely to be victims of violence (*Criminal Statistics England and Wales 1994*). The first part of table 8.9

Table 8.8 Burglary rate per 1000 households* and percentage of burglaries reported to the police, by value of stolen goods

	Social class RG SEG		
	1, 2, 3	4, 5, 6	All**
Burglary rate per 1000	43	36	40
Value of stolen goods under £200[†]	19	20	21
Value of stolen goods £200 or more	23	15	19
% of burglaries reported to police	94	79	86
Value of stolen goods under £200[†]	89	65	75
Value of stolen goods £200 or more	99	97	98

* Resident at current address for twelve months or more.
** Includes those where value was not stated.
† Includes goods of nil value or nothing stolen.
N = 9097

Devised from tables 4.5 and 4.6., General Household Survey 1991, 1993

shows that one in eight of those interviewed were not only very worried about becoming a victim of violence but also had changed their life a lot because of it. Women were twice as likely to report this as men (17 and 18 per cent compared with 7 and 8), the working classes more than the middle, and older people much more than younger – those aged 18 to 34 years, 8 and 7 per cent, those aged 55 and over, 19 and 22.

The lower part of table 8.9 shows consistent class differences in respect to concern about being out alone and becoming a victim of a range of crimes. Concern rises over the classes, with marked contrasts between AB and DE. This relationship is not readily explicable in terms of other factors (*Anxiety about Crime*, 1995). In contrast to the level of concern, as we have seen above, the incidence of burglary is higher in the working classes. The overall relationship between the known incidence of crime as opposed to fear and anxiety displays an interesting variation, those least likely to encounter it being most fearful and anxious.

Unlike crime, problems for which legal advice and services are necessary or desirable face most people at some time. However, a survey showed the use of lawyers' services closely related to social class (Royal Commission on Legal Services, 1979). The proportion using the services ranged from one in four for class (RG SEG) 1 to one in ten for class 6, with the working classes below and the middle classes above the overall average. Similarly, knowledge of the system, in this case of the existence and function of the Law Society, varied similarly and even more dramatically.

Of course, the use of legal services is related to the type of problem, together with awareness of, and willingness to use, and ability to pay

Table 8.9 Fear of being a victim of crime and anxiety about crime (percentages)

*Fear of being victim**

	Social class MR			
	ABC1	C2	DE	All
Worry all the time about being victim	8	11	19	12
Have changed life a lot	9	10	19	12

Very worried/unsafe about

	Social class MR			
	AB	C1C2	DE	All
Out alone	9	14	19	13
Mugging	14	24	28	21
Rape**	21	26	29	25
Burglary	20	28	33	26
Theft from car	18	23	26	22
Harassment	7	10	13	9

* Answers to: how often do you worry about being the victim of violence, such as being mugged, or attacked in the street? Has fear of violence made you change your way of life at all?

** Asked of women only.

N = 1000 approx.; 13,000+ (varied).

Devised from data supplied by NOP Research Group Ltd, from a poll conducted 17–19 October 1985; and table B2.8, Anxiety about Crime, 1995

for, such services. A comparison of the class profiles of persons reporting various legal problems with the overall population revealed some with a similar frequency in all social classes: the purchase of defective goods, accidents, social security and matrimonial problems. Not surprisingly, the middle classes had more concern with houses, leases, the eviction of tenants, wills and debtors, while the working classes were more involved with repairs undone, arrears in instalments, debts and employment, and juvenile court cases (Abel-Smith et al., 1973).

Some commentators have suggested that part of the reasons for the lower use of legal services by the working classes lies with the nature of the legal profession, which is better equipped to serve the middle classes (for example Zander, 1978). An interesting aspect of this thesis for our purpose is the social class composition of the profession. A review by the Royal Commission on Legal Services showed the backgrounds of law students not markedly different from those of other university students on professional courses. However, while 66 per cent of young people at that time were from working-class homes, only some

16 per cent of law students and an even smaller proportion of those becoming barristers were from such homes. Some 85 per cent of those training to be solicitors and around 90 per cent of barristers were from the middle classes, very predominantly professional and managerial backgrounds. A later study (King et al., 1990) found little change. Of a sample of law students 87 per cent were from middle-class homes (70 per cent from professional and managerial ones) and only 13 per cent from working-class homes. Ethnic minority students were somewhat more likely than 'white' students to be from the working classes (20 compared with 11 per cent). Of the students intending to practise as lawyers only 12 per cent were working class. Halpern's (1994) survey of law students had similar findings: only 18 per cent had working-class fathers (excluding those who did not answer the relevant question raised this to 23), and there was no difference in the class backgrounds of men and women students. The percentage of working-class students (excluding non-respondents) ranged from 26 in new universities, 16 in old ones, to 9 in Oxbridge. Whereas 6 per cent of the age group attended independent school at 14 years, 31 per cent of law students had done so; new universities 18, old ones 26 and Oxbridge 45. Clearly the middle-class origins of the legal profession more than match the class composition of its clients! This also provides a further reflection upon the observation made in chapter 7 that 83 per cent of High Court and Appeal judges were public school educated (see table 7.13). It is interesting to note that a small, now dated survey (Cain, 1973) of the social class backgrounds of policemen revealed none from professional and managerial backgrounds, 23 per cent from class II (RG), and 8 and 2 per cent from semi-skilled and unskilled manual backgrounds, with the remaining two-thirds from class III. Again this study underlines the differences between the social origins of professionals and those of their clients.

Politics

A popular belief is that politics is all about social class, a view shared by some academics. This is not to suggest that the situation is simple. If the working classes voted Labour, and the middle classes voted Conservative, then Britain would have had Labour government from the creation of the Labour Party until the working classes stopped being the majority. In fact the situation is confounded not only by non-conforming voters, but also by the existence of other political parties, by shifts in allegiance, and by failure to vote. Some commentators have argued that class has become a less important factor in politics in post-war Britain. However, Heath et al. (1985) concluded that while the shape of the class structure had changed, class in terms of objective inequalities,

Table 8.10 Voting intention in the 1997 general election and opinion on who would be best Prime Minister (percentages)

	Social class MR				
	AB	C1	C2	DE	All
*Final voting intention**					
Conservative	38	32	22	15	27
Labour	32	41	54	60	47
Liberal Democrat	17	18	16	16	17
Nationalist/Plaid Cymru	3	4	3	4	3
Referendum Party	5	3	3	2	3
Other	3	3	1	3	3
Who in general, do you think would make the best Prime Minister?					
John Major	33	28	21	18	25
Tony Blair	30	36	45	45	39
Paddy Ashdown	20	20	19	17	19
None of these	11	10	7	10	9
Don't know	5	6	8	10	7

* Of those naming a party and likely to vote.
N = 1292

Devised from data supplied by NOP Research Group Ltd, from a survey carried out for The Sunday Times, 25 April 1997

subjective values and party support had remained at the same level. Hence political as well as social explanations are necessary to explain the changing fortunes of political parties.

Voting behaviour is the most rigorously researched area of political activity. A growing number of commercial firms conduct polls (or surveys) of the voting intentions of samples of the public, both continuously and during election campaigns. During campaigns the polls hope to predict, and some say they affect, the outcome. They bring out some of the problems involved in this type of social research; and their predictive powers vary in accuracy, in relation both to other polls and to subsequent events. Overall, however, their track record, with the exception of the 1992 election, is quite good. Table 8.10 shows the results of a survey conducted just before the May 1997 general election, which was won by the Labour Party. The proportion of intending Conservative voters declines markedly across the classes from 38 to 15 per cent while that for Labour rises slightly less proportionally from 32 to 60 per cent. In both cases there is a clear divide between the middle and working classes, while the overall support for the two major parties – 27 and 47 per cent – clearly predicts their subsequent election performance. The table also shows that while the majority of the working classes intended to vote Labour, only between three and four in every ten middle-class

Table 8.11 Voting intention four months before the 1997 general election and voting for the two major parties in 1992 (percentages)*

	Social class MR				
	AB	C1	C2	DE	All
Voting intention, 1997					
Conservative	44	36	29	25	33
Labour	38	46	56	60	51
Liberal Democrats	13	12	10	10	11
Nationalists	2	2	2	3	2
Green Party	0.4	1	0.7	0.7	0.7
Referendum Party	2	1	1	0.9	1
Other	0.9	1	1	1	1
Voting in 1992					
Conservative	56	48	39	35	44
Labour	27	36	46	51	40

* Percentages over 1 rounded.
N = 10,585

Devised from data supplied by The Gallup Organization Inc., from a survey conducted in January 1997

voters intended to vote Conservative. The distribution of those intending to vote for the other listed parties has virtually no class pattern or difference from the overall average. The class gradients in voting intention for the two largest parties have changed considerably since 1979. For example, at that election the percentage for Conservatives declined across the classes from 60 to 31 (overall 46) and that for Labour rose from 17 to 52 (overall 38), and the pattern was similar in the election of 1987 (Gallup Polls: see Reid, 1981, table 7.1; Reid, 1989a, table 9.13). Not surprisingly, opinion on who would make the best Prime Minister follows closely the voting intention patterns – see second part to table 8.10.

Voting intention appears to be fairly volatile in both the short and the long term, as the data in table 8.11 show. The first part shows voting intention from a similar study in January 1997, which can be compared with table 8.10. While the overall class pattern in intention is similar, there was a clear indication of a shift away from the two major parties towards the others as the election approached – overall of some 10 per cent. It is also clear that there was a general movement away from Conservative voting intention and that the working classes sustained their support for Labour. The second part of table 8.11 shows the percentage of each class who voted for the two major parties in the election of 1992, allowing further comparisons to be made.

Table 8.12 Percentage of each social class voting for the main political parties in 1983

	Social class HG/C				
	I and II	III	IV	V	VI and VII
Conservative	54	46	71	48	30
Labour	14	25	12	26	49
Alliance	31	27	17	25	20
Other	1	2	–	1	1

N = 3073

Devised from table 2.3, Heath et al., 1985

Heath et al. (1985) have argued that economic interest is more important in voting behaviour than income level and life-style, and used a modified social class classification, which separated the self-employed from foremen and technicians (classes IV and V on table 8.12). As will be seen class IV was the most strongly aligned to the Conservative Party (71 per cent), a good deal more so than classes I and II combined at 54 per cent. Similarly, there is a clear difference in voting between class V and classes VI and VII combined, with almost half of the first voting Conservative and a similar proportion of the second voting Labour. The table also shows that Alliance (predecessor to Liberal Democrats) voting was somewhat more class-based than other studies, using more common class scales, have indicated. Like Conservative voting, Alliance voting was more popular in the middle than the working classes, but is least popular in class IV. In comparing the voting of the sexes the authors found a general similarity, with one exception: more working-class women than men voted Alliance (27 compared with 17 per cent). They also found few differences between the voting of married and single women.

In the past, however, many studies have shown women to be more inclined to vote Conservative than men, though often it has not been clear whether this was due to gender or to age, there being a larger proportion of older female voters, and older people being inclined to vote Conservative. A NOP (1978) survey found clear sex differences in each age group, including those aged 55 years and over. While male voting intentions were Conservative 42 and Labour 44 per cent, females were 50 and 39 per cent respectively. The Conservative lead among women was 11 per cent compared with a Labour lead among men of 2 per cent. Social class analysis revealed similar differences: the Conservative lead, in percentage terms, was ABC1, all +34, men +32, women +35; C2, all −11, men −22, women −1; and DE, all −16, men −21, women −10. It seems, as Campbell (1984) concluded at the time, that 'men have been moving to the right and women have been moving away from the right'. In any case it seems unlikely that party allegiance is determined by gender alone (see Thomas and Wormald, 1989).

Voting is for most people their only political activity; other political activities are very much minority affairs. NOP conducted several inquiries into the public's political behaviour in the 1970s (NOP 1971; 1975; 1977). 'Political activists' were identified as those who had indulged in five or more of the following: voted in the last election; helped raise funds; been elected officer of, or made a speech to, an organization or club; urged someone to vote, or to contact a councillor or an MP; written to an editor; taken an active part in a campaign or stood for public office. These activists amounted to only 7 per cent of those surveyed (NOP, 1977, p. 8). The social class profile of activists – 40 per cent from AB, 22 per cent from each of C1 and C2, and only 16 per cent from DE – was very different from that of the whole sample, whose profile was 14, 21, 37 and 28 per cent respectively. Apart from being middle-class, 'activists' were also middle-aged, some 48 per cent being in the 35 to 55 years age group. Phillips (1985) found that while three-fifths of respondents had signed a petition, only one in ten had ever attended a lawful demonstration, although a third 'might do so'. Social factors related to the likelihood of, or to the holding of favourable attitudes towards, demonstrating were age, sex and class. Those most disposed were young middle-class males, those least disposed were working-class females aged 60 and over. In the 1987 election the percentage declaring themselves unlikely to vote rose quite dramatically across the social classes AB to E, from 5 to 13 (overall 8), was similar for both sexes (men 9, women 8) and was markedly higher for those aged 18 to 22 at 20 per cent than for other age groups (Gallup Poll data: see Reid, 1989a, table 9.13).

A more up-to-date view, this time of declared interest in politics, is contained in the first part of table 8.13. It is perhaps surprising that some 54 per cent claimed either not to be interested at all or that their interest was no greater than their other interests. Overall four out of ten and nearly half the middle classes were interested but took no active part, while overall only about one in seventeen took an active interest, ranging from one in twelve of the middle class to one in thirty-three of class DE.

British Social Attitudes surveys since 1983 have invited respondents to choose up to eight courses of any political action they would take if faced with the prospect of a law they considered to be harmful or unjust. The actions were: *personal*, namely to contact their MP, speak to an influential person, contact a governmental department or the press, radio or TV; and *collective*, namely to sign a petition, raise the issue in an organization, take part in a protest/demonstration or form a group of like-minded people. Over the period 1983–91 there has been a marked

Table 8.13 Level of interest in politics (percentages) and scores on personal and collective political action indexes*

	Social class MR			
	ABC1	C2	DE	All
Interest in politics				
Take an active interest	8	8	3	6
Interested but no active part	48	26	34	39
Interest no greater than other interests	30	34	31	31
Not interested at all	14	32	32	23

	Social class RG						
	I	II	IIIN	IIIM	IV	V	All
Personal activity index	1.15	1.07	0.95	0.75	0.71	0.52	0.84
Collective activity index	1.06	1.21	1.0	0.98	0.76	1.01	1.01

* Both indexes calculated using formula: the number of actions mentioned (for details see text) minus the number of people choosing none of these actions, divided by the number of respondents in each group.

$N = 934; 2918$

Devised from data supplied by The Gallup Organization Inc., from a survey conducted in August 1996; and table on p. 190, Young, 1992

decline in the percentage saying they would do nothing. The second part of table 8.13 shows these expressed as two indexes, PAI and CAI (see note to table for explanation). PAI declines across the classes, perhaps predictably, and quite sharply. The gradient for CAI is less sharp and is disturbed in the middle classes by the relatively higher scores for class II, and in the working classes by that of class V. Men and women had closely similar scores on CAI but men had a higher one on PAI (Young, 1992).

It is clear then, that interest and involvement in politics vary along social stratification lines. These differences are clearly marked among those who become politicians and there are differences between the parties. The percentage of MPs in 1992 who had or had previously held professional occupations was Conservative 39, Labour 42, Liberal Democrat 60; those from business, Conservative 38, Labour 8, Liberal Democrat 10; manual workers, Conservative 1, Labour 22, Liberal Democrat 0; miscellaneous white collar, Conservative 22, Labour 28, Liberal Democrat 30 (Butler and Kavanagh, 1992, table 10.4). It is of interest that the proportion of Labour MPs from manual worker backgrounds was much higher at 33 per cent in 1983 (Butler and Butler,

1985), most of the change being accounted for by a rise in white-collar workers. The education of MPs is also distinctive (see table 7.13). Women continue to be under-represented in the ranks of MPs: the Parliament elected in 1987 contained the then record number of 41, that of 1992 had 60 (Butler and Butler, 1994) and that of 1997 120.

Opinion

The investigation of public opinion on a variety of matters has been a developing enterprise in Britain since the Second World War. Even the government has held referenda on the Common Market, and on devolution for Scotland and Wales. Quite apart from academic research in the field, including the annual British Social Attitudes surveys, there are a number of commercial concerns which regularly survey public opinion, particularly political opinions, and also conduct sponsored research. The possible range of research that could be reported here is, then, extremely large. The small selection presented has been chosen with a view to topicality and relevance. Several other aspects of public opinion are dealt with elsewhere in this book.

It should be noted that the term 'opinion' is used here in preference to 'attitude' because of the nature of the research involved. The data have been produced from responses to direct questions, often with a choice of responses provided. They are therefore unlikely to illuminate or explain, in any depth, the phenomena of attitudes, beliefs and understanding. There is also the factor of social group variation in response to questions and in the sensitivity to providing socially acceptable answers.

Given the range of differences between the social classes we have viewed so far, it is somewhat surprising to find that public opinion contains relatively few sharp divisions along these lines, at least as measured by surveys. The reasons for this are none too easy to identify. It could be that opinion on these subjects, especially topical ones, is shaped by the media, or that other factors are more significant. As Jowell (1984) commented, 'The term public opinion is itself misleading ... on nearly all issues there are actually several publics and many opinions ... the population's attitudes steadfastly resist being divided neatly and consistently according to age, sex, class ... They divide very differently on different issues.'

The data in table 8.14 come from several sources and have been chosen to illustrate something of the range of topics covered. It would be tedious to describe these data in any detail; they cover aspects of the welfare state, sex, the law, standard of living and what schools should teach. Hence the reader is invited to explore the data, looking for relationships and patterns. In many cases social differences are surprisingly small, and in a few cases quite different from what might be expected.

Table 8.14 Public opinion on a range of social issues (percentages)

	Social class HG/C				
	I and II	IIIN	IIIM	IV	V
*It's the government's responsibility to:**					
Provide decent housing for those who can't afford it	38	39	36	52	56
Provide a job for everyone who wants one	16	14	17	39	31
Provide health care for the sick	85	80	78	91	87
Provide a decent standard of living					
for the unemployed	25	26	23	31	38
for the old	71	77	68	87	83
Reduce differences between people with high and low incomes	13	16	19	27	23

	Social class RG			
	I and II	IIIN	IIIM	IV and V
*Disagree that employees need strong trade unions to protect their interests***	35	34	26	17
Sex before marriage				
Always/mostly wrong	24	20	17	24
Rarely/not at all wrong	49	52	59	52
Sex outside marriage				
Always/mostly wrong	80	81	84	84
Rarely/not at all wrong	2	2	3	4
Sex with same sex				
Always/mostly wrong	61	66	77	72
Rarely/not at all wrong	18	18	12	16

	Social class MR				
	AB	C1	C2	DE	All
*Taking hard drugs should be a criminal offence***					
Yes	82	90	91	91	89
No	14	8	6	6	8
Abortion law in Britain					
Too easy	36	34	40	44	39
About right	48	45	40	30	40
Still too difficult to obtain	5	10	9	11	9

Table 8.14 Continued

	Social class MR				
	ABC1		C2	DE	All
Attitude to abortion					
Women's right to choose	57	59	60	50	56
Only for strong medical reason	37	33	32	38	35
Not under any circumstances	4	6	5	11	7
Government banning most handguns					
Government was right	29	24	21	15	21
All should have been banned	54	60	61	66	61
Any ban is wrong	14	14	16	18	16
Sex in Britain					
There is an obsession	50	50	46	51	49
Things are about right	36	32	33	29	32
Should be brought out more	10	10	13	12	11
Grammar schools					
Would like to see more	51	47	40	39	44
Would like to see fewer	13	11	13	10	12

	Social class MR			
	ABC1	C2	DE	All
*Standard of living***				
Very (fairly) satisfied	20(61)	13(61)	8 (5)	15(57)
Not very (not at all) satisfied	11 (7)	17 (8)	28(20)	17(11)
Has not improved over last 5 years	53	54	70	58
Schools should try to teach: agree (disagree)**				
Christian values	70(22)	76(20)	68(27)	71(23)
Respect for people in authority	90 (7)	95 (5)	96 (2)	93 (5)
Tolerance for the opinions of others	95 (4)	96 (2)	95 (3)	95 (3)
Christian doctrine	45(42)	44(38)	50(32)	46(38)
Marriage is a good thing	76(17)	75(19)	73(22)	75(19)
Chastity before marriage	40(52)	39(48)	50(39)	42(47)
Not to tell lies	90 (7)	88 (8)	86(10)	88 (8)
Conduct a daily act of worship	52(42)	61(29)	61(31)	57(36)
Corporal punishment				
Should (should not) be reintroduced	62(31)	80(17)	67(26)	68(26)
Would allow child to have: yes (no)	63(31)	74(20)	64(30)	66(28)

* Percentage agreeing 'definitely' the government's responsibility.

** Cells/columns do not add to 100% because 'don't knows', 'refusals' and 'other' responses are not shown.

N varies between 1091 and 2797

Devised from: tables on pp. 32, 33 and 34, Taylor-Goodby, 1991; table 9.4, Airey and Brook, 1986; data supplied by NOP Research Group Ltd, from surveys conducted in November 1995, Autumn 1966 and February 1997; data supplied by The Gallup Organization Inc., from surveys conducted in July and October 1996

Table 8.15 Opinions about morality (percentages)

	Social class MR			
	ABC1	C2	DE	All
Believe that society is less moral now than 50 years ago	72	77	79	75
*Most to blame for less moral society now than 50 years ago**				
The family	30	26	25	28
Television/media	52	50	37	48
Present government	10	10	31	16
*Britain has a broadly agreed set of moral standards***	27	16	10	20
% thinking it morally acceptable to (% having done so)				
Not buy ticket on public transport	12(22)	12(17)	19(27)	14(22)
Lie to taxman	18(11)	21 (8)	27(11)	21(10)
Lie to husband/wife	19(31)	21(30)	16(28)	18(30)
Stay silent when undercharged by big chain store	28(33)	27(34)	29(27)	28(32)
Stay silent when undercharged by corner shop	12(11)	11 (8)	18(16)	13(11)
Drink-drive	3(15)	1(14)	3(13)	2(14)

* Columns do not add to 100% because church, school, other, don't know and no answer not shown.

** Alternative was: 'Or do you feel it too much left up to individuals to behave in terms of their own moral code?'

N = 601

Devised from data supplied by The Gallup Organization Inc., from survey conducted in July 1996

The explanation of these differences, even leaving aside the nature of the questions involved, is complex. In some cases it could be argued that they reflect the differing experiences and/or level of involvement or responsibility of the classes, though little consistency is to be found. Hence, in the face of the lack of clear patterns, observations must remain speculative. Little evidence exists on which to claim that any particular class is markedly and consistently more liberal, radical or conservative than the others.

Aspects of the public's views on social morality are revealed in table 8.15. Three-quarters of those interviewed thought that our society was less moral now than fifty years ago, the percentage rising across the classes from 72 to 79. Television and the media were held by just less than half of those in the study as being most to blame for this situation, ranging from over half of ABC1 to more than one-third of DE. The starkest class difference concerned the role of the present government, with almost a third of class DE, but only one in ten of others laying the blame there. There were only small class differences from the overall 28 per cent who saw the family as the cause of moral decline, the percentage falling from 30 to 25 over the classes. Only one in five felt Britain had a broadly agreed set of moral standards, ranging from more than a quarter of ABC1 to one in ten of DE, rather than that too much was left up to individuals to behave in terms of their own moral code.

The lower part of the table displays the differences between what is regarded as morally acceptable behaviour by the respondents in a number of situations and their actual behaviour (in brackets). With the exceptions of lying to the taxman and staying silent when undercharged at the corner shop, the proportion having indulged in the behaviours listed is higher than that seeing them as morally acceptable. The widest difference is in respect to drink-driving, with only 2 per cent saying it was morally acceptable, but some 14 per cent admitting to having done it – with C2 respondents having by far the greatest discrepancy. There is no clear or consistent pattern to class differences, though the middle classes are less inclined to see lying to the taxman as acceptable than are DE, yet the same proportion of both claim to have done it. Similarly fewer in DE find lying to husband/wife morally acceptable than those in other classes, but the proportion who have done it is much the same.

9

Leisure and the Media

Leisure has a range of meanings. Literally it applies to all activities other than work, but this merely shifts the problem to defining work. In any case, many activities do not fall simply into the category of work or non-work, but span both. For many people leisure is a particular set of activities, or period of time, associated with pleasure. Clearly, for survey research purposes such broad and subjective definitions would be exceedingly difficult to operationalize. Much research therefore asks questions concerning participation in specific activities. The GHS uses a somewhat different approach. Those interviewed are informed that leisure time is when they are 'not working, at school, or looking after the house or family' (GHS 1983). Informants are free to decide what they see as work and, as a consequence, activities such as gardening, DIY and sewing are included as leisure by some and not by others. Several activities however are ignored by the GHS, such as 'just sitting and thinking', 'pottering about' and 'reading the newspapers'; while other activities are excluded in analysis, such as shopping, looking after children and short walks (less than two miles). Hence, neither space, nor our present purpose, nor available research allows for a comprehensive treatment of the topic, which has been approached in a selective way.

There is also an important, further factor to be borne in mind. All leisure activities demand time, many require money and some need skill and/or opportunity for their pursuit. While such factors are not necessarily the determinants of leisure behaviour, they obviously affect it and their distribution is related to the social strata. As we saw in chapter 5, in general the manual classes spend longer at work and earn less money than the non-manual. The sexual division of labour in most homes is such that men are likely to have more time than women for

Table 9.1 Weekly household expenditure on leisure goods and services (£p)

	Social class RG					
	I	II	IIIN	IIIM	IV	V
Expenditure on leisure goods	25.91	21.41	13.55	13.79	11.07	9.25
Expenditure on leisure services	63.59	43.15	25.50	22.03	16.29	14.19
Leisure goods and services as % of total expenditure	18.3	15.6	12.8	11.8	10.8	10.9

N = 6979

Devised from table 3.5, Family Spending 1993, 1994

leisure. Retired people may have more time than others, but may have less money for, or lack access to, certain activities, as well as possibly being physically more limited. The range of facilities for leisure activities is not evenly spread and neither is availability of transport to them (see table 9.8).

Such considerations, and there are others, are very complex and have not yet received full and integrated treatment in respect to leisure. Here we have space only for a limited view of two aspects – money and time for leisure. Table 9.1 shows that the amount of money and the percentage of gross household income spent on leisure goods and services decrease across the social classes. Differences in expenditure on leisure services is more marked than that on goods – class I's amount being four and a half times that of V for the first and over two and half times for the second. The proportion of household income spent on these items ranges from just over 18 per cent for class I to almost 11 per cent for classes IV and V.

Some research has shown that, on the basis of self-report, the amount of free time available to people varies according to their economic activity (*Social Trends no. 16*). Not surprisingly, retired people had the most free time per weekday, and men in employment had more time than similarly occupied women, though housewives had almost as much as part-time male workers and more than male and female employees. It is worth noting that while employed women worked on average fewer hours than men (see also chapter 5), they spent considerably longer at domestic work and personal care, and marginally longer asleep. At weekends men had more free time than women. Of course, these overall figures hide considerable variation on factors such as family size, composition and age; type of, and distance to, work; accommodation, etc.

Table 9.2 Participation in selected leisure activities* (percentages)

	Social class RG SEG						
	1	2	3	4	5	6	All**
Watching TV	99	99	99	99	99	98	99
Visiting/entertaining	97	96	97	95	95	94	96
Listening to radio	97	92	92	88	84	81	89
Listening to records/tapes	86	79	81	73	71	64	77
Reading books	82	73	74	52	57	51	65
Gardening	59	57	50	51	42	40	48
DIY	61	53	39	54	34	30	42
Dressmaking/needlework/knitting	12	16	31	11	26	24	22

* In the four weeks prior to interview.
** Includes unclassified.
N = 17,552

Devised from table 8.16, General Household Survey 1993, 1995

Home-Based Leisure

There is a number of dimensions on which leisure can be viewed: for example, popularity, regularity, where it takes place, who is involved. Here we start with those activities indulged in at home, which are by far the commonest and within which the media are most important. Table 9.2 presents the self-reported involvement in a range of in-home leisure activities. Not surprisingly, given the near universality of household ownership of TVs (see table 6.22) and radios, watching and listening are extremely popular. And it is with these we begin our review.

Television

Research over the past three and half decades has shown TV watching to be a, if not the, major leisure-time pursuit of the population as a whole (see, for example, Sillitoe, 1969; Young and Willmott, 1973; GHS 1977; 1980; 1983; 1993). As can be seen in table 9.2, there is virtually no social class variation from the overall 99 per cent of those interviewed who were viewers. However, the continuous extensive research of the BBC makes clear that there are social differences in the amount of viewing – the overall average was 26 hours 29 minutes per week in 1996 – and what is viewed. Table 9.3 shows that the amount of time spent watching television increases across the classes (sixth row) from 20 hours

Table 9.3 Average time per week spent watching TV channels* (hours:minutes)

	Social class MR				
	AB	C1	C2	DE	All
BBC 1	8:01	8:28	8:31	9:15	8:38
BBC 2	2:49	2:53	2:44	3:05	2:54
ITV	6:09	7:59	9:30	12:15	9:18
Channel 4	2:14	2:36	2:45	3:25	2:49
Other	1:44	2:29	3:24	3:25	2:50
All TV	20:56	24:25	26:53	31:24	26:29
% BBC/terrestrial commercial viewing	56/44	52/48	48/52	44/56	49/51

* By persons aged 4 and over, classified by head of household, in fourth quarter of 1996.
N = 4500 households

Devised and calculated from table 5 TVQ, supplied by BARB/BBC Broadcasting Research 1996

56 minutes for class AB to 31 hours 24 minutes a week for class DE. These figures are, of course, averages, and the range of viewing time they represent is considerable. Viewing increases across the classes for all TV channels, but is particularly marked in respect to ITV, where the figure for DE is about twice that for AB, and for non-terrestrial (other) TV. There is a clear divide between the middle and working classes in choice of TV channel, as demonstrated by the percentages of viewing time spent on each (seventh row) which decline from 56 to 44 for BBC and increase from 44 to 56 for ITV between classes AB and DE.

On average women spend about two and a half hours a week longer than men watching TV, a difference which has closed from more than four hours in 1988. While men as a group divide their viewing time almost equally between BBC and ITV (49/51 per cent), women divide theirs 47/53 per cent.

Radio, records and tapes

Radio listening is only a little less popular than TV watching though, as table 9.2 shows, social class differences are more pronounced, the percentage declining from 97 for class 1 to 81 for class 6, with the overall at 89. Table 9.4 presents three views of radio listening. The programmes' audience profiles (second and third columns) can be compared with that of the population (bottom row): these exactly match only in respect to BBC local/regional programmes, while the most distinctive differences are for Radios 3 and 4, which have high levels of middle-class

Table 9.4 Listeners' profiles and average hours of listening to radio programmes* (percentages)

	Listeners' profile		Social class MR % reached		Hours listened	
	ABC1	C2DE	ABC1	C2DE	ABC1	C2DE
BBC						
Radio 1	49	51	24	21	7.3	10.0
Radio 2	52	48	21	16	11.0	14.4
Radio 3	68	32	8	3	3.2	3.3
Radio 4	71	29	27	9	10.5	9.2
Radio 5	59	41	14	8	4.5	5.8
Local/regional	46	54	21	21	7.2	11.1
Commercial						
National	61	49	26	22	6.6	6.5
Local	43	57	47	52	11.7	16.3
Estimated population %	46	54				

* By persons aged 15 and over, during the first quarter of 1995.
N = 14,003

Devised from data supplied by BBC Broadcasting Research from RAJAR/RSL 1995

listeners. The fourth and fifth columns show the proportion of the middle and working class reached by each programme. Local commercial stations reach the highest proportion of both at around half, and Radio 3 the lowest at 8 and 3 per cent respectively. Finally the sixth and seventh columns show the average amount of time per week spent listening to the programmes. In general they show that the working classes spend more time than the middle classes with the radio, especially with local programmes, the only real exception being Radio 4.

No such detailed data on listening to records and tapes are available. What is clear from table 9.2 is both the overall popularity of this activity and the quite dramatic decline of that popularity across the social classes, from more than four in five in class 1 to just less than two-thirds of class 6.

Reading

The most comprehensively surveyed area of reading is that of newspapers and periodicals. The *National Readership Surveys*, widely used by advertising and commercial concerns, are based on extensive and continuous research involving over 30,000 interviews each year. The data in tables 9.5(a)/(b) and 9.6(a)/(b) present the readership of selected newspaper and periodical titles (listed in order of their overall popularity) in two separate but related ways. Each (a) table shows the percentage of each social class which claims to have read or looked at a copy of the given title, in a period up to the interview corresponding to the length of time between publications: for example, in respect to weeklies, in the previous seven days. Hence, the top figure in the left-hand column of table 9.5(a) shows that 6 per cent of class A claim to have read or looked at a copy of *The Sun.* Each (b) table gives the social class and sex profiles of the readers of the same titles. Hence, the top figure in the left-hand column of table 9.5(b) shows that class A provides 1 per cent of the readers of *The Sun.* The bottom row of each part within the tables gives the readership for each type of publication, while the last row to the (b) tables gives the estimated class and sex profile for the population which allows for comparison.

There is little consistent social class pattern to readership of types of publication in general. Sunday papers have a somewhat higher readership than daily ones (65 compared with 58 per cent of those interviewed). In both cases, only classes A and E have rates markedly different from the overall figure, A being higher and E lower than the other classes. The readership of evening papers shows little variation by class. Free local weekly papers are read by around 60 per cent of classes B to E, but only 46 per cent of class A. Paid-for local weekly papers are read by a higher percentage of class A and a lower percentage of E than the overall 30 per cent (table 9.5(a)). While the readership of general weekly periodicals declines somewhat from classes A, B and C1 to C2, D and E, that for women's weeklies, with the exception of classes A and B (which are lower than the overall), shows a fairly flat pattern. Both general and women's monthlies exhibit a sharp decrease across classes A and E – from 65 to 30 per cent and from 52 to 22 per cent respectively (table 9.6(a)).

It is fairly apparent that there are major social divisions in readership of particular publications. This is best illustrated by daily newspapers, where the social classes display quite different choices. It is common practice to distinguish between so-called 'quality' papers (*The Guardian, The Independent, The Daily Telegraph, The Times, Financial Times*), which have overall readership figures of 2 to 6 per cent of the population, and 'popular' papers, which have overall readerships of 5 to 22 per cent (see right-hand column to table 9.5(a)). While 'quality' papers can be characterized as middle class – classes ABC1 constitute more than 80 per cent of their readership, and A and B more than half (table 9.5(b)) – it is also clear that the reading of such papers is only really widespread in class A. Adding together the percentage claiming to read each 'quality' paper (and thereby assuming that no individual reads more than one) reveals that 60 per cent of class A, 38 per cent of class B and 16 per cent of class C1 read such papers (table 9.5(a)).

Table 9.5(a) Percentage of each social class claiming readership of newspapers

	Social class MR						
	A	B	C1	C2	D	E	All
Daily newspapers							
The Sun	6	9	18	30	34	26	22
The Mirror	3	7	12	19	20	13	14
Daily Mail	16	15	15	9	7	5	11
The Express	8	7	8	6	4	3	6
The Daily Telegraph	21	13	6	2	2	1	6
Daily Star	1	2	3	7	8	4	5
The Times	18	10	4	1	1	1	4
The Guardian	7	7	3	1	1	1	3
The Independent	6	4	2	1	1	(–)	2
Financial Times	8	4	1	(–)	(–)	(–)	2
Any national daily*	70	58	55	61	60	50	58
Evening newspapers	21	21	23	26	25	22	24
Local newspapers							
Free	46	56	59	61	61	55	58
Paid for	37	31	30	34	28	22	30
Sunday newspapers							
News of the World	8	12	22	34	37	30	26
Sunday Mirror	4	8	14	21	22	14	16
The Mail on Sunday	21	19	18	11	8	5	14
The People	3	5	11	15	16	12	11
The Sunday Times	30	19	9	4	3	2	8
The Express on Sunday	11	9	9	7	4	3	7
The Sunday Telegraph	17	9	5	2	2	1	4
The Observer	6	7	3	1	1	1	3
Independent on Sunday	7	5	2	1	1	1	2
Any national Sunday*	73	65	64	68	66	56	65

* Includes others not listed.
(–) less than 0.5%
$N = 38{,}143$

Devised from tables 7 and 16, National Readership Survey 1996, 1997

Around a quarter of the members of each of these classes read the *Daily Mail* or *The Express* and together constitute two-thirds and more than half the readership of these papers. In contrast, between over two-thirds and three-quarters of the readership of *The Sun, The Mirror* and the *Daily Star* are from classes C2, D and E – 56, 62 and 43 per cent respectively of the members of these classes claiming to read these papers (again assuming no individual reads more than one). Table 9.5(b) also reveals sex differences. Overall, women are somewhat

Table 9.5(b) Social class profiles of the readers of newspapers (percentages)

	Social class MR						Male/
	A	B	C1	C2	D	E	female
Daily newspapers							
The Sun	1	8	22	30	26	13	56/44
The Mirror	1	9	23	31	25	11	55/45
Daily Mail	4	24	38	18	11	5	49/51
The Express	4	20	34	23	12	6	51/49
The Daily Telegraph	11	45	28	9	5	2	56/44
Daily Star	1	7	19	34	30	10	69/31
The Times	13	44	27	8	5	3	59/41
The Guardian	8	50	29	5	5	3	58/42
The Independent	9	43	31	8	6	3	60/40
Financial Times	15	47	26	5	5	1	73/27
Any national daily*	4	19	26	24	18	10	52/48
Evening newspapers	3	17	27	25	18	11	52/48
Local newspapers							
Free	2	18	28	23	18	11	48/52
Paid for	4	19	27	25	16	8	49/51
Sunday newspapers							
News of the World	1	9	23	29	24	14	52/48
Sunday Mirror	1	10	25	30	24	11	52/48
The Mail on Sunday	5	26	36	19	10	4	48/52
The People	1	8	25	30	24	12	53/47
The Sunday Times	10	42	29	10	5	3	54/46
The Express on Sunday	5	24	35	22	10	5	50/50
The Sunday Telegraph	12	40	31	9	6	2	54/46
The Observer	7	43	28	11	8	4	59/41
Independent on Sunday	9	43	30	9	5	3	54/46
Any national Sunday*	3	19	27	24	17	10	50/50
Estimated population %	3	19	28	22	17	12	49/51

* Includes others not listed
N = 38,143

Devised from tables 134 and 136, National Readership Survey 1996, 1997

under-represented in the readership profile of any daily newspaper – males 52, females 48 per cent (population, 49 and 51 respectively). The female readership of 'popular' dailies ranges from 51 per cent for the *Daily Mail* to 31 for the *Daily Star* and for 'quality' dailies from 44 per cent of *The Telegraph* to 27 for *Financial Times.* Similar observations concerning the social class readership of 'quality' and 'popular' Sunday

Table 9.6(a) Percentage of each social class claiming readership of selected periodicals

	Social class MR						
	A	B	C1	C2	D	E	All
General weeklies							
Radio Times	18	17	11	6	6	5	10
What's On TV	2	6	9	9	10	12	9
Auto Trader	3	3	5	7	5	3	5
The Big Issue	4	3	3	1	1	1	2
Any general weekly*	45	47	45	41	40	37	43
Women's weeklies							
Take a Break	2	5	10	14	16	14	11
Woman's Own	3	5	8	9	11	9	8
Bella	2	4	7	9	10	9	7
Hallo	10	7	7	4	4	3	5
Any women's weekly*	18	21	29	32	34	31	29
General monthlies							
Reader's Digest	13	13	13	11	10	8	11
National Geographic	12	8	5	3	2	1	4
What Car?	6	5	4	3	2	1	3
Any general monthly*	65	59	55	50	43	30	50
Women's monthlies							
Sainsbury's Magazine	12	10	8	5	4	3	6
Cosmopolitan	5	7	7	3	3	2	5
Homes and Gardens	8	6	4	3	2	2	4
Family Circle	3	3	3	3	2	2	3
Any women's monthly*	52	47	43	32	29	22	37

* Includes others not listed.
$N = 38{,}143$

Devised from tables 16, 25 and 34, National Readership Survey 1996, 1997

papers can be made, though it is interesting to note that sex differences in profile are less marked, with female readership ranging from 41 per cent for *The Observer* to 52 for *The Mail on Sunday*.

Some class differences in the readership of periodicals can also be found. Class differences in the readership of *What's On TV* and *Radio Times* are likely to reflect differences in viewing and listening (see tables 9.3 and 9.4) as well as differences between the publications. It is perhaps interesting that readership of *The Big Issue* is higher in the middle than the working classes. There is a somewhat more marked class pattern to reading any general monthly than to any general

Table 9.6(b) Social class profiles of the readership of selected periodicals (percentages)

	Social class MR						
	A	B	C1	C2	D	E	Male/ female
General weeklies							
Radio Times	5	33	31	14	10	6	50/50
What's On TV	1	12	27	24	20	16	40/60
Auto Trader	2	12	29	32	18	7	79/21
The Big Issue	6	27	38	14	10	6	49/51
Any general weekly*	3	20	29	22	16	10	51/49
Women's weeklies							
Take a Break	1	8	24	28	24	15	23/77
Woman's Own	1	11	28	26	22	13	14/86
Bella	1	11	26	27	22	14	17/83
Hello!	5	23	34	18	13	7	24/76
Any women's weekly*	2	14	27	25	20	13	22/78
General monthlies							
Reader's Digest	3	22	31	22	14	8	49/51
National Geographic	9	35	33	14	6	3	59/41
What Car?	6	29	33	20	9	3	80/20
Any general monthly*	4	22	30	22	15	7	57/43
Women's monthlies							
Sainsbury's Magazine	5	29	33	18	10	5	32/68
Cosmopolitan	3	26	41	15	10	4	22/78
Homes and Gardens	7	28	31	19	10	6	32/68
Family Circle	3	20	31	24	14	8	15/85
Any women's monthly*	4	24	32	20	13	7	30/70
Estimated population %	3	19	28	22	17	12	49/51

* Includes others not listed.
N = 38,143

Devised from tables 136, 138 and 140, National Readership Survey 1996, 1997

weekly. Among women's publications there are some quite marked class differences in readership: compare for example *Bella* with *Hello!* and *Homes and Gardens* with *Family Circle*.

Apart from the social differences noted above, which might be anticipated, the data also reveal considerable breadth of readership. Some members of all social classes read every newspaper: for example, very small percentages (around 1) of the working classes claim readership of the 'quality' dailies, ranging from 2 of C2 and D for *The Daily*

Telegraph to less than 0.5 in each class for the *Financial Times* and for *The Independent* in class E. On the other hand 1 per cent of class A read the *Daily Star.* The readership of women's weeklies is 22 per cent male, and of women's monthlies 30 per cent, ranging from 15 per cent for *Family Circle* to almost a third for *Homes and Gardens* and *Sainsbury's Magazine.*

In general, newspaper and periodical readership has changed considerably in the past two decades. The overall percentage claiming readership of daily newspapers fell from 75 in 1975 to 68 in 1987 and 58 in 1996 – and of Sunday newspapers from 84 to 74 and 65 per cent respectively. Readership of both general and women's weeklies fell between 1975 and 1987 – from 50 to 38 and from 37 to 26 per cent – but has risen since to 43 and 29 per cent in 1996. The readership of general monthlies increased from 36 to 50 per cent between 1975 and 1996 *(National Readership Surveys 1975*; *1987*; *1996*).

Book readership is not researched in the same detail as newspapers and periodicals. Table 9.2 shows that leisure-time reading of books is reported by almost two-thirds of the GHS respondents and that such reading is higher among women than men (71 compared with 59 per cent), with marked differences across the social classes – from 82 per cent of class 1 to 51 per cent of class 6. Similar differences exist in book purchasing, as can be seen in table 9.7, though, of course, some of these purchases will be for presents. In general both hardback and softback book purchasing declines across the classes, with classes A, B and C1 being above the overall average and the other classes below it. A similar pattern can be seen in respect to the number of each type of book purchased. This decline was somewhat sharper in respect to non-fiction than fiction. Hardbacks were purchased by about a third of those surveyed and were mainly non-fiction; paperbacks were bought by around a half and were mainly fiction.

Other home-based activities

As table 9.2 shows, gardening and DIY activity both decline across the social classes – from 59 to 40 and 61 to 30 per cent respectively. Of course, to an extent such activities are determined or affected by the type and tenure of the household's accommodation and whether or not it has a garden. As was seen in chapter 6, rented accommodation and that without a garden is more frequent in the working than the middle classes. As would be anticipated, dressmaking, needlework and knitting are distinctly female pursuits – 38 compared with 3 per cent for males. Unlike all the other activities listed, these do not decline across the social classes – classes 1, 2 and 4 having much lower incidence than the overall 22 per cent, 3 much higher (31) and 5 and 6 similar and higher

Table 9.7 Book purchases in the past twelve months* (percentages)

	Social class MR						
	A	B	C1	C2	D	E	All
Hardback							
5 or more	13	11	9	6	6	6	8
3–4	13	13	10	8	7	7	9
2 or less	28	23	18	14	12	11	16
None	47	53	64	72	75	77	67
Fiction	16		15	12	11	10	12
Non-fiction	39		28	20	17	16	25
Paperback							
10 or more	13	13	9	6	6	6	8
4–9	34	27	20	13	12	11	17
3 or less	29	27	26	21	18	14	22
None	24	31	44	60	65	69	53
Fiction	52		41	28	24	22	35
Non-fiction	35		29	21	20	15	25

* Prior to interview.
N = 25,296

Devised from data supplied by BMRB International from Target Group Index, 1994

than average. Finally, entertaining, or being entertained, in the home approaches the popularity of TV watching, 96 per cent reporting it in the four weeks before interview. Class differences are not very pronounced, though the middle classes had rates at or just above the overall, the working classes below.

Out-of-Home Activities

Motor cars

The car itself can provide leisure activity – cleaning, servicing and riding – but is probably most important in providing access to a range of other leisure pursuits. Just over three-quarters of households have a car or cars. Table 9.8 shows the social class variation, ranging from 95 per cent in class A to 42 for E. There has been a marked increase in households with a car or cars between 1987 and 1994, the percentage rising overall by 11, with the greatest increase in class E, from 27 to 43 (*Target Group Index*, 1987; 1994). Almost three in ten households had two or more cars, the percentage declining over the classes from 58 to 6, and for three or more cars from 12 to 0.6; in both cases the middle classes had

Table 9.8 Car and driving licence ownership and average weekly mileage (percentages)

	Social class MR						
	A	B	C1	C2	D	E	All
*Household car ownership**							
None	5	8	18	18	32	58	23
1 car	37	46	50	55	50	37	48
2 cars	46	38	26	23	16	5	24
3 or more cars	12	8	6	5	3	0.6	5
Adults with a full driving licence	85	83	75	69	57	40	68
Adult's average weekly driving							
Up to 179 miles	57	58	53	53	44	29	50
180 miles or more	26	22	17	14	9	4	14

* Includes company cars.
N = 25,296

Devised from data supplied by BMRB International from Target Group Index, 1994

higher and the working lower proportions than the overall. While just over two-thirds of adults surveyed held driving licences, the proportion declines across the classes – A at 85 and B at 83 per cent to D at 57 and E at 40 per cent. It is clear from the final part of the table that weekly mileage varies by class – almost certainly affected by work-related driving. The percentage driving 180 or more miles a week declines from 23 for AB to 4 for E.

Physical activities, sports and games

Involvement and participation in these types of leisure activity can be identified at several levels and in a number of ways. The GHS asks respondents an open-ended question and uses an *aide-mémoire* card about activities in the four weeks prior to interview. The first part of table 9.9 provides a view of the level of participation in physical activities and reveals that 64 per cent had indulged in at least one such activity, with a decline across the classes from 82 to 48 per cent. Excluding walking slightly sharpens the class gradient from 64 to 31 per cent. It is evident that, apart from walking, participation in physical activities such as running, jogging and training with weights is low (overall 5 per cent), and declines across the social classes (class 1 stands out as the most active in this respect). Men are more likely to take part in physical activity and sport than women, at 72 compared with 57 per cent in 1993,

Table 9.9 Participation in physical activities and selected sporting and leisure activities* (percentages)

*Physical activities***

	Social class RG SEG						
	1	2	3	4	5	6	All†
At least one activity	82	71	65	63	54	48	64
At least one activity other than walking	64	53	49	46	36	31	47
Walking††	57	46	42	39	36	31	41
Running (jogging etc.)	11	6	4	3	2	2	5
Weight lifting/training	7	5	5	6	4	3	5

Sporting and leisure activities§

	Social class MR						
	A	B	C1	C2	D	E	All
Badminton	10	10	8	6	5	4	7
Bingo	1	1	4	7	10	10	6
Bridge	6	4	2	0.4	0.4	0.7	2
Camping	8	11	10	8	7	5	8
Coarse fishing	1	2	3	4	4	3	3
Cycling	10	10	9	7	5	4	8
Dancing	7	9	15	13	14	12	13
Darts	3	3	5	7	8	7	6
Football pools	14	20	25	34	33	23	30
Golf	16	10	9	8	5	3	8
Skiing	9	6	5	1	1	0.5	3
Snooker	7	6	8	9	8	7	8
Squash	6	6	5	4	2	1	4
Swimming	25	29	25	21	17	12	22
Table tennis	7	4	4	3	2	3	3
Tennis	13	10	7	5	3	3	6

* Percentages over 1 rounded.
** In four weeks prior to interview, persons aged 16 and over.
† Includes unclassified.
†† More than 2 miles, other than to work
§ Those claiming to 'take part in or play these days'.
N = 17,552; 25,296

Devised from table 8.10, General Household Survey 1993, 1995*; and data supplied by BMRB International from Target Group Index, 1994*

though this gap has narrowed slightly from 70 and 52 per cent in 1987. This pattern is reflected in a more marked decline across the classes for women than men – 73 to 42 per cent compared with 84 to 62. Interestingly enough the largest and most consistent increase in class participation has been in class 6, rising from 42 per cent in 1987 to 48 in 1993 (GHS 1993).

The second part of table 9.9 is based on answers to the question, 'Which of these do you take part in or play yourself these days?', and for which a list was provided. Obviously such a question is likely to produce higher rates of participation. In general, as can be seen, most of the pursuits, particularly active sports, exhibit a decline in participation across the classes. There are, however, several exceptions to the overall pattern. Bingo, coarse fishing, dancing, darts and the football pools rise across the classes and are clearly more popular in the working classes; snooker has a fairly flat class profile. When considering the table, bear in mind that class E contains state pensioners whose age and economic circumstances, like casual workers who are also included, may preclude their taking part in many of the activities listed.

Voluntary work and leisure classes

As can be seen in table 9.10 almost a quarter of those surveyed had participated in some form of voluntary work in the past twelve months, ranging from 40 per cent of class 1 to 12 per cent of class 6, with the percentage of the middle classes being higher than the overall and markedly higher than the working classes. This pattern was found for both sexes, though more women than men undertook such work – 27 compared with 21 per cent. The average number of hours worked in the previous four weeks is fairly similar across the classes. There is no clear consistent class pattern to the type of voluntary activity. However, and perhaps not surprisingly, classes 1 and 2 in comparison with 5 and 6 were somewhat less likely to have collected or raised money and more likely to have taught or provided training, been involved in entertainment, given a talk or advice, served on a committee and helped with administration.

The GHS defines leisure and recreational classes as those not normally leading to examination or qualification and not designed to further people's career or job prospects. In the 1993 survey some 8 per cent of those over the age of 16 were attending such classes when interviewed – 10 per cent of the middle and 4 per cent of the working classes. Women were twice as likely to be attending as men (10 compared with 5 per cent) and both sexes displayed the overall class differences (male 6 and 3 per cent, female, 13 and 6 per cent: GHS 1993, table 8.20). Not surprisingly attendance was also related to level of education qualifications, which itself is related to class (see chapter 7). The percentage of those with a degree or equivalent attending classes was 14 compared with 4 of those without educational qualification.

Table 9.10 Participation in voluntary work* (percentages)

	Social class RG SEG 1	2	3	4	5	6	All**
% participating in last year†	40	33	30	16	17	12	24
Average hours worked in last four weeks†	14.4	16.0	15.1	17.1	14.9	15.9	15.9
Type of work undertaken in last year††							
Collected money	25	28	33	28	30	33	30
Raised money	38	44	47	45	47	47	45
Visited people in institutions	10	10	11	9	9	8	10
Teaching/training	16	16	15	16	10	10	15
Gave talks/canvassing	18	14	12	12	10	6	12
Gave advice	18	11	8	8	6	2	9
Served on a committee	46	41	31	29	21	17	32
Helped at a club	22	23	27	28	28	21	26
Administration	32	23	22	15	12	5	20
Organized/took part in entertainment	17	21	18	18	13	11	18
Other practical help	11	10	10	9	13	12	10

* By persons aged 16 and over.
** Includes unclassified.
† Prior to interview.
†† Percentages are of those undertaking voluntary work.
N = 18,179

Devised from tables 7, 19 and 32, Voluntary Work, 1993

Entertainment, food and drink

The cinema, once a major form of entertainment, has become a minority pursuit. Those who reported going once a month declined to one in ten at the end of the 1970s and to 7 per cent in 1987, since when, as can be seen in table 9.11, the figure has increased to one in eight (*National Readership Surveys 1979; 1987; 1996*). Currently just over half those surveyed never go to watch a film at a cinema. Cinema-going is clearly class related: each level of attendance declines from class A to E, that for once a month or more being three times higher in the former than the latter, while never going increases from 35 to 76 per cent. The figures for class E, which includes the retired, may seem surprising given the concessionary entrance charges at cinemas.

Somewhat less common and more strongly class-related is going to the theatre, only a third overall claiming to attend once a year or more

Table 9.11 Frequency of cinema attendance (percentages)

	Social class MR						
	A	B	C1	C2	D	E	All
Once a month or more	15	17	16	9	9	5	12
Less than once per month but at least twice a year	35	33	29	23	20	12	25
Less than twice a year	14	14	11	12	10	7	11
Never	35	36	44	56	61	76	51

N = 38,143

Devised from table 167, National Readership Survey 1996, 1997

(a 7 per cent increase since 1988) and 42 per cent ever going these days (*Target Group Index*, 1987; 1994). Table 9.12 displays very clear social class variation: among those attending more than three times per year, the proportion in class A is more than two and a half times that for C2 and six times that each of the working. The percentage never going to a theatre, overall 58, rises from 23 to 80 from class A to E. The lower part of the table lists, in order of overall popularity, based on attendance once a year or more often, attendance at differing types of performance. For each there is a clear divide between middle and working

Table 9.12 Frequency and type of theatre attendance (percentages)

	Social class MR						
	A	B	C1	C2	D	E	All
*Theatre attendance**							
More than three times a	19	13	7	3	3	3	6
Once every 2–3 months	12	8	5	2	2	2	4
Two to three times a year	20	19	15	9	5	5	12
Once a year	12	15	13	10	6	6	11
Less than once a year	10	12	11	6	6	4	9
*Type of performance***							
Plays	42	34	21	9	6	7	17
Popular/rock concerts	16		19	13	9	7	14
Classical concerts	24	19	10	3	3	3	8
Ballet	8	8	5	1	1	1	4
Opera	11	10	4	1	1	1	4

* Based on answer to question 'About how often these days do you go to . . . ?'
** Attendance once a year or more often.
N = 25,296

Devised and calculated from data supplied by BMRB International from Target Group Index, 1994

Table 9.13 Frequency of use of pubs, licensed clubs, wine bars and restaurants and of consuming alcoholic drink (percentages)

	Social class MR						
	A	B	C1	C2	D	E	All
Public house							
Twice or more a week	12	13	16	15	16	11	15
More than once a month	25	26	26	24	23	17	24
Once a month or less	44	41	36	36	32	28	36
Any use	81	80	78	75	71	56	74
Licensed club							
More than once a month	12	13	18	21	23	17	18
Any use	28	30	39	43	43	34	38
Wine bar							
More than once a month	8	7	7	5	5	3	6
Any use	34	30	28	20	17	11	23
*Restaurants**							
Day	63		52	44	37	34	48
Evening	78		71	61	52	33	62
Alcoholic drink							
Once a day	19		11	8	6	8	11
Two or three times a week	35		33	29	26	18	29
Never	6		7	8	11	16	8

* Any use.
N = 25,296

Devised from data supplied by BMRB International from Target Group Index, 1994

classes, with only plays and popular or rock concerts having any real following in the latter. The general decline across the classes is not present in respect to popular or rock concerts where the percentage of C1 is higher than AB. Ballet and opera stand out as being almost exclusively middle class choices: in both, classes A and B stand out in terms of attendance.

Eating and drinking can either be leisure activities in their own right or an aspect of other activities. The self-reported use of pubs, clubs, wine bars and restaurants is presented on table 9.13. The use of public houses declines across the classes – from 81 per cent of A to 56 of E – though the range to class D (71 per cent) is much less. With the exception of E it is clear that classes A and B are less frequent pub users than classes C1, C2 and D, their percentage for 'twice or more a week' being lower and for 'once a month or less' higher. The second and third parts of the table suggest that while wine bars are used more often by the middle classes, licensed clubs are used most by classes C2 and D. Eating

Table 9.14 Outings to places of interest in the last twelve months (percentages)

	Social class MR						
	A	B	C1	C2	D	E	All
Beauty spots/gardens	43	47	38	28	22	20	33
Museums	48	43	33	22	18	19	28
Stately homes/castles	37	37	27	16	13	12	22
Art galleries/exhibitions	39		28	14	9	11	22
Nature reserves	24	23	19	15	10	10	16
Archaeological sites	14	15	9	4	3	3	7
Alton Towers	3	6	7	8	8	5	7
Safari parks	2	4	6	7	6	4	5

N = 25,296

Devised from data supplied by BMRB International from Target Group Index, 1994

in restaurants declines across the classes, the decline being somewhat more marked for evening than day visits. While the overall percentage of those reporting use of licensed clubs and wine bars has remained stable, that for pubs increased by 4 between 1987 and 1994 and that for restaurants by 6 for day and 5 for evening use (*Target Group Index*, 1987; 1994).

As was seen in chapter 3 (table 3.11) the level of alcohol consumption is class-related. The final part of table 9.13 shows that self-reported daily drinking is more frequent in the middle classes, especially A and B, and that while drinking two or three times a week declines across the classes, never drinking rises. As might be expected, tastes in alcohol vary. For example, bottled wine is more popular among the middle classes: 67 per cent of those who drink at least three bottles of table wine a month belonged to classes A, B and C1 (*Target Group Index*, 1994). In contrast, 63 per cent of those who drank 20 or more pints of beer and 65 per cent of those who drank the same quantity of lager a week were from classes C2, D and E. Similar class differences exist among all drinkers. Lager is somewhat more popular than beer in the younger age groups and among women. While men constitute 84 per cent of all beer and 65 per cent of all lager drinkers, the sex profile of wine drinkers is similar to the population at large.

Outings and holidays

Table 9.14 provides a view of outings to selected places of interest, listed according to their overall popularity. There are clear and perhaps expected social class differences in visits to such places as museums, art

Table 9.15 Holidays in the last twelve months* (percentages)

	Social class MR					
	AB	C1	C2	D	E	All
Any holiday	78	68	62	54	40	63
Three or more holidays	17	11	7	6	4	10
Holiday in UK	44	40	39	35	27	38
Holiday camp	5	8	10	10	7	8
Holiday abroad	52	40	30	23	16	34
Package tour abroad	28	24	20	16	9	21

* Prior to interview; excludes short visits to relatives.
N = 25,296

Devised from data supplied by BMRB International from Target Group Index, 1994

galleries and stately homes, which decline across the classes, with the middle being above and the working below the overall averages. At the same time places like Alton Towers and safari parks appear, with the exception of class A, to be of similar attraction to all. There are also some studies of the class composition of visitors to specific places, for example the National Portrait Gallery in London, where eight out of ten visitors were middle class – six out of ten from classes I and II (RG) – and only 7 and 1 per cent respectively from classes IV and V (*Visiting the National Portrait Gallery*, 1987, table 3.11).

As would be expected from the data on car ownership (table 9.8) the working classes, especially IV and V, use other modes of transport, particularly scheduled buses, taxis and walking, for leisure day trips more than the middle classes (*Leisure Day Visits in Great Britain 1988/89*, tables 2.27 and 3.24). Trips taken by members of classes D and E were more likely than others to be to visit friends and relatives.

Holidays had been taken in the previous year by 63 per cent of those interviewed in 1994, with the percentage declining across the classes from 78 to 40 (see table 9.15). One in ten had had three or more holidays, the percentage declining much more sharply over the classes from 17 to 4. The class differences are wider for those holidaying abroad than those in Britain, where the use of holiday camps is highest in classes C2 and D. Overall some 45 per cent had travelled by air for holiday or pleasure purposes in the past three years, ranging from 62 per cent of class AB to 22 of E.

10

Class in a Classless Society

This book has presented what amounts to a catalogue of social class differences in Britain. This catalogue is based on, and some might say limited by, the exclusive use of data from empirical research. The book's presentation is matter-of-fact; for example, it does not present only those data which exhibit the extremes of difference or inequality. It has not elaborated either these or what might be seen as the attendant injustices to the disadvantaged. It provides no description or first-hand account of the varying situations and conditions of the classes surveyed. Doubtless had this been done a much starker and more dramatic picture would have been presented. Nevertheless, an abiding impression must be that the classes in the Britain of the 1990s experience not only differing life-styles but also differing life-chances. Both the quality and quantity of life of the classes are affected by their level of ownership of, and access to, forms of social wealth, particularly the economic and that of power, but also to others. Further, however much the life-chances and life-styles of the disadvantaged may have improved in absolute terms, relative differences have resolutely remained, and in some cases widened.

Indeed, it can be argued that relative differences between the classes not only have been sustained or increased but are potentially of greater importance. As Runciman (1966) argued, relative deprivation is likely to be a more serious social and political problem than abject deprivation since the disadvantaged in the latter situation have few concerns other than about survival. If the desirable aspects of life continue to grow in number and their desirability is heightened through political activity and advertising, then there may well be two consequences. First, on the assumption that such aspects of life remain scarce, competition for them will increase along with the feeling of deprivation by those without. Second, the mechanisms by which they are distributed will come under increasing scrutiny and the bases of inequality of opportunity will be questioned, and perhaps challenged.

The dimensions and extent of the class differences revealed in this book are limited by its reliance on social survey data. This implies that the view of class obtained is neither as comprehensive nor as detailed or continuous as might be expected or desirable. This situation reflects the facts that much of the surveyed research was designed for purposes other than the exploration of class differences *per se*, and that research is subject to both changes and inertia in fashion. In other words, like that which it studies, it is socially produced. To a great extent, shifts in social research mirror shifts in society's interest in, and recognition of, problems. This accounts for the rise in research activity in respect to gender and ethnicity, and its slackening in class. The central focus of the book togther with the nature of much of the research reviewed in it has meant that our view of class has generally been separated from the other forms of social stratification. Yet, as we have seen, where more than one stratum has been viewed simultaneously there is evidence of cumulative advantage and disadvantage and the exposed differences are often extenuated.

Those who have read this book are now in an informed position from which to judge both the usefulness of categorizing society into classes and the importance and nature of the exposed differences between them. For example, the actual differences between the separate classes have varied in magnitude and importance. What is clear is the very substantial extent of the differences between the middle (non-manual) and the working (manual) classes, and of the stark differences between the extremes – the professional and the unskilled manual classes. Readers would find it relatively simple to compile a list of contrasting differences from either a middle-class or a working-class perspective. Further, they have some knowledge both of the size of such differences and of the basis on which the evidence rests.

So equipped, they should have no difficulty in evaluating claims that Britain is moving towards being a classless society or that class analysis is becoming sterile or out of date. There have long been those who have seen or predicted the coming of a classless society, though their visions have been varied. In the 1990s one of these, perhaps because of his biography, or from political motive, was John Major:

> I think we need a classless society, and I think we need to have what I refer to as social mobility. And what I mean by social mobility is the capacity of everybody to have the help necessary to achieve the maximum for their ability. (*The Guardian*, 28 November 1990)

This was far from being a new idea and may well be part of the ideology of late twentieth-century capitalism, involving beliefs in civil equality, equality of opportunity and individual success. His statement certainly echoes that of the Conservative, then Leader of the House of Commons, Norman St John-Stevas, when he said:

> I think that class is largely an irrelevancy in contemporary British society. Some people may use it as an excuse for their own failures, but I think we have very largely a mobile society, a society open to talent. The talented child or young person is able to reach the top of any profession or activity to which that child sets his or her mind, provided that the ability is there . . . We talk a lot about class in British society, but I think its social significance is very small. (*The Listener*, 1980)

Likewise New Labour appear to have lost the term 'social class' from their political vocabulary. How widespread views of classless Britain may be is not easy to ascertain. While opinion polls find that most people disagree (see p. 37), Hoggart (1995) has described the claim that we are all classless now as 'one of the most commonly voiced misconceptions' and states that it has been said for at least half a century.

There is little evidence that government action in the 1990s provided the help which John Major saw as necessary for all to achieve the maximum for their ability. More importantly, he and many others failed to recognize the need for political action to remove the range of inequalities and barriers which stand in the way of achieving the equality of opportunity identified. Indeed, some would argue that, for example, the reintroduction and extension of selection and diversity in schooling (following the 1988 Education Reform Act) simultaneously increased opportunity for some and limited it for others. They may well go on to reflect that in general those for whom opportunity was heightened were more likely to be those already socially advantaged. To be sure of the effects both sides would need to have access to carefully conducted research or monitoring, which was not undertaken. While changes in taxation and income differentials may have provided opportunities for some, the overall effect (as is illustrated in chapter 4) has been to widen the economic differentiation between the richest and poorest groups in Britain.

It is not easy to see what a classless society as envisaged by politicians and other advocates would entail. However, Ossowski (1963) has provided a clear view of the concept. In a classless society the social and economic status of individuals would not be inherited, and the highest positions in society would be open to anybody even if they did not have an equal start. There would be no distinct barriers to the social status scale which would be a continuum rather than a series of strata. The various parts of the scale would have no clear privileges attached to them and there would be no permanent conflicts of interest between them. Social contacts between those of differing social status would be neither restricted nor separated.

There is a range of ideas about a classless society. One is that envisaged by Marx as the final stage of communist revolution, where there would be simply no classes at all. This was to be achieved through the abolition of private property and inheritance, state provision for social needs and the prevention of any group having the political power to indulge their own interests. Another idea is that there will be only one, single social class in society. This might be a working or a middle class. The latter reflects the claims of some that everyone in Britain is, or is becoming, middle class, by virtue of the reduction of differences in income and wealth leading to identical patterns of consumption, shared interests and a lack of conflict. As we have seen there is no evidence that this has happened or is happening in Britain in the 1990s. Finally, there is a view of the possibility of a classless society which has a number of classes in which the structure of these is breaking down, consciousness of them declining and mobility between them increasing. It is this concept that is used by politicians and others in respect to Britain.

It is fairly obvious that there are clear contradictions in a concept of classlessness in a society with classes, since if all were equal there would be no place to move to, or from. Everybody cannot be successful so that there would continue to be a balance of winners and losers. In any case as we have seen economic and social differences continue to be characteristic of Britain towards the new millennium – the evidence suggesting greater economic differentiation. Together with fairly constant levels of individual social mobility, these factors indicate the continuing importance of inherited cultural and economic capital in a society whose structure and politics also support social class. Readers of this book are likely to be more impressed with attempts to explain why social class continues to be such a significant aspect of their society, rather than with those which argue that it is in decline and about to disappear.

There have been a number of critics of class analysis also from within sociology, for example Pahl (1989) who stated that 'class as a concept is ceasing to do any useful work for sociology' (and see for example Holton and Turner, 1989). However, Goldthorpe and Marshall (1992) have argued that much of these criticisms stem from an assumption that class analysis needs to be related to a general theory of class – typically Marxist. They argue that class analysis is better seen as a research programme which is about examining the effects of class in shaping life-chances and social action and in the monitoring of change, and that as such it has a promising future. Their review of the outcomes of class analysis, in social mobility, education and political partisanship, leads them to conclude that what is revealed is the stability of class inequalities and class patterns of social action within periods of rapid change in economic structure and social institutions. This situation they see as posing a problem for those who see class as withering away, and calling for a reorientation from explanations of social change based on class to an understanding of the processes involved in the stability observed.

In the face of the data contained in this book it would be difficult to deny that social class, in spite of the considerations discussed here and in the first two chapters, is a meaningful and useful concept. If it were only a spurious and artificial concept of social scientists it is difficult to imagine that its research application would so consistently turn up differences. However uncomfortable it may be, however incongruent with values concerning individuality and individual responsibility, the evidence clearly shows that in reality most of life's opportunities and its experiences are vitally affected and mediated by the dimensions of social class. Of course, readers will form, or have formed, their own views and reactions to the differences exposed in this book. As discussed at the outset, facts do not speak for themselves: they are available for differing interpretation and receive an almost infinite range of reaction. It seems unlikely, however, that many will be able to dismiss all or even the majority of the facts and differences as inconsequential and of no concern to themselves or others.

As we have seen, there are intimate relationships between the forms of social stratification, much in the same way as we are all members of each. What remains somewhat contentious since it is not clearly demonstrated in research is whether the forms of stratification vary in their significance. This book was written on the assumption that social class is the most fundamental form of social stratification. Mainly this is due to the fact that most of the vital social differences can be seen to have an economic base. Just as important, however, is the clear indication that both the conditions of the other strata and their relationships vary according to class context. Put as boldly as possible, being Black, female or elderly and middle class is different from being Black, female or elderly and working class. Again, the relationships between the sexes, ethnic groups and age groups are not identical in the different classes. This is not to deny the importance of gender, ethnicity and age either objectively or subjectively, or to suggest that changes in class would necessarily end the differences between them. It is rather, again, to assert the necessity of properly viewing all forms of social stratification, and to underline once more the inherent dangers in ignoring social class. It is to return to the basic claim that social groups are differentiated mainly by their ownership of or access to various forms of social wealth. Consequently, real change in their situations is dependent upon the redistribution of that wealth, however that may be achieved.

Our view has been of Britain in the immediate past (most of the data being from the 1990s and almost all from the last two decades) in empirical research terms, and, for most practical purposes, that is the here-and-now. At the same time it is clear that the differences both have a history of persistence and vary in the amount of change that can be discerned. It is difficult to escape from the realization that the basic facts of class are very far from being dynamic. For those with investment of hope in change, the lack of change observed in areas where the rhetoric for equality abounds – like health and education – may be galling. Indeed there is some evidence to suggest that class differences in some areas may be widening. At the same time, in some few cases change towards greater equality can be discerned. However, such changes do not relieve the overall picture of the stability of relative class differences within a context of general change in society. It is difficult to see that political activity and social change in the 1980s and 1990s has done much other than to sustain, or even increase, existing class differences. Indeed, the large body of unemployed, especially the long-term, may be seen as a new class whose deprivations are many and severe. There is, in short, no evidence to suggest that class differences are anything but alive and well at present and that they will feature prominently, along with those of gender, ethnicity and age, into the 2000s and beyond. Despite the cut-backs in academic and governmental agencies' research funding, together with a shift away from research interest in class, there will be more than enough data on which to base a similar review to this one in the future.

Among the most significant and rapid changes reported in this book is that in the educational performance of the sexes, especially as it is in contrast to the continuing class differences (see chapter 7). While the effects have yet to reach the related areas of employment and earnings to the same degree, the fact that girls now out-perform boys in school and that the sexes are equally represented on degree courses is a significant social change – and one achieved in a comparatively short time. While the precise ingredients and process of this change are not well understood, for those dedicated to greater equality this achievement serves as an encouragement.

As we have seen, the disadvantaged and advantaged often share a common view of the appropriateness and justice of each other's position. Perhaps the assumed inevitability of inequality has had a profound effect on all, even on the proponents of equality. As Le Grand (1982) commented,

> If greater equality of whatever kind is desired, it is necessary to reduce economic inequality. To do this successfully, however, it is necessary to reduce the hold of the ideology of inequality on people's values and beliefs, and this can only be done by challenging the factual underpinnings of that ideology.

He further observed that in the social services the strategy of equality through public provision failed primarily because the policies implicitly accepted the ideology of inequality.

It is ironic that the empirical approach to social class, which reveals so much by way of differences, at the same time disguises some. Though obviously effective in disclosing between-class variations, it can overlook within-class variation, which can be considerable, and more difficult to explain. While this was illustrated, for example, in respect to earnings and income, it needs to be borne in mind elsewhere. A further interesting effect of the approach is how little we know about the most powerful and rich – what we might call the upper class of our society. Not only are they relatively rare in the population and hence extremely so in any sample, however drawn, but it is open to speculation how such people declare themselves, or are coded by researchers, in terms of occupation. Some have several 'occupations', none of which is necessarily revealing for, or within, a social class classification based on occupation. Other, perhaps less exotic, groups within the recognized classes – including the poor, the unemployed, the sick and the disabled, to mention the obvious – are similarly hidden. Both the strengths and limitations of operationalizing social class on the single criterion of occupation need, then, to be fully recognized.

Many, if not most, social differences can be seen to stem from, or be related to, basic economic inequalities, and their effects, both long- and short-term, on the people involved. In spite of changes in our society, the realities of life for people in different social classes have remained pretty constant. Field's (1973) comment still rings true: 'Despite the growth in national wealth the age-old inequalities remain. The position of the poor has improved. But so, too, has that of the rich.' Somebody who read an earlier book by the author on class remarked, 'What does it tell us other than that there are some very big economic differences in our society?' However tempting such a conclusion may be, it is almost certainly only partially true. Many social differences are difficult to explain directly, if at all, in such terms. It is by no means clear that we would all be middle class if we could afford to be, or working class if we could not afford to be middle class. For example, a study of affluent factory workers showed they were selective about which aspects of middle-classness they adopted and that they maintained some important aspects of traditional working-class life (Goldthorpe et al., 1969). Again, the relative increase in wealth (in real terms) of many working-class people, together with increased opportunities for higher education, appear not to have significantly affected the proportion of working-class university students. This proportion has remained stubbornly constant. If equality in the paid labour market or even economic equality between the sexes were to be achieved, it would profoundly affect the nature of gender differences and roles, but not necessarily heighten their similarity. Much the same case could be made in respect to ethnic and age groups. What would be achieved, however, would be the removal of the economic constraints on life-chances, life-styles and choices – releasing them from the present level of economic determinism to become more the product of individuals and their society.

If social class differences were related to the existence of closed groups with vastly different amounts of power, wealth and so on, within a political context of unmitigated self-interest, then they would be unremarkable and, perhaps, unexpected. However, as we have seen, there is social mobility in our society, and its social classes are not entirely closed, self-recruiting, stable and self-conscious groups. Very few institutions in our society completely exclude any social stratum, although representation and power in them vary greatly. Between the Second World War and the 1990s there have been shifts in power between political parties which had apparently differing social interests and policies. Women have gained and are gaining access to many domains that were once exclusively male. However, the extent to which these facts indicate that our society is an open one is a subject for debate. What is clear is that such facts and changes are intriguingly related to the existence and persistence of social class differences. The fact that class differences are created and exist within relatively open, widely recruiting and dynamic social groups, in a context of apparent political diversity and democracy, and show little if any sign of changing, is perhaps more than surprising. The evidence in this book clearly indicates that, however hazy the concept of class may be, the realities of social class, together with those of the other forms of social stratification, are obtrusive enough at present to be unavoidable.

It seems reasonable to conclude, then, by accepting that economic differentiation is a root factor in, or cause of, social differences. At the same time, we can appreciate that such differentiation, on its own, is not a sufficient, let alone a complete, explanation. Only to a limited extent, then, may the continued existence of class and stratification differences be seen as due to the fact that the economic structure of our society has not changed dramatically and appears unlikely to do so. Even if it were to change, the concepts of class and stratification would still have considerable utility. In societies which claim more economic equality than our own, social differences similar to ours have far from disappeared. Indeed the fundamentals of the existence of social stratification appear inescapable. What is almost infinitely variable and open to change are their cultural manifestations.

Finally, then, the book provides some basis for the identification of those areas in which change might or ought to be sought. Almost regardless of political or ideological belief, some aspects of class differences and inequality can be seen as undesirable or objectionable. As Tawney (1931) so aptly pointed up, to desire and work for social equality is not a romantic or an idle pursuit, but a hallmark of civilized society:

> So to criticize inequality and to desire equality is not, as is sometimes suggested, to cherish the romantic illusion that men [sic] are equal in character and intelligence. It is to hold that, while their natural endowments differ profoundly, it is the mark of a civilized society to aim at eliminating such inequalities as have their source not in individual differences, but in its own organization: and that individual energies, which are a source of social energy, are more likely to ripen and find expression if social inequalities are, as far as practicable, diminished.

As society creates social differences so it can affect, change and perhaps abolish them. There seems little incapable of change or avoidance in the social manifestations of social class. There is, however, little if any evidence of any profound change taking place, together with few if any signs of social and political interest in attempting to achieve significant change.

Appendix A

List of Abbreviations and Acronyms

BARB	British Audience Research Bureau
BBC	British Broadcasting Corporation
BEC	Business Education Council
BMI	body mass index
BMRB	British Market Research Bureau (International)
BSAG	Bristol Social Adjustment Guide
BTEC	Business and Technology Education Council
CHES	Child Health and Education Study
CSE	Certificate of Secondary Education
CSO	Central Statistical Office
CTC	City Technology College
DES	Department of Education and Science
DfE	Department for Education
DfEE	Department for Education and Employment
DHSS	Department of Health and Social Security
DIY	do it yourself
DoE	Department of Employment
DSS	Department of Social Security
EOC	Equal Opportunities Commission
FE	further education
FES	Family Expenditure Survey
GB	Great Britain (England, Scotland and Wales)
GBA	Association of Governing Bodies of Public Schools
GBGSA	Association of Governing Bodies of Girls' Public Schools
GCE	General Certificate of Education
GCSE	General Certificate of Secondary Education
GHS	General Household Survey
GP	general practitioner
GROS	General Register Office for Scotland
HE	higher education
HMC	Head Masters' Conference

HMSO	Her Majesty's Stationery Office
HNC	Higher National Certificate
HND	Higher National Diploma
ILO	International Labour Organization
IQ	intelligence quotient
ISIS	Independent Schools' Information Service
IUD	intra-uterine device
LEA	local education authority
LFS	Labour Force Survey
LS	Longitudinal Study
MORI	Market and Opinion Research International
MP	Member of Parliament
NCDS	National Child Development Study
NDHS	National Dwelling and Housing Survey
NHS	National Health Service
NISRA	Northern Ireland Statistics and Research Agency
NOP	(National Opinion Polls) NOP Research Group Ltd
NSHD	National Survey of Health and Development
OAPs	old age pensioners
ONC	Ordinary National Certificate
OND	Ordinary National Diploma
ONS	Office for National Statistics
OPCS	Office of Population Censuses and Surveys
PGCE	Postgraduate Certificate in Education
RG	Registrar General
RJAR	Radio Joint Audience Research Ltd
RSL	Research Services Ltd
SATs	Standard Attainment Tasks (tests)
SC	School Certificate
SCE	Scottish Certificate of Education
SCOTBEC	Scottish Business Education Council
SCOTECH	Scottish Technical Education Council
SCOTVEC	Scottish Vocational Education Council
SLC	Scottish Leaving Certificate
SMR	standardized mortality ratio
SOC	Standard Occupational Classification
SSC	Scottish School Certificate
SSD	Social Surveys Division
SUPE	Scottish Universities Preliminary Examination
TEC	Technical Education Council
UCAS	Universities and Colleges Admissions Service
UCCA	Universities Central Council on Admissions
UK	United Kingdom (England, Scotland, Wales and Northern Ireland)
WHR	waist–hip ratio

Appendix B

Social Class Classifications

The following is an outline of the classifications of occupations into social classes used in empirical research reviewed in this book. These are listed below together with a reference code allowing the readers to refer from each table in this book to the classification of social class.

Code	*Source*	*See pages*
RG	Registrar General's social class	246–50
RG SEG	Registrar General's socio-economic groups	250–2
HJ	Hall–Jones	252–3
HG	Hope–Goldthorpe	253–6
MR	Market research	256
UC	Universities Central Council on Admissions	257

The classification of occupations into social classes is an extremely complex business, because there are so many occupations. In 1980 the Registrar General had a list of around 25,000 separate occupational titles, which were grouped into 350 occupational codes, each of which had a social class classification *(Classification of Occupations,* 1980). Presently there are some 22,900 titles organized into 371 unit groups, 77 minor groups (each of which has a social class and socio-economic group designation) and 9 major groups (*Standard Occupational Classification*, 1990). Space dictates that only brief outlines of the classifications be presented below. Interested readers will find that the full classifications, and instructions for their use, are generally available, and sources for these are included.

Registrar General

The census contains two classifications of occupations which are of direct relevance to the present text.

Social class (RG)

Since the census of 1911 it has been the practice to group the occupational units of the census into a small number of broad categories known as social classes. The present categories derive from the 1921 census (see Stevenson, 1928; Leete and Fox, 1977). Indeed, as has been pointed out above, and as will be obvious from the rest of this appendix, the Registrar General's social classes form the basis of all the commonly used social class classifications in Britain.

The basis and rationale of this categorization has changed somewhat during the period in which the data reported in this book have been collected, as follows.

Classification of Occupations, 1970

> The unit groups included in each of these categories (i.e. Social Classes) have been selected so as to ensure that, so far as is possible, each category is homogeneous in relation to the basic criterion of the general standing within the community of the occupations concerned. This criterion is naturally correlated with, and its application conditioned by, other factors such as education and economic environment, but it has no direct relationship to the average level of remuneration of particular occupations. Each occupational unit group has been assigned as a whole to a Social Class, and is not a specific assignment of individuals based on the merits of a particular case.
>
> (a) Each occupation is given a basic Social Class.
> (b) Persons of foreman status whose basic Social Class is IV or V are allotted to Social Class III.
> (c) Persons of manager status are allocated either to Social Class II or III, the latter applying if the basic class is IV or V.

Until the census of 1971 the social classes were titled as follows:

I Professional etc. occupations
II Intermediate occupations
III Skilled occupations
IV Partly skilled occupations
V Unskilled occupations.

The Registrar General recognized that social class I was wholly non-manual and that social class V was wholly manual *(Classification of Occupations,* 1960). The other social classes contained both manual and non-manual occupations. Researchers usually ignored the mixed nature of classes II and IV, normally treating II as non-manual and IV as manual. There was some concern about social class III, which clearly contained a large proportion of both types of occupation – some 49 per cent of the occupations of economically active persons in Great Britain in 1971. Researchers quite commonly subdivided this class into IIIN (non-manual) and IIIM (manual). This practice was sometimes indulged in by census and government researchers, who on occasion extended the process to classes II and IV as well. The 1971 census adopted the division of social class III as a standard procedure. Hence the social classes became as follows:

I	Professional etc. occupations
II	Intermediate occupations
IIIN	Skilled non-manual
IIIM	Skilled manual
IV	Partly skilled occupations
V	Unskilled occupations.

Classification of Occupations, 1980

> These categories have been selected in such a way as to bring together, so far as is possible, people with similar levels of occupational skill. In general each occupation group is assigned as a whole to one or another Social Class and no account is taken of differences between individuals in the same occupation group, e.g. differences of education or level of remuneration. However persons of a particular employment status within occupational groups are allocated . . . by the following rules.
>
> The Social Class appropriate to any combination of occupation and status is derived by the following rules:
>
> (a) Each occupation is given a basic Social Class.
> (b) Persons of foreman status whose basic Social Class is IV or V are allotted to Social Class III.
> (c) Persons of manager status are allocated to Social Class II except for the following: Social Class I for General Administrators, national government (Deputy Secretary and above); Social Class III for club stewards, scrap dealers, general dealers, rag and bone merchants.

Standard Occupational Classification, 1990

> The occupation groups included in each of these categories have been selected in such a way as to bring together, as far as is possible, people with similar levels of occupational skill. In general, each occupation group is assigned as a whole to one or other Social Class and no account is taken of differences between individuals in the same occupation group, for example, differences in education. However, for persons having the employment status of foreman or manager the following additional rules apply:

(a) Each occupation is given a basic Social Class.
(b) Persons of foreman status whose basic Social Class is IV or V are allotted to Social Class III.
(c) Persons of manager status are allocated to Social Class II with certain exceptions.

The term 'social class' was extended to 'social class based on occupation' and the title of class II changed from Intermediate to Managerial and Technical.

There have been changes from one census to another in the allocation of occupations to the social classes. Details of these changes are to be found in the relevant volumes of *Classification of Occupations* (1960; 1966; 1970; 1980) and *Standard Occupational Classification* (1990; 1991; 1995). The most extensive changes occurred between the census of 1951 and that of 1961. The most important change in the classification was the total exclusion of members of the armed forces in 1961. The net result was to increase significantly the 'unclassified' groups. Other changes reflected a reordering of occupations in order to retain the basic social gradient of the classifications within the changing economic and social structure of Britain. The changes that occurred in the 1970 and 1980 classifications were comparatively minor. 'Social class and socio-economic groups [see below] were retained unchanged and the only changes in the allocation of individual occupations have been necessitated by the revision of the classification of occupations' (*Classifications of Occupations*, 1980).

The *Standard Occupational Classification* of 1990 had as its objective to group together, using job titles, those occupations similar in two respects: the level of skill and/or experience and/or formal qualification required to competently carry out the work involved; and the nature of the work. In doing this a choice was faced between adjusting to change and preserving continuity with the previous classification. A maximum continuity rule was adopted in order to achieve the greatest formal continuity. As a result the most salient changes were of a decrease of 1.2 per cent in cases assigned to class IV, and an increase of 1.4 per cent in class V (the effects on SEG – see below – were similar). At the time of writing a number of new social class classifications are under consideration for possible inclusion in the census of 2001 (*Constructing Classes*, 1997).

Modifications In some studies, for a variety of reasons, certain of the classes are combined. These combinations are clearly indicated in tables and text – for example, I and II. The descriptive terms 'non-manual' and 'middle' obviously refer to classes I, II and IIIN, while 'manual' and 'working' refer to classes IIIM, IV and V.

RG/A The DoE in the *New Earnings Survey* classifies employees as non-manual or manual using the following Major Groups from the

Table B.1 Typical occupations* in each RG social class

I	*Professional, etc.* Accountant, architect, barrister, business analyst, chemist, clergy, dentist, doctor, engineer, judge, lawyer, management consultant, optician, psychologist, scientist, solicitor, surveyor, university teacher, veterinarian.
II	*Intermediate/managerial and technical* Author, aircraft pilot or engineer, chiropodist, farmer, fire service officer (station officer or above), journalist, laboratory assistant/technician, manager, nurse, proprietor, publican, police officer (inspector or above), probation officer, schoolteacher, social worker.
IIIN	*Skilled non-manual* Cashier, clerk, computer operator, draughtsperson, fire service officer (leading fire officer and below), playgroup leader, police officer (sergeant and below), sales representative, secretary, sales assistant, receptionist, typist, telephone supervisor.
IIIM	*Skilled manual* Baker, bus driver, butcher, bricklayer, carpenter, cook, electrician, hairdresser, miner (face trained worker), motor mechanic, nursery nurse, railway engine driver, upholsterer, van salesperson.
IV	*Partly skilled/semi-skilled* Farm worker, barstaff, bus conductor, care assistant, fisherman, gardener, hospital porter, machine sewer, market and street traders, packer, postman, security guard, shelf filler, traffic warden, telephone operator, tyre and exhaust fitter.
V	*Unskilled* Cleaners/domestics, docker, kitchen hand, labourer, lift/car park attendant, driver's mate, messenger, railway station staff, refuse collector, road construction and maintenance worker, road sweeper, water and sewerage plant attendant, window cleaner.

*In alphabetical order. These are standard occupational classification unit groups; foremen and managers in occupations listed are allotted to different classes (see above).

Devised from table A1, Standard Occupational Classification, Vol 3 (1991)

Standard Occupation Classification 1990 (*New Earnings Survey* 1996, appendix 1 and appendix 4).

1 Managers and administrators
2 Professional occupations
3 Associate professional and technical occupations
4 Clerical and secretarial occupations
5 Craft and related occupations
6 Personal and protective service occupations
7 Sales occupations
8 Plant and machine operatives
9 Other occupations.

The job title and description of the main duties of each employee given by the employer is used to allocate the employee to one of the above groups; apprentices and trainees are allocated by the occupation for which they are training. Non-manual occupation is accorded to those in SOCs 1 to 4, together with those in 6 and 7 not marked with a M (denoting manual). Manual occupation is accorded to those in SOCs 5, 8 and 9 together with those in 6 and 7 marked with M.

RG/B A modification by Routh (1965; 1980) divided RG classes into seven classes, two of which are further subdivided (A and B).

Routh class	*RG class*	*Descriptive definition*
1A	I	Higher professional
1B	II	Lower professional
2A	II	Employers and proprietors
2B	II	Managers and administrators
3	III	Clerical workers
4	III	Foremen, supervisors, inspectors
5	III	Skilled manual
6	IV	Semi-skilled
7	V	Unskilled

Socio-economic Groups and Social Class (RG SEG)

Since the 1951 census, occupations have also been classified into socio-economic groups. In 1961 the original thirteen groups were replaced by seventeen and these have been used since. The aim of the grouping is laid out as follows:

> Ideally each socioeconomic group should contain people whose social, cultural and recreational standards and behaviour are similar. As it is not practicable to ask direct questions about these subjects in a population census, the allocation of occupied persons to socioeconomic groups is determined by considering their employment status and occupation. (*Classification of Occupations*, 1960)

> to bring together people with jobs of similar social and economic status. The allocation of occupied persons to socioeconomic groups is determined by considering their employment status and occupation. (*Classification of Occupations*, 1980; *Standard Occupational Classification*, 1991)

The groups are as follows. Changes and additions made to the 1980 descriptions in 1990 are in italics.

1 *Employers and managers in central and local government, industry, commerce, etc.* Large establishments (with twenty-five or more employees).
   1.1 Employees in industry, commerce, etc. Persons who employ others in non-agricultural enterprises.
   1.2 Managers in central and local government, industry, commerce etc. Persons who generally plan and supervise in non-agricultural enterprises.

2 *Employers and managers in industry, commerce, etc.* Small establishments (with fewer than twenty-five employees).
   2.1 as in 1.1; 2.2 as in 1.2.

3 *Professional workers – self-employed* In work normally requiring qualifications of university degree standard.
4 *Professional workers – employees* In work as for 3.
5 *Intermediate non-manual workers* Employees engaged in non-manual occupations ancillary to professions but not normally requiring university degree standard qualifications; artistic workers not employing others; self-employed nurses, medical auxiliaries, teachers, work-study engineers and technicians; foremen and supervisors (non-manual), i.e. employees other than managers in occupations included in 6, who formally and immediately supervise others engaged in those occupations.
   5.1 Ancillary workers and artists. Employees engaged in non-manual occupations ancillary to the professions, not normally requiring qualifications of university degree standard. Persons engaged in artistic work and not employing others therein. Self-employed nurses, medical auxiliaries, teachers, work study engineers and technicians are included.
   5.2 Foremen and supervisors non-manual. Employees (other than managers) engaged in occupations in group 6, who formally and immediately supervise others engaged in such occupations.
6 *Junior non-manual workers* Employees, not exercising general or supervisory powers, engaged in clerical, sales and non-manual communications and security. *Excluding those who have additional and formal supervisory functions (these are included in 5.2).*
7 *Personal service workers* Employees engaged in service occupations caring for food, drink, clothing and other personal needs.
8 *Foremen and supervisors – manual* Employees, other than managers, who formally and immediately supervise others engaged in manual occupations, whether or not themselves engaged in such occupations.
9 *Skilled manual workers Employees engaged in manual occupations which require considerable and specific skills.*
10 *Semi-skilled manual workers Employees engaged in manual occupations which require slight but specific skills.*
11 *Unskilled manual workers Other employees engaged in manual occupations.*
12 *Own-account workers (other than professional)* Self-employed in any trade, personal service or manual occupation not normally requiring training of university degree standard and having no employees other than family workers.
13 *Farmers – employers and managers* Persons who own, rent or manage farms, market gardens or forests, employing people other than family workers.
14 *Farmers – own account* Persons who own or rent farms, market

gardens or forests and have no employees other than family workers.

15 *Agricultural workers* Employees who tend *Persons engaged in tending* crops, animals, game or forests, or operate agricultural or forest machinery.

16 *Members of the armed forces*

17 *Occupations inadequately described*

The last two groups are generally disregarded, but the rest of the classification is extensively used. Government research, including the census and the GHS, makes use of a collapsed version referred to here as socio-economic class. This collapse is achieved, as shown below, by placing the fifteen groups into six categories. These are not identical with social classes, but are clearly parallel, and in the present text the groups are referred to as social classes. They are distinguished both by a separate code (RG SEG), and by the use of Arabic numerals as opposed to the Roman numerals used for RG social class.

Socioeconomic class	*Socioeconomic groups*	*Descriptive definition*
1	3, 4	Professional
2	1, 2, 13	Employers and managers
3	5, 6	Intermediate and junior non-manual
4	8, 9, 12, 14	Skilled manual (with own account, professional)
5	7, 10, 15	Semi-skilled manual and personal service
6	11	Unskilled manual

Modifications In some cases a sevenfold classification is used, obtained by separating intermediate and junior non-manual workers from 3 into 3 and 4, and renumbering 4 to 6 above as 5 to 7. In other cases combinations of classes are used. Both these are clearly indicated in tables and text.

Hall–Jones Scale (HJ)

This scale was developed in the late 1940s and was based on a scale used in the pre-war Merseyside survey (Jones, 1934). Its development involved a consideration of the subjective social grading of occupations (Hall and Jones, 1950). Subsequently it has been used and modified by other researchers. The resulting classification of occupations was into seven social classes:

1 Professional and high administrative
2 Managerial and executive
3 Inspectional, supervisory and other non-manual higher grade
4 Inspectional, supervisory and other non-manual lower grade
5 Skilled manual and routine grades of non-manual
6 Semi-skilled manual
7 Unskilled manual.

Modification

HJ/A Townsend (1979, appendix 6) divided Hall and Jones's class 5, producing eight classes, and reallocated some manual occupations from their original coded level of skill to that in the RG's scale.

1 Professional
2 Managerial
3 Supervisory – higher
4 Supervisory – lower
5 Routine non-manual
6 Skilled manual
7 Partly skilled manual
8 Unskilled manual.

Hope–Goldthorpe scale (HG)

This scale was derived from a modified set of the 223 unit groups of occupations used by the OPCS *(Classification of Occupations,* 1970), ordered in relation to the results of ranking exercises according to their 'social standing' (see pp. 41–3 above). From the complete scale of 124 categories a collapsed version of 36 was derived. These were achieved without combining major employment status divisions (employer/manager/employee) or types of occupation (professional/technical/non-manual/manual) and resulted in the following (devised from Goldthorpe and Hope, 1974, table 6.6):

1 Self-employed professionals
2 Salaried professionals: higher grade
3 Administrators and officials: higher grade
4 Industrial managers: large enterprises
5 Administrators and officials: lower grade
6 Technicians: higher grade
7 Large proprietors
8 Industrial and business managers: small enterprises
9 Self-employed professionals: lower grade

10 Salaried professionals: lower grade
11 Farmers and farm managers
12 Supervisors of non-manual employees: higher grade
13 Small proprietors
14 Managers in services and small administrative units
15 Technicians: lower grade
16 Supervisors of non-manual workers: lower grade
17 Supervisors of manual workers: higher grade
18 Skilled manual workers: higher grade
19 Self-employed workers: higher grade
20 Supervisors of manual employees: lower grade
21 Non-manual employees in administration and commerce
22 Skilled manual workers in manufacturing; intermediate grade
23 Skilled manual workers in construction
24 Smallholders without employees
25 Service workers: higher grade
26 Skilled manual workers in manufacturing
27 Skilled manual workers in transport/communications/services/extraction
28 Service workers: intermediate grade
29 Self-employed workers: intermediate grade
30 Skilled manual workers in manufacturing: lower grade
31 Agricultural workers
32 Semi-skilled manual workers in construction and extraction
33 Semi-skilled manual workers in transport/communication/services
34 Service workers: lower grade
35 Unskilled manual workers
36 Self-employed workers: lower grade.

Officers, NCOs and other ranks in the armed forces are assigned to categories 3, 17 and 22 respectively.

A social class scale was derived by combining these thirty-six categories into seven classes, as follows (Goldthorpe et al., 1980, pp. 39–41):

Class	*Hope–Goldthorpe categories*	*Descriptive definition*
I	1, 2, 3, 4, 7	All higher-grade professionals, self-employed or salaried higher-grade administrators/officials in central/local government and public/private enterprises (including company directors), managers in large industrial establishments, large proprietors
II	5, 6, 8, 9, 10, 12, 14, 16	Lower-grade professionals/administrators/officials, higher-grade technicians,

		managers in small business/industrial/ service establishments, supervisors of non-manual workers
III	21, 25, 28, 34	Routine non-manual, mainly clerical, sales, and rank-and-file employees in services
IV	11, 13, 19, 24, 29, 36	Small proprietors, including farmers/ smallholder/self-employed artisans/own-account workers other than professional
V	15, 17, 20	Lower-grade technicians (whose work is to some extent manual), supervisors of manual workers
VI	18, 22, 23, 27, 30	Skilled manual wage-workers, all industries
VII	26, 31, 32, 33, 35	All manual wage-workers in semi- and unskilled grades, agricultural workers

Modifications

HG/A An eight-class modification achieved by removing HG category 24 from HG class IV and category 35 from class VII (Halsey et al., 1980). With these changes the modified scale then reads as the original with the addition of:

Class	*Hope–Goldthorpe categories*	*Descriptive definition*
VIII	24, 35	Agricultural workers, including smallholders

HG/B A collapsed version of three classes (Goldthorpe et al., 1980) as follows:

Class	*HG classes*
Service class	I and II
Intermediate class	III, IV and V
Working class	VI and VII; or VI, VII and VIII

HG/C A collapsed four-class version, which separates the self-employed and foremen and technicians as classes (Heath et al., 1985):

Class	*HG classes*
Salariat	I and II
Routine non-manual	III

Petty bourgeoisie	IV
Foremen and technicians	V
Working class	VI and VII

Market Research (MR)

Most commercial social, advertising and consumer research enterprises whose work is reported in this book use the following social grading of occupations originating from the Institute of Practitioners in Advertising. Fuller details of this grading can be found in Monk (1985).

A *Upper middle class* Successful business persons (e.g. self-employed, manager/executive of large enterprise); higher professionals (e.g. bishop, surgeon/specialist, barrister, accountant); senior civil servants (above principal) and local government officers (e.g. chief, treasurer, town clerk).

B *Middle class* Senior, but not the very top, people in same areas as A.

C1 *Lower middle class* Small trades people, non-manual, routine administrative, supervisory and clerical (sometimes referred to as 'white-collar' workers).

C2 *Skilled working class*

D *Semi-skilled and unskilled working class*

E *Those at the lowest levels of subsistence* Including OAPs, those on social security because of sickness or unemployment, and casual workers.

The national percentages of informants falling into these classes are: A, 3; B, 14; Cl, 22; C2, 28; D, 18; E, 15.

An interesting feature of this classification is the inclusion of armed forces personnel, in contrast to their exclusion by the Registrar General. Indeed it provides a good illustration of the grading involved. For example, army personnel are allocated as follows: lieutenant-colonels and above, A; captains and majors, B; sergeants, sergeant-majors, warrant officers and lieutenants, Cl; corporals and lance-corporals, C2; privates, D.

Modifications

The full classification of six classes is not always used. Combinations of classes – for example, A and B, and D and E – are clearly indicated in tables and text.

Universities Central Council on Admissions (UC)

Until the 1980s this body used a four-category division of occupations devised from the classification in *Classification of Occupations*, appendix B, which lists twenty-seven orders. The unusual feature of the UCCA scale was its complete lack of differentiation of manual occupations. Non-manual occupations were divided, however, so that there is some correspondence between these and the RG's non-manual social classes, though, for example, UCCA's class 1 contained occupations in RG classes I and II.

UCCA social class	*RG's occupational order*	*Descriptive definition*
1	XXV	Professional, technical and artists
2	XXIV	Administrators and managers
3	XXI–XXIII, XXVI	Clerical, sales, service, sport and recreation workers
4	I–XX	All manual occupations

Appendix C

Definitions of Household, Head of Household and Educational Qualifications

Household

Until 1980 the GHS used the following definition of household:

> one person living alone or a group of people, who all live regularly at the address ... and who are all catered for at least one meal a day by the same person. (Atkinson, 1971).

Thus members of a household need not be related by blood or marriage, though the term 'household' includes families. From 1981 the GHS definition changed, bringing it in line with the census definition, to:

> one person or a group of people who have the accommodation as their only or main residence and ... who *either* share at least one meal a day or share the living accommodation. (McCrossan, 1984)

A group of people would not be counted as a household solely on the basis of a shared kitchen or bathroom.

The GHS is concerned with 'private households', therefore excluding institutional dwellings such as hotels, hospitals, boarding schools, barracks, prisons, etc.

Head of Household

Research using the household as its basic unit normally classifies it by the head of household and may so classify its members (for example, by social class). Heads of household are defined by the GHS by the relationship between one of its members and the household accommodation.

> The head of the household is a member of the household and (in order of precedence) either the husband of the person, or the person, who:
>
> (a) owns the household accommodation, or
> (b) is legally responsible for the rent of the accommodation, or
> (c) has the accommodation as an emolument or perquisite, or
> (d) has the accommodation by virtue of some relationship to the owner in cases where the owner or lessee is not a member of the household.
>
> When two members of a different sex have equal claim, the male is taken as head of household. When two members of the same sex have equal claim, the elder is taken as head of household (GHS 1994).

Obviously such a definition results in a clear preponderance of male heads of household. For example, the GHS *Introductory Report* (1973) found that four-fifths of heads were male, and that three-fifths of female heads were heads by virtue of being the only member of a household. GHS 1985 revealed little change: 76 per cent of heads of household were male, and 65 per cent of female heads were the sole member of their household, while in 1995 the respective figures were 74 and 63 (unpublished table from GHS 1995 supplied by ONS).

Educational Qualifications

There is a considerable range of qualifications, with some changes over time. The following outlines the terms used in tables and text and defines their equivalents. (Appendix A is a key to the abbreviations.)

16+ examinations

Until 1988 these were of two main types: O level GCE/SCE and CSE. Each of these had five grades of pass: A–E and 1–5 respectively. Until 1975 GCE/SCE O levels were pass/fail only. Subsequently CSE grade 1 was equivalent to an O level pass (grades A–C). A distinction was drawn between higher and other grades (see below). GCE and CSE were replaced by GCSE.

Educational categories

The tables in chapter 7 use the following categories.

Degree or equivalent Higher degrees; first degrees; university diplomas and certificates, qualifications from colleges of technology etc. and from professional institutions, of degree standard.

Higher education below degree level Non-graduate teaching qualifications; HNC/HND; City and Guilds Full Technological Certificate; BEC/TEC/BTEC Higher, SCOTECH Higher; university diplomas and certificates, qualifications from colleges of technology etc. and from professional institutions, below degree but above GCE A level standard; nursing qualifications.

GCE A level or equivalent One or more subjects at GCE A level, AS level, Scottish Certificate of Education (SCE) Higher; Scottish Universities Preliminary Examinations (SUPE) Higher and/or Higher School Certificate; Scottish Leaving Certificate (SLC) Higher; Certificate of Sixth Year Studies; City and Guilds Advanced/Final level; ONC/OND; BEC/TEC/BTEC/National/General certificate or diploma.

GCSE grades A–C or equivalent One or more subjects at GCE O level (grades A–C), GCSE (grades A-C), CSE (grade 1), SCE Ordinary (bands A–C); SUPE Lower or Ordinary and/or School Certificate; SLC Lower; City and Guilds Craft/Ordinary level; SCOTVEC.

GCSE grades D–E or equivalent GCSE (grades D–E), CSE (grades 2–5), GCE O level (grades D and E), SCE Ordinary (bands D and E); clerical and commercial qualification; Apprenticeship.

Foreign and other qualifications Those from outside the UK and other.

None Excludes those who never went to school (omitted from the classification altogether).

Qualified persons

The Census defines a qualified person as one who holds at least one of the following:

(a) higher degrees of UK standard
(b) first degrees and all other qualifications of UK first degree standard
(c) qualifications that are:
(i) generally obtained at 18 and over; (ii) above GCE A level standard; and (iii) below UK first degree standard.

Level (c) includes most nursing and many teaching qualifications, although degrees in education (including PGCE) will be classified as level (b).

References and Author Index

All these sources are followed by page references (in bold) which show where they are discussed or mentioned in the text. Figures in italics refer to tables. Works are referenced, wherever possible, by author(s)/editor(s) and otherwise by title or body responsible for publication. Appendix A is a key to abbreviations used.

Abbott, P. and Sapsford, R. (1987) *Women and Social Class*. London: Tavistock. **32**, **34**, **36**, **40**, **115**, **117**, *5.13, 5.14*

Abel-Smith, B., Zander, M. and Brooke, R. (1973) *Legal Problems and the Citizen*. London: Heinemann. **202**

Abrams, M. (1951) *Social Surveys and Social Actions*. London: Heinemann. **45**

Airey, C. (1984) Social and moral values. In *British Social Attitudes, The 1984 Report*. Social and Community Planning Research. London: Gower. **32**

Airey, C. and Brook, L. (1986) Interim report: social and moral issues. In *British Social Attitudes, The 1986 Report*, Social and Community Planning Research, London: Gower. *8.14*

Alberman, E. (1994) Pre-maturity: epidemiology, prevalence and outcome. In I. B. Pless (ed.), *The Epidemiology of Childhood Disorders*, New York: Oxford University Press. **47**

Alderson, M. R. (1971) Social class and the health service. *The Medical Officer*, 124, 50–2. **70**

A National Health Service (1944) Command 6502. London: HMSO. **67**

Anxiety about Crime (1995) Findings from the 1994 Crime Survey. Home Office Research and Planning Report no. 147. London: Home Office. **201**, *8.9*

Arber, S. (1989) Gender inequalities in health: understanding the differentials. In A. J. Fox (ed.), *Health Inequalities in European Countries*, Aldershot: Gower. **53**

Arber, S. (1990) Revealing women's health: re-analysing the General Household Survey. In H. Roberts (ed.), *Women's Health Counts*, London: Routledge. **53**

Arber, S., Dale, A. and Gilbert, G. N. (1986) The limitations of existing classifications for women. In A. Jacoby (ed.), *The Measurement of Social Class*, Guildford: Social Research Association. **40**

Atkinson, A. B. (1980) *Wealth, Income and Inequality*. Oxford: Oxford University Press. **87**

Atkinson, A. B. (1996) Seeking to explain the distribution of income. In J. Hills (ed.), *New Inequalities*, Cambridge: Cambridge University Press. **83**

Atkinson, A. B. and Harrison, A. J. (1978) *The Distribution of Personal Wealth in Britain*. Cambridge: Cambridge University Press. **88**

Atkinson, J. (1971) *A Handbook for Interviewers*. OPCS. London: HMSO. **258**

Audit Commission (1993) *Unfinished Business: Full-Time Educational Courses for 16 – 19 year olds*. Audit Commission Local Government Report no. 2. London: HMSO. **177**

Banks, O. (1968/1971) *The Sociology of Education*. London: Batsford. **158**

Barker, D. T. P. (1990) Foetal and infant origins of adult disease. *British Medical Journal*, 301 (6761), 1111. **78**

Barker, D. T. P. (1991) Foetal and infant origins of inequalities of health in Britain. *Journal of Public Health Medicine*, 13 (2), 64–8. **78**

Batey, B. and Brown, P. (1997) *The Influence of Neighbourhood Type of Participation in Higher Education (Interim Report)*. The Higher Education Funding Council for England. **175**

Benn, C. and Chitty, C. (1996) *Thirty Years On: Is Comprehensive Education Alive and Well or Struggling to Survive?* London: David Fulton. **177**, *7.10*

Ben-Shlomo, Y., Sheiham, A. and Marmot, M. (1991) Smoking and health. In *British Social Attitudes, The 8th Report*, Social and Community Planning Research, Aldershot: Gower. **61**

Beral, V. (1979) Reproductive mortality. *British Medical Journal*, 1979 (2) (6191), 632–4. **67**

Beral, V. (1985) Long term effects of childbearing on health. *Journal of Epidemiology and Community Health*, 39 (4), 343–6. **68**

Berent, J. (1954) Social mobility and marriage: a study of trends in England and Wales. In D. V. Glass (ed.), *Social Mobility in Britain*, London: Routledge and Kegan Paul. **128**

Birth Statistics 1984 (1985) OPCS Series FM1 no. 11. London: HMSO. **133**

Birth Statistics 1994 (1996) ONS Series FM1 no. 23. London: HMSO. **132**, **133**, *6.6, 6.7, 6.8*

Black, D. (1980) *Inequalities in Health: Report of a Research Working Group*. London: DHSS. **70**, **78**

Blane, D., Smith, G. D. and Bartley, M. (1990) Social class differences in years of potential life lost: size, trends, and principal causes. *British Medical Journal*, 301 (6749), 150–3. **75**

Bloomfield, D. S. F. and Haberman, S. (1992) Male social class mortality differences around 1981: an extension to include ages. *Journal of the Institute of Actuaries*, 119 (III), 545–9, *3.18*

Bone, M. (1973) *Family Planning Services in England and Wales*. OPCS. SSD for DHSS, SS 467. London: HMSO. **134**

Bone, M. (1977) *Pre-School Children and the Need for Day-Care*. OPCS. SSD for DHSS, SS 1031. London: HMSO. **134**

Bone, M. (1978) *Family Planning Services: Changes and Effects*. OPCS. SSD for DHSS, SS 1055. London: HMSO. **144**

Bottomore, T. B. and Rubel, M. (1963) *Karl Marx: Selected Writings in Sociology and Social Philosophy*. Harmondsworth: Penguin. **9**

Bradshaw, J. (1993) *Budget Standards for the United Kingdom*. Aldershot: Avebury. **94**

Brierley, P. and Wraight, H. (1995) *UK Christian Handbook 1996/97*. London: Christian Research/Evangelical Alliance/Bible Society. **190**

Briggs, A. (1960) The language of class in early nineteenth century England. In A. Briggs and J. Saville (eds), *Essays in Labour History in Memory of G.D.H. Cole*, London: Macmillan. **8**

Britain's Workforce (1985). OPCS Census Guide no. 3. London: HMSO. **109**

British Lending Library Supplementary Publication Number 90, 119 (CHES). Unpublished appendix to N. R. Butler and J. Golding, 1986, *From Birth to Five*, Oxford: Pergamon. *6.13, 6.15*

Britten, N. (1984) Class imagery in a national sample of women and men. *British Journal of Sociology*, 15 (3), 406–34. **40**

Brockington, F. and Stein, Z. (1963) Admission, achievement and social class. *Universities Quarterly*, 18 (1), 52–73. **186**

Brotherston, J. (1976) Inequality: is it inevitable? In C. O. Carter and J. Peel (eds), *Equalities and Inequalities in Health*, London: Academic Press. **68**, **72**

Brown, A. and Kiernan, K. (1981) Co-habitation in Great Britain: evidence from the General Household Survey. *Population Trends*, no. 25, 4–10. **127**

Brown, C. (1984a) *Black and White in Britain: The Third PSI Study*. Aldershot: Gower. **27**

Brown, C. (1984b) Patterns of employment among black and white people in Britain. *Employment Gazette*, July. **27**

Buchan, I. and Richardson, I. (1973) *The Study of Consultations in General Practice*. Scottish Home and Health Department Study no. 27. Edinburgh: HMSO. **69**

Bulmer, M. (1977/1984) *Sociological Research Methods*. London: Macmillan. **44**

Burnhill, P. (1981) The relationship between examination performance and social class. *Centre for Educational Sociology, Collaborative Research Newsletter*, no. 8. *7.5*

Burt, C. (1937) *The Backward Child*. London: University of London Press. **157**

Burt, C. (1943) Ability and income. *British Journal of Educational Psychology*, 13 (2), 83–98. **157**

Burton, L. (1975) Social class in the local church: a study of two Methodist churches in the Midlands. In M. Hill (ed.), *A Sociological Yearbook of Religion in Britain*, vol. 8, London: Student Christian Movement. **197**

Butler, D. and Butler, G. (1985) *British Political Facts 1900–85*. London: Macmillan. **209**

Butler, D. and Butler, G. (1994) *British Political Facts 1900–94*. London: Macmillan. **209**

Butler, D. and Kavanagh, D. (1984) *The British General Election of 1983*. London: Macmillan. *7.13*

Butler, D. and Kavanagh, D. (1992) *The British General Election of 1992*. London: Macmillan. **208**

Butler, D. and Stokes, D. (1969) *Political Change in Britain*. London: Macmillan, Harmondsworth: Penguin. **33**

Butler, D. and Stokes, D. (1974) *Political Change in Britain*, 2nd edn. London: Macmillan. **34**

Butler, N. R. and Bonham, D. G. (1963) *Perinatal Mortality*. London: Livingstone. **47**

Butler, N. R. and Golding, J. (1986) *From Birth to Five*. Oxford: Pergamon. **144**

Cain, M. E. (1973) *Society and the Policeman's Role*. London: Routledge and Kegan Paul. **203**

Cairns, E. (1992) Political violence, social values and the generation gap. In P. Stringer and G. Robinson (eds), *Social Attitudes in Northern Ireland: The Second Report 1991–92*, Belfast: Black Staff. 192, *8.3*

Cambridge University Reporter (1996) *Undergraduates: Statistics of Applications and Acceptances for October 1996*. Special no. 7, vol. CXXVII. *7.14*

Campbell, B. (1984) *The Iron Ladies*. London: Virago. **206**

Carr-Hill, R. A. and Pritchard, C. W. (1992) *Women's Social Standing: The Empirical Problem of Female Social Class*. London: Macmillan. **41**

Carstairs, V. (1966) Distribution of hospital patients by social class. *Health Bulletin*, 24, 59–64. **65**

Cartwright, A. (1978) *Recent Trends in Family Building and in Contraception*. OPCS Studies on Medical and Population Subjects no. 34. London: HMSO. **134**

Cartwright, A. (1987) Trends in family intentions and the use of contraception among recent mothers, 1967–84. *Population Trends*, no. 49, 31–4. **134**

Cartwright, A. and O'Brien, M. (1976) Social class variations in health care and in the nature of GP consultations. In M. Stacey (ed.), *The Sociology of the National Health Service*, Sociological Review Monograph no. 22. **69, 70**

Census 1991. See under report title.

Census News (1996) no. 37. ONS, GROS. London: HMSO. **79, 160**

Census News (1997) no. 38. ONS, GROS, NISRA. London: HMSO. **189**

Chapman, A. D. (1984) *Patterns of Mobility among Men and Women in Scotland: 1930–1970*. Unpublished PhD thesis, Plymouth Polytechnic. **117**

Chester, R. and Streather, J. (1972) Cruelty in English divorce. Some empirical findings. *Journal of Marriage and the Family*, 34 (4), 706–12. **126**

Children's Dental Health in the United Kingdom 1993 (1993) OPCS SSD. London: HMSO. **64**

Classification of Occupations (1960, 1966, 1970, 1980) Published year before census. OPCS. London: HMSO. **245, 246, 247, 248, 250, 253**

Commission of the European Communities (1991) *Final Report on the Second European Poverty Programme 1985–1989*. Luxembourg: Office for the Official Publications of the European Communities. **91**

Comprehensive Education (1978) DES. London: HMSO. **176**

Constructing Classes: Towards a New Social Classification for the UK. (1997) ESRC: Essex University. **248**

Consumer Council (1967) *Living in a Caravan*. London: HMSO. **150**

Country of Birth, 1971 Census, Great Britain (1978) Supplementary Tables (10% sample), Part 2, OPCS. London: HMSO. **27**

Coxon, A. P. M. and Jones, C. L. (1974) Occupational similarities. *Quality and Quantity*, 8, 139–58. **42**

Coxon, A. P. M. and Jones, C. L. (1978) *The Images of Occupational Prestige*. London: Macmillan. **42**

Coxon, A. P. M. and Jones, C. L. (1979) *Class and Hierarchy*. London: Macmillan. **42**

Coxon, A. P. M., Davies, P. M. and Jones, C. L. (1986) *Images of Social Stratification*. London: Sage. **42**

Criminal Statistics England and Wales 1994 (1995) Command 233, Home Office. London: HMSO. **198, 200**

Crompton, R. (1993) *Class and Stratification: An Introduction to Current Debates*. Cambridge: Polity Press. **12**

Cullen, M. J. (1975) *The Statistical Movement in Early Victorian Britain*. London: Harvester Press, New York: Barnes and Noble. **8**

Dale, A., Gilbert, N. and Arber, S. (1985) Integrating women into class theory. *Sociology*, 19 (3), 384–409. **41**

Dale, R. R. (1963) Reflections on the influence of social class on student performance at university. In P. Halmos (ed.), *Sociological Studies in British University Education*, Sociological Review Monograph no. 7. **186**

Davie, R., Butler, M. and Goldstein, H. (1972) *From Birth to Seven*. London: Longman. **47, 139, 140, 142, 143, 144, 155**

Davis, H. H. (1979) *Beyond Class Images*. London: Croom Helm. **42**

Day Care Services for Children (1994) OPCS SSD. London: HMSO. *6.14*

Dean, C. (1997) Social class linked to results. *Times Educational Supplement*, 18th April, 2. **174**

Demographic Review 1977 (1979) *A Report on Population in Great Britain*. OPCS Series DR 1. London: HMSO. **131**

Demographic Review 1984 (1987) *A Report on Population in Great Britain*. OPCS Series DR 2. London: HMSO. **131, 132**

Douglas, J. W. B. (1948) *Maternity in Great Britain*. London: Oxford University Press. **47, 140**

Douglas, J. W. B., Ross, J. M. and Simpson, H. R. (1968) *All Our Future*. London: Peter Davies. **170**

Douglas, J. W. B., Ross, J. M., Hammond, W. A. and Mulligan, D. G. (1966) Delinquency and social class. *British Journal of Criminology*, 6, 294–302. **198**

Drever, F., Whitehead, M. and Roden, M. (1996) Current patterns and trends in male mortality by social class (based on occupation). *Population Trends*, no. 86, 15–20. **70**, *3.14, 3.15*

Drudy, S. (1991) The classification of social class in sociological research. *British Journal of Sociology* 42 (1), 21–42. **10**

Drug Misuse Declared (1996) Results of the 1994 British Crime Survey. Home Office Research Study no. 151. London: Home Office. *8.7*

Duke, V. and Edgell, S. (1987) The operationalisation of class in British sociology. *British Journal of Sociology*, 38 (4), 445–63. **10**

Dunnell, K. (1979) *Family Formation 1976*. OPCS SSD. London: HMSO. **123**

Economic Activity, 1981 Census, Great Britain (1984) OPCS. London: HMSO. **21**

Economic Activity, 1991 Census, Great Britain (1994) OPCS and GROS. London: HMSO. *2.1, 2.2, 2.3, 2.4, 2.5, 2.7, 2.9*

Education: A Framework for Expansion (1972) London: HMSO. **167**

Education for All (1985) The Swann Report. Report of Committee of Inquiry into the Education of Children from Ethnic Minority Groups. Command 9453. London: HMSO. **159**

Education Statistics for the United Kingdom 1993 (1994) GSS. London: HMSO. **172**

Education Statistics for the United Kingdom 1994 (1995) DFE. London: HMSO. **177**, *7.14*

Education Statistics for the United Kingdom 1995 (1996) DFEE. London: HMSO. **164**

Education Tables (10% sample), 1961 Census, England and Wales (1966) General Register Office. London: HMSO. **160**

Edwards, E. G. and Roberts, I. J. (1980) British higher education: long term trends in student enrolment. *Higher Education Review*, 12 (2), 7–43. **183**, *7.15*

Employment Gazette (1982) Vol. 90, November. DoE. London: HMSO. **109**

Employment Gazette (1991) Vol. 99 (6), May. Special feature, *Characteristics of the Unemployed*. DoE. London: HMSO. **165**

Ethnic Group and Country of Birth, 1991 Census, Great Britain (1993) OPCS and GROS. London: HMSO. *2.6*

Family Spending 1993 (1995). *A Report on the 1993 Family Expenditure Survey*. CSO. London: HMSO. **95**, *4.3, 4.13, 9.1*

Fenner, N. (1987) Leisure, exercise and work. In *The Health and Lifestyle Survey*, London: Health Promotion Research Trust. **59**

Field, F. (1973) *Unequal Britain*. London: Arrow. **240**

15–18 (1960) The Crowther Report. Central Advisory Council for Education. London: HMSO. **176**

Fogelman, K. and Goldstein, H. (1976) Social factors associated with changes in educational attainment between 7 and 11 years of age. *Educational Studies*, 2 (2), 95–109. **168**

Fogelman, K., Goldstein, H., Essen, J. and Ghodsian, M. (1978) Patterns of attainment. *Educational Studies*, 4 (2), 121–30. **168**

Forster, D. P. (1976) Social class differences in sickness and general practitioner consultations. *Health Trends*, 8, 29–32. **69**

Francis, L. J., Pearson, P. R. and Lankshear, D. W. (1990) The relationship between social class and attitude towards Christianity among 10 and 11 year old children. *Personality and Individual Differences*, 11 (10), 1019–27. **196**

Gaine, J. J. (1975) *Young Adults Today and the Future of the Faith*. Upholland: Secretariat for Non-Believers. **189**, **197**

Gallup Polls (1979) Report no. 662. London: Social Surveys (Gallup Polls) Ltd. **195**

Gavron, H. (1966) *The Captive Wife*. London: Routledge and Kegan Paul. **123**

George, V. (1970) *Foster Care*. London: Routledge and Kegan Paul. **139**

Gerard, D. (1985) Religious attitudes and values. In M. Abrams, D. Gerard and N. Timms (eds), *Values and Social Change in Britain*. London: Macmillan. **195**

GHS *Introductory Report* (1973) *General Household Survey, Introductory Report*. OPCS Series GHS no. 1. London: HMSO. **150**, **151**, **259**

GHS 1972 (1975) *General Household Survey 1972*. OPCS Series GHS no. 2. London: HMSO. **151**

GHS 1976 (1978) *General Household Survey 1976*. OPCS Series GHS no. 6. London: HMSO. *3.7*

GHS 1977 (1979) *General Household Survey 1977*. OPCS Series GHS no. 7. London: HMSO. **106**, **149**, **151**, **216**, *7.11*

GHS 1979 (1981) *General Household Survey 1981*. OPCS Series GHS no. 9. London: HMSO. *3.7*

GHS 1980 (1982) *General Household Survey 1980*. OPCS Series GHS no. 10. London: HMSO. **216**

GHS 1981 (1983) *General Household Survey 1981*. OPCS Series GHS no. 11. London: HMSO. **56**, **63**, **69**, **258**

GHS 1982 (1984) *General Household Survey 1982*. OPCS Series GHS no. 12. London: HMSO. *6.23*

GHS 1983 (1985) *General Household Survey 1983*. OPCS Series GHS no. 13. London: HMSO. **107**, **108**, **134**, **214**, **216**, *3.13*

GHS 1984 (1986) *General Household Survey 1984*. OPCS Series GHS no. 14. London: HMSO. **134**

GHS 1985 (1987) *General Household Survey 1985*. OPCS Series GHS no. 15. London: HMSO. **165**, **259**

GHS 1988 (1990) *General Household Survey 1988*. OPCS Series GHS no. 18. London: HMSO. *4.7*

GHS 1989 (1991) *General Household Survey 1989*. OPCS Series GHS no. 20. London: HMSO. **53**, *3.4, 3.5, 7.6, 7.7*

GHS 1991 (1993) *General Household Survey 1991*. OPCS Series GHS no. 22. London: HMSO. **105**, *6.17, 6.22, 8.8*

GHS 1992 (1994) *General Household Survey 1992*. OPCS Series GHS no. 23. London: HMSO. **151**, *7.1, 7.2, 7.3, 7.4*

GHS 1993 (1995) *General Household Survey 1993*. OPCS Series GHS no. 24. London: HMSO. **216**, **228**, *3.7, 9.2, 9.9*

GHS 1994 (1996) *General Household Survey 1994*. ONS Living in Britain. London: HMSO. **53**, **60**, **61**, **62**, **63**, **64**, **123**, **148**, *3.6, 3.7, 3.10, 3.11, 5.1, 5.5, 5.9, 6.18*

Gibson, C. (1974) Divorce and social class in England and Wales. *British Journal of Sociology*, 25 (1), 79–93. **124**

Gibson, H. M., Francis, L. J. and Pearson, P. R. (1990) The relationship between social class and attitudes towards Christianity among 10 and 15 year old adolescents. *Personality and Individual Differences*, 11 (6), 631–5. **196**

Giddens, A. (1973) *The Class Structure of the Advanced Societies*. London: Hutchinson. **14**

Gilmour, I. (1992) *Dancing with Dogma: Britain under Thatcherism*. London: Simon and Schuster. **93**

Glass, D. V. (1954) *Social Mobility in Britain*. London: Routledge and Kegan Paul. **111**

Goldthorpe, J. H. (1983) Women and class analysis: in defence of the conventional view. *Sociology*, 17 (4), 465–88. **12**, **40**

Goldthorpe, J. H. and Hope, K. (1974) *The Social Grading of Occupations: A New Approach and Scale*. Oxford: Clarendon Press. **41**, **253**

Goldthorpe, J. H., Llewellyn, C. and Payne, C. (1980) *Social Mobility and Class Structure in Modern Britain*. Oxford: Clarendon Press. **111**, **112**, **254**, **255**, *5.11, 5.12*

Goldthorpe, J. H., Llewellyn, C. and Payne, C. (1987) *Social Mobility and Class Structure in Modern Britain*, 2nd edn. Oxford: Clarendon Press. **111**, **115**

Goldthorpe, J. H., Lockwood, D., Bechhofer, F. and Platt, J. (1969) *The Affluent Worker*. Cambridge: Cambridge University Press. **240**

Goldthorpe, J. H. and Marshall, G. (1992) The promising future of class analysis: a response to recent critiques. *Sociology*, 26 (3), 381–400. **237**

Goldthorpe, J. H. and Payne, C. (1986) On the class mobility of women: results from different approaches to the analysis of recent British data. *Sociology*, 20 (4), 531–55. **117**

Gorer, G. (1971) *Sex and Marriage in England Today*. London: Nelson/Panther. **123**

Gosling, A., Machin, S. and Meghir, P. (1996) What has happened to the wages of men since 1966? In J. Hills (ed.), *New Inequalities*. Cambridge: Cambridge University Press. **83**

Gray, P. G. and Russell, R. (1962) *The Housing Situation in 1960.* London: HMSO. **151**

Gray, P. G., Todd, J. E., Slack, G. L. and Bulman, J. S. (1970) *Adult Dental Health in England and Wales in 1968.* OPCS SSD for DHSS. London: HMSO. **56**

Greenhalgh, C. and Stewart, M. B. (1982) *Occupational Status and Mobility of Men and Women.* Warwick Economic Papers no. 211. Warwick: University of Warwick. **117**

Grey, E. (1971) *A Survey of Adoption in Great Britain.* Home Office Research Studies no. 10. London: HMSO. **138**

Haberman, S. and Bloomfield, D. S. F. (1988) Social class differences in mortality in Great Britain around 1981. *Journal of the Institute of Actuaries*, 115, 495–517. **76**

Hall, J. and Jones, D. C. (1950) The social grading of occupations. *British Journal of Sociology*, 1, 31–5. **41**, **252**

Halpern, D. (1994) *Entry into the Legal Profession.* London: The Law Society. **203**

Halsey, A. H. (1978/1981/1986/1995) *Change in British Society from 1900 to the Present Day*, 1st to 4th edns. Oxford: Oxford University Press. **15**

Halsey, A. H. (1972/1988) *Trends in British Society since 1900*, 1st and 2nd edns. London: Macmillan. **14**, **15**

Halsey, A. H., Heath, A. F. and Ridge, J. M. (1980) *Origins and Destinations.* Oxford: Clarendon Press. **180**, **183**, **255**, *7.11*

Hanks, P. (1979) *Collins Dictionary of the English Language.* London: Collins. **120**

Harbury, C. D. and McMahon, P. C. (1980) Inheritance and the characteristics of top wealth leavers in Britain. In A. B. Atkinson (ed.), *Wealth, Income and Inequality*, Oxford: Oxford University Press. **88**

Harding, S. (1995) Social class differences in mortality of men: recent evidence from the OPCS Longitudinal Study. *Population Trends*, no. 80, 31–8. **73**

Harris, J. and Jarvis, P. (1979) *Counting to Some Purpose.* London: Methodist Church Home Mission Division. **197**

Harrop, M. (1980) Popular conceptions of social mobility. *Sociology*, 14 (1), 99–112. **119**

Hart, J. T. (1971) The inverse case law. *The Lancet*, 1, 405–12. **68**

Haskey, J. (1983) Social class patterns of marriage. *Population Trends*, no. 34, 12–19. **129**, *6.1, 6.4*

Haskey, J. (1984) Social class and socio-economic differentials in divorce in England and Wales. *Population Studies*, 38 (3), 419–38. **124**, *6.2*

Haskey, J. (1986) Grounds for divorce in England and Wales – a social and demographic analysis. *Journal of Biosocial Science*, 18 (2), 127–53. **126**, *6.2*

Haskey, J. (1987) Social class differentials in remarriage after divorce: results from a forward linkage study. *Population Trends*, no. 47, 34–42. **127**, *6.3*

Haskey, J. (1991) Estimated numbers and demographic characteristics of one-parent families in Great Britain. *Population Trends*, no. 65, 35–47. **128**

Haskey, J. (1993) *First Marriage, Divorce and Remarriage: Birth Cohort Analysis. Population Trends*, no. 72, 24–33. **128**

Haskey, J. and Coleman, D. (1986) Cohabitation before Marriage: a comparison of information from marriage registration and the General Household Survey. *Population Trends*, no. 43, 15–30. **124**

Haskey, J. and Kiernan, K. (1989) Co-habitation in Great Britain: characteristics and estimated numbers of co-habiting partners. *Population Trends*, no. 58, 23–32. **124**

Hatch, S. and Reich, D. (1970) Unsuccessful sandwiches? *New Society*, 15 (389), 842–5. **186**

Health in England 1995 (1996) ONS. London: HMSO. **136**, *6.10*

Health Survey for England 1993 (1995) OPCS SSD. London: HMSO. **59**

Health Survey for England 1994 (1996) *Volume 1: Findings*. Joint Health Surveys Unit, University College London. London: HMSO. **53**, **54**, **58**, **64**, *3.9*

Heath, A. and Britten, N. (1984) Women's jobs do make a difference. *Sociology*, 18, 475–90. **41**

Heath, A., Jowell, R. and Curtice, J. (1985) *How Britain Votes*. Oxford: Pergamon. **203**, **206**, *8.12*

Hedges, B. (1994) Work in a changing climate. In *British Social Attitudes, The 11th Report*, Social and Community Planning Research. London: Gower. *5.6*

Higher Education (1963) The Robbins Report. Command 2154. London: HMSO. **169**, **181**, **182**, **183**, **186**

Hills, J. (1996) *New Inequalities*. Cambridge: Cambridge University Press. **82**, **85**

Hodge, R. W., Trieman, D. J. and Rossi, P. H. (1966) A comparative study of occupational prestige. In R. Bendix and S. M. Lipset (eds), *Class, Status and Power*, 2nd edn, New York: Free Press, London: Routledge and Kegan Paul. **42**

Hoggart, R. (1995) *The Way We Live Now*. London: Chatto and Windus (1996) Pimlico. **236**

Hoggarth, T., Maguire, M., Pitcher, J., Purcell, K. and Wilson, R. (1997) *Participation of Non-Traditional Students in Higher Education*. University of Warwick: Institute for Employment Research. **186**

Holman, R. (1975) *Trading in Children*. London: Routledge and Kegan Paul. **139**

Holton, R. J. and Turner, B. S. (1989) Has class analysis a future? Max Weber and the challenge of liberalism to *gemeinshaftlich* accounts of class. In R. J. Holton and B. S. Turner (eds), *Max Weber on Economy and Society*, London: Routledge and Kegan Paul. **237**

Home Office Research Unit (1978) *Research Bulletin no. 5*. London: HMSO. **198**

Hospital In-Patient Inquiry 1983 (1985) *Summary Tables*. DHSS OPCS Series MB4 no. 22. London: HMSO. **65**, **70**

Household Composition Tables, 1971 Census, Great Britain (1975) OPCS. London: HMSO. **123**

Household and Family Composition, 1991 Census, Great Britain (1994) OPCS and GROS. London: HMSO. **128**, *4.5, 6.5*

Households below Average Income (1994) *A Statistical Analysis 1979–1991/2*. DSS. London: HMSO. **85**

Housing Deprivation and Social Change (1994) ONS Series LS no. 8. London: HMSO. *6.20, 6.21*

Hunt, K. and Annandale (1990) Predicting contraceptive method usage among women in West Scotland, *Journal of Biosocial Science* 22 (4), 405–21. **136**

Hymns Ancient and Modern (1950) Revised 1950 edition, original 1861. London: Clowes. **8**

Infant Feeding 1980 (1982) OPCS SSD. London: HMSO. **140**

Infant Feeding 1990 (1992) OPCS SSD. London: HMSO. **141**, *6.11, 6.12, 6.13*

Jones, D. C. (1934) *Social Survey of Merseyside*. Liverpool: Liverpool University Press. **252**

Joseph, J. and Sumption, J. (1979) *Equality*. London: John Murray. **91**

Jowell, R. (1984) Introducing the survey. In *British Social Attitudes, The 1984 Report*, Social and Community Planning Research, London: Gower. **209**

Kahan, M., Butler, D. and Stokes, D. (1966) On the analytical division of social class. *British Journal of Sociology*, 17 (2), 122–32. **32, 33, 34**

Kelsall, R. K. (1963) Survey of all graduates. In P. Halmos (ed.), *Sociological Studies in British University Education*, Sociological Review Monograph no. 7. **186**

Kelsall, R. K., Poole, A. and Kuhn, A. (1972) *Graduates*. London: Methuen. **186**

King, M., Israel, M. and Goulbourne, S. (1990) *Ethnic Minorities and Recruitment to the Solicitors' Profession*. Report by the Department of Law, Brunel University. London: The Law Society. **203**

Knight, I. and Eldridge, J. (1984) *The Heights and Weights of Adults in Great Britain*. OPCS SSD. London: HMSO. **57**, *3.8*

Labour Force Survey 1990 and 1991 (1992) OPCS Series LFS no. 9. London: HMSO. **100, 165**

Labour Force Survey 1996 (1996) ONS. London: HMSO. *5.3, 5.7, 5.8, 5.10*

Lambert, L. and Streather, J. (1980) *Children in Changing Families*. London: Macmillan. **139**

Lee, D. J. and Turner, B. S. (1996) *Conflicts about Class: Debating Inequality in Late Industrialism*. London: Longman. **10**

Le Grand, J. (1978) The distribution of public expenditure: the case of health care. *Economica*, 45 (178), 125–42. **68**

Le Grand, J. (1982) *The Strategy of Equality*. London: Allen and Unwin. **69, 239**

Leete, R. (1979) *Changing Patterns of Family Formation and Dissolutions in England and Wales 1964–76*. OPCS Studies on Medical and Population Subjects no. 10. London: HMSO. **121, 129**

Leete, R. and Anthony, S. (1979) Divorce and remarriage: a record linkage study. *Population Trends*, no. 16, 5–16. **127**

Leete, R. and Fox, J. (1977) Registrar General's social classes: origins and uses. *Population Trends*, no. 8, 1–7. **246**

Leisure Day Visits in Great Britain 1988/89 (1991) OPCS SSD. London: HMSO. **233**

Lomas, G. B. G. and Monck, E. (1977) *The Coloured Population of Great Britain*. London: The Runnymede Trust. **27**

McCallum, I. (1996) The chosen ones? *Education*, 187 (3), 12–13. **174**

McCrossan, L. (1984) *A Handbook for Interviewers*. OPCS. London: HMSO. **258**

Macfarlane, A. (1980) Official statistics and women's health and illness. In *Women and Government Statistics*. EOC Research Bulletin no. 5. Manchester: Equal Opportunities Commission. **46**

McGregor, O. R. (1957) *Divorce in Britain*. London: Heinemann. **124**

Macintyre, S. (1994) Understanding the social patterning of health: the role of the social sciences. *Journal of Public Health Medicine*, 16 (1), 53–9. **78**

McPherson, A. and Willms, J. W. (1987) Equalization and improvement: some effects of comprehensive reorganization in Scotland. *Sociology*, 21 (4), 509–39. **159**

McPherson, A. and Willms, J. W. (1988) Comprehensive schooling is better and fairer. *Forum*, 30 (2), 39–41. **159**

Mack, J. and Lansley, S. (1985) *Poor Britain*. London: Allen and Unwin. **93**

Marriage and Divorce Statistics 1990 (1992) OPCS Series FM2 no. 18. London: HMSO. **121**, **122**

Marriage and Divorce Statistics 1992 (1994) OPCS Series FM2 no. 20. London: HMSO. **124**, **126**

Marsh, D. C. (1965) *The Changing Structure of England and Wales 1871–1951*. London: Routledge and Kegan Paul. **15**

Marshall, G., Rose, D., Newby, H. and Vogler, C. (1988) *Social Class in Modern Britain*. London: Hutchinson Education. Reprinted in 1993 by Routledge. **32**, **34**, **35**, **117**, *2.11*

Martin, F. M. (1954) Some subjective aspects of social stratification. In D. V. Glass (ed.), *Social Mobility in Britain*. London: Routledge and Kegan Paul. **32**, **35**

Martin, J. (1978) *Infant Feeding 1975: Attitudes and Practice in England and Wales*. OPCS SS 1064 for DHSS. London: HMSO. **140**

Martin, J. and Roberts, C. (1984) *Women and Employment: A Lifetime Perspective*. OPCS Studies on Medical and Population Subjects no. 47. London: HMSO. **117**

Marwick, A. (1980) *Class, Image and Reality*. London: Collins. **8**

Marwick, A. (1990) *Class, Image and Reality*. London: Macmillan. **8**

Matthijsen, M. A. J. M. (1959) Catholic intellectual emancipation in the Western countries of mixed religion. *Social Compass*, 6, 91–113. **189**

Mays, J. B. (1970) *Crime and its Treatment*. London: Longman. **198**

Metcalf, A. (1997) *Class and Higher Education: the participation of young people from lower socio-economic groups*. Interim Report to National Committee of Inquiry into Higher Education. **186**

Migration, 1991 Census, Great Britain (1994) OPCS and GROS. London: HMSO. *6.24*

Milne, S. (1997) Facts that fail to fit the figures. *The Guardian*, 16 April. **108**

Monk, D. (1970) *Social Grading on the National Readership Survey*. London: Joint Industry Committee for National Readership Surveys. **2**

Monk, D. (1985) *Social Grading on the National Readership Survey*. London: Joint Industry Committee for National Readership Surveys. **256**

Morbidity Statistics from General Practice 1981–82 (1990) Royal College of General Practitioners. OPCS DoH Series MB5 no. 2. London: HMSO. **12**, **70**, *3.12*

Morris, J. N. (1975) *The Uses of Epidemiology*, 3rd edn. London: HMSO. **78**

Mortality and Geography (1990) OPCS Series DS no. 9. London: HMSO. *3.17*

Mortality Statistics 1991 (1993) *Mortality Statistics, Perinatal and Infant: Social and Biological Factors, England and Wales 1991*. OPCS Series DH3 no. 25. London: HMSO. **47**, *3.1*

Moser, K. A., Goldblatt, P. O., Fox, A. J. and Jones, D. R. (1987) Unemployment and mortality: comparison of the 1971 and 1981 Longitudinal Study census samples. *British Medical Journal*, 294 (6564), 86–90. **74**

Moser, K. A., Goldblatt, P. O., Fox, A. J. and Jones, D. R. (1990) *Unemployment and Mortality in Longitudinal Study 1971–1981*. OPCS Series LS no. 6. London: HMSO. **73**

Moulin, Leon de Saint (1968) Social class and religious behaviour. *The Clergy Review*, 53, 20–35. **196**

Murgatroyd, L. (1982) Gender and occupational stratification. *Sociological Review*, 30 (4), 574–602. **41**

Musgrove, F., Cooper, B., Derrick, T., Foy, J. M. and Willig, C. J. (1967) Preliminary studies of a technological university. Mimeograph. Bradford: Bradford University. **186**

National Readership Survey 1975 (1976) London: Joint Industry Committee for National Readership Surveys. **224**

National Readership Survey 1979 (1980) London: Joint Industry Committee for National Readership Surveys. **229**

National Readership Survey 1987 (1988) London: Joint Industry Committee for National Readership Surveys. **224**, **229**

National Readership Survey 1996 (1997) London: National Readership Survey Ltd. **224**, **229**, *9.5(a)(b)*, *9.6(a)(b)*, *9.11*

New Earnings Survey 1979 (1980) Part D, Analysis by Occupation. DoE. London: HMSO. **80**

New Earnings Survey 1987 (1988) Part F, Hours and Earnings of Part-Time Employees: Holiday Entitlements. DoE. London: HMSO. **80**, *5.4*

New Earnings Survey 1995 (1995) Part A, Streamlined and Summary Analyses: Description of the Survey. CSO. London: HMSO. **102**

New Earnings Survey 1996 (1996a) Part A, Standard Analysis: Description of the Survey. ONS. London: The Stationery Office. **249**

New Earnings Survey 1996 (1996b) Part D, Analysis by Occupation. ONS. London: The Stationery Office. *4.1*

New Earnings Survey 1996 (1996c) Part F, Distribution of Hours. ONS. London: The Stationery Office. *5.2*

Newfield, J. G. H. (1963) Some factors related to the academic performance of British university students. In P. Halmos (ed.), *Sociological Studies in British University Education*, Sociological Review Monograph no. 7. **186**

Newson, J. and Newson, E. (1963) *Infant Care in an Urban Community*. London: Allen and Unwin. **139**

Newson, J. and Newson, E. (1968) *Four Years Old in an Urban Community*. London: Allen and Unwin. Harmondsworth: Penguin, 1970. **139**, **145**

Newson, J. and Newson, E. (1976) *Seven Years Old in the Home Environment*. London: Allen and Unwin. **139**, **145**, **146**, *6.16*

Newson, J. and Newson, E. (1977) *Perspectives on School at Seven Years Old*. London: Allen and Unwin. **139**

NOP (1971) *National Opinion Polls, Bulletin*, no. 101. London: NOP Market Research Ltd. **207**

NOP (1972) *National Opinion Polls, Bulletin*, no. 109. London: NOP Market Research Ltd. **32**, **190**

NOP (1975) *National Opinion Polls, Political Social Economic Review*, no. 3. London: NOP Market Research Ltd. **207**

NOP (1977) *National Opinion Polls, Political Social Economic Review*, no. 13. London: NOP Market Research Ltd. **207**

NOP (1978) *National Opinion Polls, Political Social Economic Review*, no. 16. London: NOP Market Research Ltd. **34**

Northern Ireland Census 1991, Religion Tables (1993) DHSS/RG. Belfast: HMSO. **189**

Occupational Mortality, Childhood Supplement (1988) OPCS Series DS no. 8. London: HMSO. **49**, *3.2, 3.3*

Occupational Mortality (1971) *The RG's Decennial Supplement for England and Wales 1961*. OPCS. London: HMSO. **71**

Occupational Mortality (1978) *The RG's Decennial Supplement for England and Wales 1970–2*. OPCS Series DS no. 1. London: HMSO. **76**

Occupational Mortality (1986) *The RG's Decennial Supplement for England and Wales 1982–3*. OPCS Series DS no. 2. London: HMSO. **70**, *3.16*

OPCS (1987) *The Family*. Occasional Paper no. 31, British Society for Population Studies, Conference Papers. London: HMSO. **120**

Osborn, A. F. and Morris, T. C. (1979) The rationale for a composite index of social class and its evaluation. *British Journal of Sociology*, 30 (1), 39–60. **41**

Osborn, A. F., Butler, N. R. and Morris, A. C. (1984) *The Social Life of Britain's Five Year Olds*. London: Routledge and Kegan Paul. **147**

Ossowski, S. (1963) *Class Structure in the Social Consciousness*. London: Routledge and Kegan Paul. **8**, **236**

Oxford University Gazette (1996) Supplement (2), no. 4421, *Oxford Colleges: Statistics*. *7.14*

Pahl, R. E. (1989) Is the emperor naked? Some comments on the adequacy of sociological theory in urban and regional research. *International Journal of Urban and Regional Research*, 13 (4), 709–20. **237**

Pahl, R. E. and Wallace, C. (1985) Household work strategies in economic recession. In E. Mingione and N. Redclift (eds), *Beyond Employment*. Oxford: Blackwell. **41**

Phillips, D. (1985) Participation and political values. In M. Abrams, D. Gerard and N. Timms (eds), *Values and Social Change in Britain*. London: Macmillan.

Pierce, R. M. (1963) Marriage in the fifties. *Sociological Review*, 11 (2), 215–40. **123**

Platt, J. (1971) Variations in answers to different questions of perceptions of class. *Sociological Review*, 19, 409–19 (3). **38**

Playford, C. and Pond, C. (1983) The right to be unequal: inequality in incomes. In F. Field (ed.), *The Wealth Report 2*. London: Routledge and Kegan Paul. **83**

Pond, C. (1983) Wealth and the two nations. In F. Field (ed.), *The Wealth Report 2*. London: Routledge and Kegan Paul. **87**, **90**

Population Trends no. 86 (1996) London: HMSO. *3.18*

Power, C., Manor, O. and Fox, A. J. (1991) *Health and Class: the Early Years*. London: Chapman and Hall. **57**

Prais, S. J. and Schmool, M. (1975) The social class structure of Anglo-Jewry, 1961. *Jewish Journal of Sociology*, 17 (1), 5–15. **197**

Psychiatric Morbidity amongst Homeless People (1996) OPCS Report no. 7. London: HMSO. *6.19*

Public Schools Commission (1968) *First Report*. DES. London: HMSO. **179**

Regional Trends 1996 (1996) ONS. London: HMSO. **186**

Reid, I. (1969) *An Analysis of Social Factors in Children's Educational Experience between 11 and 17 Years of Age in Two LEA Areas*. Unpublished MA thesis, University of Liverpool. **175**

Reid, I. (1977) *Social Class Differences in Britain*, 1st edn. London: Open Books. **1**, **111**

Reid, I. (1978) What you had to say about life in Britain today. *Home and Gardens*, 9 (59), 65–71. **32**

Reid, I. (1979) *Sunday Schools as Socialisation Agencies*. In G. White and R. Mufti (eds), *Understanding Socialisation*, Driffield: Nafferton. **197**

Reid, I. (1980a) *Sunday Schools: A Suitable Case for Treatment*. London: Chester House. **197**

Reid, I. (1980b) *Teachers and Social Class*. Westminster Studies in Education no. 3, 47–58. **38**

Reid, I. (1981) *Social Class Differences in Britain*, 2nd edn. London: Grant McIntyre. **1**, **169**, **205**

Reid, I. (1986) *The Sociology of School and Education*. London: Fontana. **158**

Reid, I. (1989a) *Social Class Differences in Britain*, 3rd edn. London: Fontana. **1**, **27**, **31**, **123**, **151**, **169**, **182**, **192**, **205**, **207**

Reid, I. (1989b) Vital statistics. In I. Reid and E. Stratta (eds), *Sex Differences in Britain*, Aldershot: Gower. **67**, **70**

Reid, I. (1992) *The Sociology of School and Education*. London: Paul Chapman. **158**

Report for Great Britain, 1991 Census (1993) OPCS and GROS. London: HMSO. *2.8*

Report of the Committee on the Working of the Abortion Act (1974) Vol. 2, Statistical Volume. Command 5579–1. London: HMSO. **136**

Retirement and Retirement Plans (1992) OPCS SSD. London: HMSO. **105**

Roberts, H. (1981) *Women, Health and Reproduction*. London: Routledge and Kegan Paul. **68**

Roberts, H. (1987) *Women and Social Classification*. Brighton: Wheatsheaf. **41**

Roberts, H. (1990) *Women's Health Counts*. London: Routledge. **68**

Roberts, K., Cook, F. G., Clark, S. C. and Semeonoff, E. (1977) *The Fragmentary Class Structure*. London: Heinemann. **32**, **34**

Robertson, D. and Hillman, J. (1997) *Widening Participation in Higher Education for Students from Lower Socio-Economic Groups and Students with Disabilities*. Report no. 6, National Committee of Enquiry into Higher Education. London: HMSO. **184**, **185**, *7.16*

Robinson, P. and White, P. (1997) *Participation in Post-Compulsory Education*. London: Centre for Education and Employment Research. **174**, **177**, **184**, **186**

Rogers, R. (1980) The myth of 'independent' schools. *New Statesman*, 4 January. **178**

Rosser, C. and Harris, C. C. (1965) *The Family and Social Change*. London: Routledge and Kegan Paul. **32**

Routh, G. (1965) *Occupation and Pay in Great Britain 1906–60*. Cambridge: Cambridge University Press. **15**, **250**, *4.2*

Routh, G. (1980) *Occupation and Pay in Great Britain 1906–79*. London: Macmillan. **15**

Royal College of Psychiatrists (1986) *Alcohol: Our Favourite Drug*. London: RCP. **62**

Royal Commission on Legal Services (1979) *Final Report*, vol. 2. Command 7648–1. London: HMSO. **201**, **202**

Royal Commission on the Distribution of Income and Wealth (1979) *Report no. 7*, Command 7595. *Report no. 8*, Command 7679. London: HMSO. **82**, **88**, *4.2*

Runciman, W. G. (1964) Embourgeoisement, self-rated class and party preference. *Sociological Review*, 12 (2), 137–54. **32**

Runciman, W. G. (1966) *Relative Deprivation and Social Justice*. London: Routledge and Kegan Paul. **234**

Russell, B. (1997) System squeezes on the working class early on. *Times Educational Supplement*, 8th August, 3. **174**

Rutter, M., Maugham, B., Mortimore, P., Ouston, J. with Smith, A. (1979) *Fifteen Thousand Hours*, London: Open Books. **170**, **198**

Sampson, A. (1982) *The Changing Anatomy of Britain*. London: Hodder and Stoughton. **15**, *7.13*

Seglow, J., Pringle, M. K. and Wedge, P. (1972) *Growing Up Adopted*. Slough: NFER. **138**

Sex, Age and Marital Status, 1991 Census, Great Britain (1994) OPCS and GROS. London: HMSO. **127**

Sheiham, A., Marmot, M., Rawson, D. and Ruck, N. (1988) Food value: health and diet. In *British Social Attitudes, The 1987 Report, Social and Community Planning Research*, London: Gower. **59**

Sillitoe, K. (1969) *Planning for Leisure*. Government Social Survey. London: HMSO. **196**, **216**

Silver, H. (1973) *Equal Opportunity in Education*. London: Methuen. **157**

Sissons, P. L. (1973) *The Social Significance of Church Membership in the Borough of Falkirk*. Report to the Hope Trust and Church Ministry Department. **197**

Skeggs, B. (1989) *Gender Differences in Education*. In I. Reid and E. Stratta (eds), *Sex Differences in Britain*. Aldershot: Gower. **172**

Small Area Statistics, 1981 Census (1985) OPCS. London: HMSO. **31**

Social Trends no. 16 (1986) CSS. London: HMSO. **82**, **215**

Social Trends no. 17 (1987) CSS. London: HMSO. **68**, *3.13*

Social Trends no. 23 (1993) CSO. London: HMSO. **120**, **124**

Social Trends no. 24 (1994) CSO. London: HMSO. **83**, **88**, **98**, **178**

Social Trends no. 25 (1995) CSO. London: HMSO. *4.6*

Sparks, J. (1986) Marital condition estimates 1971–85: A New Series. *Population Trends*, no. 45, 18–25. **127**

Standard Occupational Classification (1990) Vols 1 and 2, Structure and Definition of Major, Minor and Unit Groups. OPCS. London: HMSO. **245**, **248**, **249**

Standard Occupational Classification (1991) Vol. 3, Social Classifications and Coding Methodology. OPCS. London: HMSO. **248**, **250**, *B.1*

Standard Occupational Classification (1995) Vol. 2, Structure and Definition of Major, Minor and Unit Groups, 2nd edn. OPCS. London: HMSO. **248**

Stanworth, M. (1984) Women and class analysis: a reply to John Goldthorpe. *Sociology*, 18 (2), 159–70. **40**

Statistical Bulletin 13/84 (1984) DES. London: HMSO. **174**

Statistical Review of England and Wales 1967 (1971) Part 3, Commentary. RG. London: HMSO. **124**, **129**

Statistics of Education 1961, Supplement (1962) Ministry of Education. London: HMSO. **170**

Statistics of Education 1979 (1981) DFE. London: HMSO. **167**

Stevenson, T. H. C. (1928) The vital statistics of wealth and poverty. *Journal of the Royal Statistical Society*, 91, 207–30. **41**, **45**, **246**

Stott, D. H. (1963) *The Social Adjustment of Children*. London: London University Press. **143**

Stratta, E. (1989) Involvement in crime. In I. Reid and E. Stratta (eds), *Sex Differences in Britain*. Aldershot: Gower. **198**

Studies in Sudden Infant Deaths (1982) OPCS. London: HMSO. **48**

Survey of the Physical Health of Prisoners 1994 (1995) OPCS SSD. London: HMSO. **198**

Target Group Index (1987) London: British Market Research Bureau. **225**, **230**, **232**

Target Group Index (1994) London: British Market Research Bureau. **225**, **230**, **232**, *4.8, 6.22, 9.7, 9.8, 9.9, 9.12, 9.13, 9.14, 9.15*

Tawney, R. H. (1931) *Equality*. London: Unwin. **99**, **241**

Taylor-Goodby, P. (1991) Attachment to the welfare state. In *British Social Attitudes, The 8th Report*, Social and Community Planning Research, Aldershot: Dartmouth. *8.14*

The Health and Lifestyle Survey (1987) London: Health Promotion Research Trust. **53**, **54**, **58**, **59**, *3.8*

The Health of Our Children (1995) *Decennial Supplement*. OPCS Series DS no. 11. London: HMSO. *3.1*

The Health of the Nation (1992) Command 1986. London: HMSO. **78**, *3.1*

The National Prison Survey 1991 (1992) OPCS SSD. London: HMSO. **198**, *8.6*

The Prevalence of Psychiatric Morbidity among Adults Living in Private Households (1995). OPCS Surveys of Psychiatric Morbidity in Great Britain. Report no. 1. London: HMSO. **56**, **57**

The Times House of Commons (1964–84). London: Times Newspapers. *7.13*

Thomas, L. and Wormald, E. (1989) Political participation. In I. Reid and E. Stratta (eds), *Sex Differences in Britain*, Aldershot: Gower. **207**

Thompson, K. (1988) How religious are the British? In T. Thomas (ed.), *The British*. London: Routledge and Kegan Paul. **190**

Titmuss, R. M. (1968) *Commitment to Welfare*. London: Allen and Unwin. **68**

Townsend, P. (1979) *Poverty in the United Kingdom*. Harmondsworth: Penguin. **32**, **33**, **34**, **35**, **39**, **91**, **105**, **118**, **253**, *2.11, 4.9*

Townsend, P. (1993) *The International Analysis of Poverty*. Hemel Hempstead: Harvester Wheatsheaf. **91**

Townsend, P. (1996) The struggle for independent statistics on poverty. In R. Levitas and W. Guy (eds), *Interpreting Official Statistics*. London: Routledge. **93**

Townsend, P., Corrigan, P. and Kowarzik, U. (1987) *Poverty and Labour in London*. London: Low Pay Unit. **83**, **93**

Townsend, P. and Davidson, N. (1982) *Inequalities in Britain*. Harmondsworth: Penguin. **70**

Townsend, P., Gordon, D. and Gosschalk, B. (1996) *The Poverty Line in Britain Today: What the Population Themselves Say*. Bristol: Bristol Statistical Monitoring Unit, School for Policy Studies, University of Bristol. **85**, **94**, *4.4*

Treiman, P. J. (1977) *Occupational Prestige in Comparative Perspective*. London: Academic Press. **42**

UCAS (1994) *31st Report 1992–3*. Cheltenham: UCCA. **186**, *7.14, 7.17*

UCAS (1996) *Annual Report 1995 Entry*. Cheltenham: UCAS. **187**, *7.16*

Unemployment Unit Bulletin (1986) London: Unemployment Unit. **108**

Visiting the National Portrait Gallery (1987) OPCS SSD. London: HMSO. **233**

Voluntary Work (1993) OPCS SSD. London: HMSO. *9.10*

Wadsworth, M. E. J. (1975) Delinquency in a national sample of children. *British Journal of Criminology*, 15 (2), 167–74. **198**

Walby, S. (1986) Gender, class and stratification. In R. Crompton and M. Mann (eds), *Gender and Stratification*. Cambridge: Polity Press. **40**

Ward and Civil Parish Monitor (various dates following 1991 census) OPCS. London: HMSO. **31**

Webb, D. (1973) Some reservations on the use of self-rated class. *Sociological Review*. 21 (2), 321–30. **38**

Webb, M. (1989) Sex and gender in the labour market. In I. Reid and E. Stratta (eds), *Sex Differences in Britain*, Aldershot: Gower. **164**

Wellings, K., Field, J., Johnson, A. and Wadsworth, J. (1994) *Sexual Behaviour in Britain: The National Survey of Sexual Attitudes and Lifestyles*. Harmondsworth: Penguin. **136**, *6.9*

Wellings, K. and Wadsworth, J. (1990) AIDS and the moral climate. In *British Social Attitudes, The 7th Report*, Social and Community Planning Research, Aldershot: Gower. **138**

Wells, N. (1987) *Women's Health Today*. London: Office of Health Economics. **46**, **59**, **78**

Werner, B. (1984) Fertility and family background: some illustrations from OPCS Longitudinal Study. *Population Trends*, no. 35, 5–10. **131**

Werner, B. (1985) Fertility trends in different social classes. *Population Trends*, no. 41, 5–12. **133**

Werner, B. (1988) Birth intervals: results from the OPCS Longitudinal Study 1972–84. *Population Trends*, no. 51, 18–24. **132**

West Indian Children in Our Schools (1981) The Rampton Report. Interim Report of the Committee of Inquiry into the Education of Children from Ethnic Minority Groups. Command 8273. London: HMSO. **159**

Whitaker's Almanac 1984 (1984) 116th edn. London: Whitaker. *7.13*

Whitburn, J., Mealing, M. and Cox, C. (1976) *People in Polytechnics*. Guildford: Society for Research into Higher Education. **186**

Who's Who (1984) London: A. and C. Black. *7.13*

Yarrow, M. R., Campbell, J. D. and Burton, R. V. (1964) Reliability of maternal retrospection: a preliminary report. *Family Process*, 3, 207–18. **139**

Young People's Intentions to Enter Higher Education (1987) OPCS SSD. London: HMSO. **172**, *7.8, 7.9, 7.12*

Young, K. (1992) Class, race and opportunity. In *British Social Attitudes, The 9th Report*, Social and Community Planning Research, Aldershot: Dartmouth. **32**, **208**, *2.10, 8.13*

Young, M. and Willmott, P. (1956) Social grading by manual workers. *British Journal of Sociology*, 7, 337–45.

Young, M. and Willmott, P. (1973) *The Symmetrical Family*. London: Routledge and Kegan Paul, Harmondsworth: Penguin, 1975. **216**

Zander, M. (1978) *Legal Services for the Community*. London: Temple Smith. **202**

Subject Index

Numbers in italics refer to tables.